Sundowner

Robin Lamb

Sundowner

Olympia Publishers
London

www.olympiapublishers.com
OLYMPIA PAPERBACK EDITION

A CIP catalogue record for this title is
available from the British Library.

ISBN: 978-1-78830-584-6

First Published in 2020

Olympia Publishers
Tallis House
2 Tallis Street
London
EC4Y 0AB

Printed in Great Britain

An Idea in Ithaca

The idea started to germinate during a balmy Mediterranean afternoon in September, with the scent of pine fresh in the air. We had each been trying to make one cold beer last the afternoon — and the cold beer may have contributed to this particular flight of fancy.

"We should have another," I complained, "It's unnatural to make one beer last all afternoon."

"It's practice for when we retire and you aren't able to throw the stuff down your throat with such gay abandon," Helen responded.

"I wish you wouldn't use that word."

"Gay?"

"No. Retire," I said, "I'm not going to — can't afford to."

"You'll have to. You're sixty-five next year and you should. How much longer do you think the Americans are going to keep you in work?"

She was referring to my single remaining customer, a company that had felt the need to 'downsize' several times in the past few years. I had so far managed to survive the successive culls, but had been invited to share some of the pain. I had been asked to 're-examine' my charges (American for reduce them — apparently) and my workload had been pared back due to their currently declining business.

Other customers had vanished from my books for one reason or another but, truth be told, I was accepting, nay enjoying, the slowdown. There was enough money coming in as I had managed to pay off the mortgage on the house in my own personal celebration of the turn of the century.

I contemplated the condensation on the two fresh bottles of beer that suddenly appeared in front of us and looked up at the smiling weathered countenance of Tzanetos. We had made it a rule during our years of wandering around Greece — and other parts of the world —

not to favour a particular watering hole — they came to expect you and you had to endure their baleful looks and worse if you fancied a change. Tzanetos was an exception we had made to that rule. He was the proprietor of our favourite watering hole in this particular port and now a friend of some years standing.

"Why, thank you, Tzanetos."

"Is from me," he told us, his voice rich with Greek gravel. "Your house? Good?" He was asking about a house we had looked at that morning with a view to buying.

"No. It was bad… And very expensive."

"Yes. Is crazy. Last year, house prices… wooosh," and he made an upwards gesture indicating prices going through the stratosphere.

In years of backpacking around the Greek islands, and other places, we had often met Brits who had bought property for a song and settled down there. "How nice," we had thought and then, "but not for us."

Why not? Well, on holiday in the Greek islands, like many other backpackers, we enjoyed being able to pull up sticks after a few days and move on to somewhere new, or to look up an old friend elsewhere. The tie of owning a house in an admittedly idyllic setting and the commitment to spend most — if not all — of our limited holidays in the one place, probably much of the time with paintbrush, screwdriver or hammer in hand, was not for us. Not now. Maybe later in life. But, all of a sudden, here we were. 'Later in life' had suddenly arrived. Where had it come from? The children had grown up, found jobs, had children of their own and it would not be long before those children started the cycle yet again. In fact, at the time of going to press, — they have!

"The agents," Tzanetos continued. "Those bastards have put prices up. I hear they take more than half the price as a commission. They don't tell the seller, but the word — the word — gets around." He tapped his nose conspiratorially. "Maybe true, maybe not. But, anyways, they see Germans, Dutch, English, and now Russians and…" here he shrugged and looked up at the heavens "…even rich Athenians that look for houses on the island and they push up prices. Now the local people cannot afford!"

Here, it must be said, that for some of the islanders, the 'rich Athenian' is well up on the grockle scale of tourists they could do without; —however, on some islands, most of the population returns to Athens outside the tourist season. So there it is: one of the many delightful dichotomies of Greek island life.

Tzanetos warmed to his theme. Certain predictable subjects easily launched him into a tirade — the usual: politicians, the local authority, taxes... "Politicians..." his hand outstretched with his palms facing upwards and his blue eyes looked up to the blue sky "...I'm telling you, those bastards need..." And some suitable grisly end was nominated for the politician — local or Athenian. It seemed estate agents and escalating house prices had joined them this year.

"How much? The house... how much?" Tzanetos prompted.

"Three hundred and thirty thousand euros." This was about two hundred and twenty thousand pounds and, at the time, not so far different to a similar house in the UK.

"And it was a tip," I continued "Nice garden... Big garden with olive trees and peach trees. A nice view across the water to Keffalonia too. But the house needed pulling down and re-building. It looked like he kept goats in it."

"Ah, Stavros, he most likely did." Tzanetos chuckled fruitily, and then, spotting one of the local fishermen coming in, "Live well" (his standard goodbye) as he hurried off to get the choice of the catch before the other taverna owners homed in on the fishing boat that was approaching its quayside mooring.

I returned to contemplating the bottle of beer wondering how long I could resist it. A large exotic butterfly landed on the neck of the bottle and stamped several of his feet up and down presumably to keep them warm as the bottle was fresh out of Tzanetos very cold display fridge. The clonk of bells and bleating announced the arrival of a dozen goats picking their way down the impossibly vertical rock face on the north west side of the harbour. A new quayside there lured the unsuspecting visitor to lay his boat alongside and get it damaged by the swells that came sweeping in from the distant ferries hurrying to make time between Patras and Igoumenitsa. There was no swell at the moment though, and the late afternoon katabatic wind that could howl down the valley behind the port had yet to arrive. It was calm. It was peaceful. It was warm.

"Nice here," I said, as I stretched up and plucked some leaves from the overhanging eucalyptus, crumpled them in my hand to release the scent of the leaves, and held them under Helen's nose.

"Mmmm, nice," she said dreamily and then, conversationally, "The answer is a boat you know."

"What was the question?"

"Getting a place in Greece for our retirement, of course. With a boat, we can anchor in beautiful bays at no cost at all. When we get tired of one place, we can move on as we have always liked to — 'Another day, another bay', to quote Sailing Holidays. A boat is the answer. I don't want to sell our house in England. Not yet. I want to go back and see the family in the winter. I don't want to spend the winter on my own in Greece."

"You wouldn't be on your own. You'd have me."

She looked at me appraisingly, "Yes. Quite."

"And, anyway, if you don't want to sell the house what do we buy a boat with?"

"You retire. You get some cash from your pensions."

"We need that. We need to invest it. That won't give us enough for a boat and the pensions are not enough for us to live on."

"You can sell Tethera."

A bombshell. A silence descended. Dried leaves shifted uneasily like spindthrift on the ground, and the air took a chilly turn.

Tethera was my 28-foot Countess. An Essex-built boat designed for comfort rather than speed. It had bilge keels; two shallow, stubby, side-by-side keels instead of a single deep keel. This meant less performance, but it also gave the boat less draft than those with a fixed single keel so it could get into interesting creeks and shallow places that the owners of deep keel boats found difficult or impossible. Additionally, if a miscalculation put you on the putty, so to speak, you could usually sit there quite comfortable and upright until the next tide gently lifted you off. Not a practice endorsed by the teaching schools, no doubt, but it works providing you don't sit it on a rock. It is not quite the same with a deep keel boat where, if it goes aground on a falling tide, it cants over and the wall becomes the floor and the floor a wall... so to speak.

"Sell Tethera? Over my dead body!"

Selling Tethera

Less than a week later, my dead body was challenged. We looked over Alex, a 41 ft Bavaria. Helen fell in love with the boat. I had to admit that it was in good nick. Bavaria is a German company building boats using, it is said, 'production line techniques'. Perhaps the Ford of the boating world in that you get a lot of boat for your money. There is less of the boat hull-thickness-wise than, for example, a Countess. One result of this is a lighter, faster, boat that handles — let's face it — much easier than my cantankerous Countess. It is a low-cost boat (a relative term — in truth, there is no such thing as a low-cost boat) but, as such, it suffers a certain amount of snooty disdain from those who can afford higher cost boats — much as it is with all things. Do BMW drivers spring to mind?

Alex was berthed in Lefkas marina. The owner, Nikos, a thoroughly charming Greek, met us at the boat and showed us over. It was impressive, but we apologetically explained that it was all a bit premature as we had a boat to sell before we bought: "But we are definitely interested," Helen told him. We even agreed the price if we managed to sell Tethera. Helen promised to keep in touch via his broker.

I was not as sure as Helen, "What do I want a 41 ft boat for?" I grumbled, "It's an enormous boat."

"Don't be so negative. It's much roomier than Tethera and I bet it's faster too."

"Speed isn't everything. Tethera is built for comfort not speed. I'm very happy with Tethera."

"That's not what you say when you're trying to get back along the Solent against the falling tide and Ryde Church spire is gaining on you each time you tack."

It was true enough. Even if we were not on a beat and the prevailing Solent south-westerly was up our tail, the trip home could be quite arduous in our chubby little Countess if we left it late, and the wind died, and the tide set against us. Even the reliable little Volvo engine found it difficult to best the Solent tide in full flow.

"Yes, but a Bavaria though. It won't take the sort of punishment that Tethera takes. It's made out of rice paper. Hit a pile and it'll crumple."

"Then you'll have to stop hitting things, won't you?"

My protests, at the quite unnecessary slur on my abilities, hit stony ground. We looked at other boats in the boatyards that faced Preveza, across the water, but none of them came up to snuff. We phoned a John Smith in Corfu having picked up his name on the internet. I outlined our requirements. It was a 'we want a boat; a bloody good one, and it's got to be dirt cheap' sort of a specification.

"I am down in your direction on Monday. Let's meet up. I have some boats that might interest you."

We obtained the details of three boats from him. "I will show you over them when I come down on Monday," he said.

"Oh, you are not making a special journey? It's really quite a casual enquiry; we have a boat to sell yet."

"No, no. I'm coming down anyway."

We got the names and whereabouts of the boats out of him. We rather sneakily persuaded the office wallahs at the boat yards to give us keys, and then crawled all over the boats and rejected them. John sounded miffed when we phoned his mobile early on Monday to tell him that we were not interested, and he was quite obviously upset that the keys had been handed over to us. Ah well. We had little time before our plane back and Helen had seen and fallen in love with Alex, so his boats didn't stand a chance. However, Alex was not to be.

Alex was not to be because we had a boat to get rid of first. Owning one boat is a kind of madness; to own two would be total insanity. American yachtsman, Denis Connor, and former British Prime Minister, Ted Heath, have both been accredited with describing sailing as 'like standing in a cold shower and tearing up bank notes as fast as you can'. I don't know which of them coined this quip, but it is commonly held that a boat is a 'hole in the water into which you shovel money'. Mooring fees, maintenance, the frequent repair of this or that, craning the thing in or out of the water — all are a never-ending demand on your resources — mental and financial.

On our return to the UK, Tethera was booked into one of the 'bring and buy' sales that boatyards around the Solent hold near the time of the Southampton boat show. There was interest, but there were no offers. I had it craned back into the water on the last day of the thirty days ashore that the sale agreement had offered, and puttered down the Hamble between trots of far more stylish and expensive yachts. It was a warm October day. I engaged the autohelm and put up the mainsail when the width of the river and the direction of the wind permitted. Tethera and I motorsailed out of the Hamble and into Southampton Water. There were very few other sails in sight — quite a contrast to the height of the season in these parts. Out on Southampton Water, I unfurled the Genoa (the big foresail) and Tethera romped along. With the sword of Damacles hanging over her, she was being as sprightly and co-operative as possible. I was on my own on the boat, but the Solent was deserted enough and the weather benign enough that I could briefly leave the steering to the autohelm and make a cup of coffee. I sat drinking it in the cockpit and savoured the Solent in autumn for the last time.

During the following months, I put the boat on the internet, stuck it in a couple of popular sailing magazines, and registered it with a broker. I also set about looking for cheaper moorings for Tethera in case the boat was not sold by the start of the next sailing season when my berthing agreement with Hasler marina in Gosport expired. In the end, I sold the boat before I had to commit to a new mooring, but it was a close-run thing. In fact, I overstayed at the marina by half a week (for which they graciously, and to my surprise, waived their fees). Finally, I sailed Tethera up Southampton Water and the River Itchen to a boatyard that was to be her new home. It was opposite a quay where scrap metal was noisily being loaded on to a freighter for eventual shipment to the Chinese who, at the time, were in the market for all the scrap metal that they could lay their hands on.

Before that, Tethera had a sea trial in Southampton Water in the snow. We had to renegotiate the price after the purchaser's dastardly surveyor discovered the dreaded 'osmosis'. Similar, but not the same, as the osmosis that you learned about in school biology lessons; this condition seems to have the reputation in the boat world that cancer does in the human world, but with much less justification. It is more a mechanism for surveyors to justify their charges by enabling their customers to negotiate a hefty price reduction. However, in spite of the price reduction that we agreed to, we had a deal and that enabled us to set out in our ageing Toyota a month or so later. The car, crammed with useful stuff, was to take us across France through Italy, and by ferry into Greece to spend the first summer of our retirement looking for, and hopefully buying, a boat and living aboard it.

Into Europe

We had idly mused that one day, when we had the opportunity to have more than the usual two weeks off, we would take off for Greece and just backpack around the country and see how long it would be before we got bored with this. Effectively, this was what we were now embarking on, but with an aim—: to buy a boat.

'Operation live-aboard' started when we left the house, shortly before six o'clock, on the morning of Tuesday 10th June. The reading on the car speedometer was 61496 miles. It had averaged about seven and a half thousand miles a year since new. We were about to give it a treat. In half a week, we were to cover over 1200 miles — about two months' worth of motoring, going by previous years. At this initial stage of the journey, the traffic was nice and light. Two hours of easy driving got us from Reading to Dover.

Dover brought back a flood of memories as it must for a lot of people. Recently, we met an uncle and aunt of mine there after they had brought their boat (another Countess, but a 37 ft version) across from France, and we sailed with them along the south coast for a while. We had sheltered from a storm in Rye, just inside the river mouth, with the bulky 37 ft boat perched precariously up against the quay on its long fin keel as the tide dropped away. My bunk was on the outside (starboard side), and I remember being wary of walking over to it feeling that my weight might be enough to tip the balance and bring the boat crashing into the river.

I remembered too, many years back, bringing Debue, a 20 ft plywood-built Debutante, into Dover harbour on a dark and stormy night when I was seventeen. Again, I was in the company of David, my uncle. It was his first boat, but he was convulsed with seasickness and not much use when it came to specific directions.

"Where do I aim for?" I asked him.

"Just get it into the harbour between the harbour lights. See there and there," he pointed. "Red and green."

"How do you know which is which?" I asked. David is red-green colour blind — a bit inconvenient for a sailor.

"The light signature — I count the flashes."

"I see. It doesn't look like a very wide entry from here."

"The car ferries are managing. We've only got a small boat," he moaned.

The only other member of the crew, my schoolmate, 'Hutch', had not responded to my entreaties to take his watch. He had made the mistake of going below to sleep and been gripped with bad seasickness. The cabin was still imbued with the cloying smell of resins that a new boat sometimes takes its time to shake off. The light plywood boat was being tossed about like a cork in seas drummed up by winds that were being reported as force nine. With the noise of the seas crashing against the plywood hull, it was rather like sailing in a kettle drum. Hutch was jammed into a nook next to the galley. He was nursing a saucepan that he had grabbed off the galley and vomited into shortly before passing out. Both David and Hutch still sail, and suffer seasickness, to this day. Such is the pull of the sea.

The harbour entry had been plenty big enough, but there were ferries and other monsters about. The lights of Dover town annihilated my night vision — it's amazing what you can see by starlight in mid-channel, but the lighting in a harbour like Dover puts a stop to all that. As we entered the harbour, I could pick out a large dark shape with strange protuberances silhouetted against the town lights. It seemed to be coming towards me whichever way I went. Eventually, I deduced that it was moored up within the harbour. The strange protuberances were that of a dredger named, appropriately it seemed to me, Dracula.

David came back to life as the water flattened within the harbour. He started the motor to take us into the inner harbour and then into the small boats harbour where the conditions, although raining, seemed positively benign and David positively cheery. We tied up the boat and then David was shouting for me. He couldn't find me and couldn't think where I had got to but then he stepped on me. Exhausted, I had fallen asleep among the oilskins discarded into the small cockpit. We got below, sorted out Hutch and found a bunk apiece. We had just drifted off again and were awoken by a knocking on the hull. Customs were wanting to know who we were, where we had come from and what our intentions were!

Back to the present day... I followed signs for the ferries in the eastern docks. The entry seemed unchanged and that took me, once again, off to the memory of a hot June day in 1975.

We arrived, then, in the small lorry that we had hired from a garage in Eindhoven. It was packed with most of the content of the Chelmsford house that we had been living in at the time. Our belongings: clothes, bedding, domestic appliances, books and, not to put too fine a point on it, junk. All of it had seemed important at the time. Fortunately, the truck we had hired was the modern equivalent of a covered wagon, canvas sides with plenty of give which gave to accommodate our junk — just. And there was room in the cab for all five of us — just.

"What if they stop us and say there are too many in the cab? We have only three seat belts."

"One of us will have to walk — we'll draw lots — except me, I'm driving."

"No seriously."

"It'll be all right. They don't worry about things like that on the continent and, if they do, we'll sort something out."

"What?"

"Something; we'll, we'll improvise."

"What make a lot of noise like your bloody jazz records?"

We were then (as now, I suppose) like a bunch of nomads, except that on that occasion, we were off to a life in Holland.

The lorry, though small, was tall enough that it was considered a tall vehicle and so had to go in an area in the ferry where the ceiling was high enough to accommodate her. I was directed to park on the harbourside among huge articulated lorries that dwarfed ours.

I wandered about the harbourside and got into conversation with a bunch of lorry drivers gathered around their big rigs. Usual men's talk — football, sex, and tales of derring-do. All good fun. I was one of the lads. During the conversation, one of the port officials in neatly pressed trousers and smart dazzling clean white shirt with epaulettes approached us — wanting to take part in the smutty conversation I supposed. But no, he beckoned one of the drivers over. After a brief exchange, the driver climbed into the cab of his massive lorry gunned the engine and drove the beast with its large trailer in an arc across the concrete concourse. He stopped and then reversed it smartly, and without any suggestion of hesitation, into the black maw of the ferry.

"Blimey. He's done that before," I said open mouthed.

"A few times," chuckled a big Geordie driver. "Don't worry, bonny lad, it'll be your turn soon."

"Yeah. I won't be reversing in like him though."

"Oh, yes you will. All tall vehicles have to on this boat."

"Oh, shhhiiiitt." I croaked.

"Why, which one is yours?"

"That one over there." I pointed out my truck which, although tall by the definition of the ferry operator, was diminutive compared to the massive machines that towered over it, and it didn't have the complication of a trailer.

The other lorry drivers collapsed in laughter and down too went any kudos that my story telling may have garnered.

"Don't worry, Sonny," laughed a large cockney. "We'll see you in," and he had the effrontery to ruffle my hair — but he was big so I let him.

"Yeah, I'll just go over and get our pal in the uniform to take you in next," said the Geordie with tears of laughter running down his cheeks. "Just so we can all help you... see."

I managed to avoid that particular indignity and re-joined the family to be greeted with, "Fell out with your friends then?"

But, to return again to the present, Helen and I drove towards the east end of Dover harbour. At the docks, signs and lane markings led us to a booth where a man took the email print-out and read the reference. He gave us a sticker to hang from the mirror and some other bits of paper. We drove onward, following signs for lane 189, and were parked awaiting the ferry two hours after leaving the house. Here, another man presented us with another bit of paper. This one warned us that there were obligations for motorists going abroad, some of them were legal requirements. Transgression, it seemed, was likely to invite the full brute force of the law. The leaflet was pretty uninformative when it came to defining exactly which countries insisted on what, but had the consoling message that all these things would be available on the boat. For a modest outlay (a small fortune), one could buy a complete kit that would safeguard you from the stern attention of the gendarmerie in any European country that you cared to think of.

I knew of the red triangle and had bought one from Halfords a week or so back. I had forgotten about the GB sticker; indeed, I had assumed that now the plates carried the legend GB, it was no longer required. However, I bought a magnetic sticker that would doubtless fall off the car later. A set of spare bulbs for the rear lights seemed like a good idea. The man behind the counter said the French insisted on them and, indeed, manned a machine gun post just outside the exit from Calais port that would check for them in every car and gun down any that attempted to jump the queue. He sold us a suitable set.

"They do not look like the bulbs for my car," I said.

"Yep, 2002 Toyota Avensis you said?"

"Yes, but it says Nissan on the packet," I replied.

He assured us that it was just a 'Printing error'.

Similar arguments were presented for the bright green/yellow dayglow jackets. "If you have a car accident and have to get out of the car, especially on a motorway, you have to wear them. The French insist that you have them on board, and they man a machi—"

"All right, all right, we'll have one."

"You have to have one each, and besides, we only sell them in threes."

"I'm not wearing one of those, I will look like a road sweeper," chimed in Helen. "Is it really compulsory if you have an accident?" she continued.

"Oh yes — it makes you an easier target for the French motorist," he explained. So we had two — his and hers — sweet.

"That's the first days' budget shot to pieces," said Helen who had produced all sorts of elaborate spreadsheets that proved that we could do this summer on £4... 19s... 6d per day "and what's the point? I'm not wearing one of those jackets even if we do have an accident."

"We are not going to have an accident. Not when I have just spent all that money on having the wing, the headlight and the rear light cluster replaced."

"Bloody daft if you ask me. Over a thousand pounds on a car just before we are planning on driving it through France, over the Alps, through Italy and then all over Greece. You're just bound to hit something. You took the rear light cluster out by reversing into that pillar in a Chinese restaurant car park."

"It was very dark."

"Yes, but the pillar had a light on it!"

La Belle, France

We drove on to the Ferry at nine o'clock and it left a quarter of an hour later. The French coast loomed large by ten o'clock. I cannot remember exactly when we docked, but I know that when I got down to the car deck, I discovered that I did not have my car keys with me.

"That was the announcement I was trying to get you to listen to."

"What announcement?"

"The one that said 'A set of car keys have been handed in. Will the owner please pick them up from the bursar's office'. I asked you whether you were sure that you had your keys and you said 'Yes'."

"Well, I thought I had."

"But you didn't check, did you?"

"All right, all right. Guilty as charged," I said, defending myself.

As I had packed the spare key, and we were near front of the queue, I used the spare to drive the car off the boat and pulled to the right at the foot of the ramp. I told the officials standing there that the keys were on the boat. They motioned us to park well clear of the exiting traffic and they would remedy the situation. One of them unclipped his hand-held radio and had a conversation with the crew on the boat; a conversation that was doubtless not very complimentary with respect to English motorists, and me in particular. Once all the traffic was off the boat, the young man who had been dealing with the situation jumped into a little white VW Golf and shot up the ramp returning half a minute later with the keys. Once again, we were on our way.

The drive through France was fairly uneventful, but fast. Helen took the wheel at Reims at about two thirty. I was navigator and watcher of the speedometer; frequently reminding her of the speed limit, and the fact that it was the inner ring of figures on the speedometer that gave kilometres/hour, as well as the fact that I had just spent over £1,000 on the car. The latter was indeed beginning to seem a daft decision on my part.

France was exciting at first, then boring, as the flat fields with their occasional outcrops of trees and farm buildings sped past. Fortunately, the terrain began to get a bit crinkly once we were past Dijon and, before long— as we approached the Alps — the scenery was edging toward spectacular. A thunderstorm with great branches of forked lightning added a touch of drama.

Peter, a regular at my sister's pub in Suffolk, had a boat in Greece that he shared with two other owners and when my sister had learned of my plan to buy a boat out there, she put the two of us in touch. Peter was most helpful. He gave us a list of contacts for when we got out there, advice on local conditions and hazards and so on. Among other things, he recommended the 'Formula 1' chain of motels as being economic but clean and generally satisfactory if all you were after was somewhere to put your head down en-route. Helen had picked out a number of them on the web, but the one we were aiming for was in France just south of Geneva at a place called St Cergues a couple of miles north east of Annemasse and within spitting distance of Lake Geneva.

We took a wrong turning and got involved in a traffic jam after Dijon, but eventually cleared it and picked up the A40 for Annemasse, south of Dijon. The directions from the website enabled us to find the place quite easily about twenty minutes after leaving the motorway. By now, we were looking forward to getting our heads down and making an early start in the morning. We were about sixty euros poorer due to toll charges, and tired from a long day. We had not booked up the hotel as we were not sure exactly how far we would get on our first day. I could, I suppose, have measured distances on maps and estimated, but I didn't, so we were pleased to have made our target albeit having driven on for longer than we had planned in order to do so.

The hotel was full. We asked the proprietor for his suggestions for other likely hotels in the price range.

"All full. Even expensive 'otels."

"What! Why?"

"Euro football's in Geneva."

It was the start of the 2008 UEFA European Championship jointly hosted by Switzerland and Austria. There was an opening match in nearby Geneva that night. All accommodation was taken by spectators, reporters, TV crews and the like. 'Oh, ballcocks' was my immediate thought, but when we waxed a bit more constructive, we headed back to the A40 rejoined the route south about an hour behind ourselves by now.

I had red-bulled myself a bit during the late afternoon, so I was, by now, fairly alert and with it. Helen was mortified, but we decided to put some distance between us and the European Championship and its full 'otels. We now drove on through spectacular countryside, viaducted roads high above valleys and snow-capped crests high above them. The unfortunate thing was that the light was failing, and it was pouring with rain. It would have been so much nicer to have seen this in the early light of morning the following day.

After an hour or so, we drove into the Mont Blanc Tunnel then out the other end, and into yet more tunnels. Tunnels, tunnels, tunnels, for the next hour or so.

The night was dark. I had not an ounce of sleep in me. Traffic was light as we continued down the Italian side of the Alps. What a pity we were doing all this in the dark. The scenery, if only we could see it, was probably spectacular. We pulled into a service area that was far from spectacular, however. Helen surmised that, although I was up and running, she was knackered and we were both likely to be little piles of poo tomorrow if we carried on, so we started to look for somewhere to sleep. A picture of a bed was shown at a roadside sign preceding a service area, so we pulled in but we could see nothing that resembled a hotel or bunkhouse. We thought about sleeping in the car, but the area was brightly lit and lavishly littered with cans and packets. A bunch of unsavoury youths were kicking some of the cans around.

"Bugger it, these pull ins seem fairly frequent, let's try the next." The next had an expensive hotel. Paying through the nose for a few hours' sleep did not appeal. So, on we went.

I was still buzzing, but Helen was knackered and unable to sleep with the car in motion. I don't know why that is, I frequently do, but not while driving — well, not often. Even a couple of hours in the car in a car park would be better than nothing she insisted.

"How about this layby?" I said, slowing down and pulling in.

"Anything," was the response.

We found that we were sharing the layby with a car and a couple of lorries. The car moved off shortly after we arrived. One of the lorries was hitched to a long trailer full of livestock. Horses? Cows? It was difficult to tell. The noise was unearthly and whatever was entrapped in the trailer was kicking the bejasus out of the sides of the trailer with hard shod or hooved feet. Christ knows what they were going to do when they burst out as seemed inevitable. The driver presumably slept through it all in the cab. Helen could not. This was partly because of the noise level, but mainly because the general shindig suggested distressed animals, something that she does not put up with. I had a hard job persuading her that it was probably not a good idea to let them out to play on the motorway — particularly in the early hours of a pitch-black, moonless night. I started the car and we wearily got back on the road.

At the next service area, we found a parking place but then another lorry full of livestock turned up and, although not the same lorry, the inmates were similarly kicking shit out of their prison. At the next one, it was chickens or maybe it was pigs. I don't know; delirium was setting in. They were not as noisy as the bigger animals, but Helen's 'distressed-animal syndrome' had kicked in with a vengeance and she was not going to be able to sleep.

The entire livestock of Italy seemed to be travelling in convoy with us that night — being transported and objecting to it loudly. I turned off the motorway at one point between Milan and Turin following signs that clearly indicated that there were beds to be found in a nearby town. The town name should be emblazoned on my memory, but some sort of safety mechanism has erased it. We drove through the town. It was deserted, dark, and alien. I don't think I would have accepted a bed if it had been on offer. The place had the air of a mad axe man's territory. We could not see any place that looked like it would offer a bed. One bar had been brightly lit when we arrived. I tried to find my way back to it so I could enquire about accommodation.

"At two thirty in the morning and in Italian?" Helen asked, "when your only Italian seems to be *Ciao*, *Due biglietti per Roma por favor* and *gelato*" ('Hello/goodbye', 'Two tickets to Rome please', and 'Ice cream' for the benefit of those who do not have my linguistic skills!)

The bar was unlit as we retraced our route, so we desperately tried to extricate ourselves from the hell hole of a town. Everywhere we drove, we ended up in the same industrial estate where strange industrial plant loomed sinisterly against the faint light of the early morning sky. Plant that was doubtless used to melt down tourists to make glue, or else particularly bad Italian cheese — this perhaps explained the smell of bad feet that parmesan exudes. Heavy industrial smoke was visible in the dim lit sky and even more evident to our olfactory systems.

"Do you think we've wandered into Chernobyl?"

"Anything's bloody possible."

We found a service area that was no better or worse than the others, and may have had lorry loads of livestock doing the Charleston for all we knew. We rearranged stuff in the back of the car so that we could recline the seats and slept until five thirty. Bliss. Or it would have been, but some sort of nightmare had us running in slow motion pursued by pigs, demented sheep, mad cows, giant chickens with blood dripping from their beaks as they pecked each other grotesquely featherless. I imagined horses frothing at the mouth in the dark and kicking hell out of their enclosures. Italian punks wearing Italian National Football Team's strip and playing football with empty beer cans entered the fray somewhere too.

Italia

While the traffic had been light during the early hours, at half past five in the morning it was already busy and working its way towards furious. In the daylight, the road was a concrete toilet enclosed with concrete walls with yet more concrete, and industry and railyards peering over the walls that contained us in this madhouse of a road. The lorries were humungous and trying for land speed records. They were the sort of lorries that would eat a Toyota Avensis for breakfast without the lorry driver realising he had done any more than run over an irregularity in the road surface (of which there were plenty). Occasionally, beyond the concrete, we would see a green field, flat and seductively shrouded in the early morning mist. But then it would be back again to railyards, factories and grimy warehouses.

There were roadworks too that suddenly forced two or three lanes of traffic into one. Oncoming lorries were suddenly sharing our side of the dual carriageway. To warn us of this there would be a man waving a dirty orange flag about while his mate fiddled with a cone and scratched his arse apparently unaware of the vehicular ordinance hurtling past to left and right and pretty much over him. The wartime joke about the lack of courage of the Italian army seemed not to hold too much water with the evidence of these arse scratching Eyties, nonchalant in the face of certain death.

The lorries were from Spain, France, the UK, Germany, Poland, almost everywhere you could think of. All of them hurtling west to east, or vice versa, across the top of Italy. Why? What sort of trade route is this? I need to do a bit of reading when I get home.

"Where are we?"

"Tuscany?"

"Can't be — nowhere near."

"We must be in Tuscany."

"Why?"

"It's the only province in Italy that I know by name."

The roads, though still busy, had become quieter and cars had started to replace lorries as we went past Piacenza. We were starting to get more glimpses of fields of vines and other produce with occasional outcrops of farm buildings interspersed with two or three trees. It was all very redolent of numerous watercolours of rustic Italy.

At about eight o'clock, we pulled into a service area just after Forti about an hour and a half away from Ancona. Although the motorway was still an eyesore, even by the normal standards of motorways, there were mainly fields to either side. Fields as far as the eye could see. The situation was reversed. Industry was now the rarity. Small towns ambled past the motorway from time to time with the occasional warehouse or factory. We started to envisage ourselves bumbling along long straight deserted country roads leaving the expensively tolled autostrada and taking to the friendly untolled rustic road that ran a parallel course. Perhaps we would stop at some roadside place to sit and take coffee and croissants in rural Italy amidst lots of agricultural inactivity.

We pulled off the Autostrada at Cesena straight into a small but crowded town. Everything was suddenly at a standstill. We crawled at a snail's pace between pavements that spilled pedestrians onto the road. People were shopping, standing talking, sitting talking, drinking coffee, shouting across the street at each other. Charming, Italian, and slow, oh so slow. The road signs that might help us through were difficult to spot and then difficult to understand. The scale of our motorist's road map of Europe did not acknowledge the existence of pretty much all of the towns on the signs.

After a few minutes of driving at 0.8 mph, rather than 80, Helen, who was at the wheel at the time instructed me to get her back on the f***ing motorway, autobahn, autostrada or whatever they called it in this neck of the world. Actually, she was a bit more ladylike than that, but I feel that summarised her sentiments in a nutshell.

"Easier said than done, Your Gorgeousness."

It took some time to pick up a sign for the *autostrada*. I did not see it at the next junction, picked it up again at the following one but then had to double back because we had overshot and so on. We ended up at the junction that we had left forty minutes earlier. The whole exercise had been a waste of diesel and time. We were back on the boring autotoiletstrada, but Helen was now happy with her foot on the floor, her teeth gritted and challenging the death and destruction brigade to take her on. Lorry drivers were in the ascendancy again now we had Rimini in our sights.

A place called San Marino was marked on the map just inland and south(ish) of Rimini. On the map, it was encircled with a thick purple line strangely similar to the lines that marked the border between countries in our Motorists Road Atlas of Europe. The letters RSM were in a little ellipse of the same purple colour. RSM? Regimental Sergeant Major? Hardly. Could a town, or whatever the place was, be an RSM? Perhaps a British RSM had fought bravely and released the town from the evil clutches of 'Il Duce' during World War Two so they had named the town after him. Did the British army declare the town to be a Regimental Sergeant Major after the town had provided the allies with heroic support during WWII? This seemed possible given the anachronistic habits of our armed forces where, for example, the navy call what is clearly a plot of land with buildings on it, 'Her Majesty's Ship such and such'.

When we got nearer, the truth turned out to be that RSM indicated the 'Republic of San Marino', a little purple boil in the otherwise clear skin of Italy. Perhaps it didn't join in when all the disparate warring factions were merged into one benign, harmonious, law-abiding (apart from the mafia) modern country. Even today, inside their high-walled citadel all the population — each of whom was obviously called Regimental Sergeant Major San Marino — defended their tiny republic against the outside world by manning the battlements and hurling old hard smelly cheeses, ancient ancestors of parmesan, at any one who approached.

We hurtled past without a single cheese hitting our car, but the venerable Toyota was by now covered with the samples of the insect life from most of the regions of France and Italy that we had driven through. Perhaps I could offer the car up for research. They could tell what was picked up where by the depth it was buried on the surface of the car.

But I digress. Where was I? Ah yes, driving from Rimini to Ancona.

"I thought we were going to see the sea from here," Helen muttered.

"Well, according to the map, we're running alongside it."

"All I can see is the concrete walls of the motorway."

"Well, perhaps if we dropped down on to the little red road that runs beside the motorway."

"No fear."

We found the ferry port in Ancona in time to catch a 'Superfast' ferry that was leaving for Greece. Signs for the car ferry port were easy to spot as they showed an outline of a boat with the shape of a car within it and the words, 'Car Ferry', in English. However, they sometimes seemed to contradict each other and sometimes seemed to direct you the wrong way up a one-way street. Just as Helen's patience was beginning to run out, we arrived at the port. It was crammed with cars, coaches and lorries. Where do you go for tickets? Who do you ask? I parked in a place that said 'No Parking' in half a dozen languages. It's usually the way to get someone's attention. Sure enough, a man in uniform came to see us and remonstrated demonstrating that he had perfectly good English and couldn't play the 'No speak English' card.

"We want to get the ferry for Igoumenitsa."

"Then get in the ferry queue, please," he said as he pulled his hat off and ran his hand exasperatedly across his brow.

"Where is it?"

"There. There," he said pointing with his hat at a mass of untidily parked cars. It was hardly a queue. At least not in the British sense of the word.

"Where do we get the tickets?"

"In the ticket office of course!"

"Where is that?"

"You see the big building with the word TICKETS written on it in enormous letters. Do you know, I think it must be in there?"

Within ten minutes, we had tickets for the car ferry to Greece that would drop us at Igoumenitsa the following morning before continuing on its way to Patras near the Gulf of Corinth.

Igoumenitsa is the most northern port on the west coast of mainland Greece. Large ferries to and from Patras in the Gulf of Corinth and the Italian ports of Venice, Ancona, Brindisi and Bari dock in the large new harbour while an assortment of car ferries use the old town harbour to transport vehicles and foot passengers to and from the popular islands of Corfu and Paxos.

Boats and Brokers in Corfu

We arrived in Igoumenitsa about six thirty in the morning having slept where we could on the crowded ferry.

"We'll get a cabin next time," I told a dishevelled looking Helen.

"Too right," she croaked.

Once on shore, we stopped for a strong, dark cup of coffee at one of the tavernas facing the port from across the street. What to do next? After some deliberation, we got the first ferry to Corfu. Searching various websites, we had spotted a couple of possible boats that were laying in Corfu. There would be others in boatyards around Corfu Town and the large marina at Gouvia, which was on the east coast of Corfu to the north of Corfu town. In any case, a couple of days 'chilling' would not do us any harm after our headlong rush through France and Italy. European Championship? Pah. What had it got to do with Switzerland? What did they know about football?

The Corfu ferry was far more our style than the Superfast Ferries monster that had brought us from Ancona to Igoumentisa. The Superfast had been bright lights, waiters in bum freezer jackets, a la carte restaurants and a casino. It had been pleasant sitting on the top deck, at the stern, nursing a brandy in the dying hours of the evening, feeling the wind roughing my hair and watching the straight ferry wake disappear to a point. But the ferry to Corfu — great. No waiters tutting when you walked to the bar because you were cutting them out of the action. Just a surly half shaven general dogsbody who grunted at you when you said "Nescafe"? and barked "sugar-milk?" back at you.

The ferry crossing was one-and-a-half hours, or thereabouts, so we found ourselves gently entering the harbour under the Venetian ramparts of Corfu town as nine o'clock approached. The sun was beating down with that benevolent Greek morning warmth as we eased the Toyota out of the gates of the new port and into the hurly burly of traffic heading north along the coast out of Corfu town. A few hundred yards and we were outside a Corfu boatyard. We parked under a eucalyptus tree and wandered in. There was a 37 ft Jeanneau sporting a big 'for sale' notice and someone fussing over her. There was a smell of new paints and resins. The Jeaneau was the only boat we could immediately see that advertised the fact that it was for sale, so we explored further scrambling between the tightly packed boats in the yard trying not to trip over the beams, props, heavy chain and other boatyard impedimenta. There were many boats crammed into the relatively small yard, but no others that advertised the fact that they were for sale and looked like the sort of boat we were interested in. However, there was one that, while it was not adorned with a "for sale" notice, was shown as for sale on a website that we had looked at recently.

A dusty notice at the boat yard entrance had identified the yard as, among other things, brokers. There was one black building with none of the signs of modern brokerage that we are used to in the UK where the high-profile brokerages operate from glass-fronted offices furnished with modern desks and computers. This tar black building had no windows but inside the smell of hemp, resin, paint, and old sails suggested a general workshop though there was little evidence of work actually being done. A battered bench was strewn with boat and engine parts which in turn were strewn with dust. Wind surfers, plastic dinghies, sails and other oddments were hauled up into the rafters. The dust and detritus of ages was everywhere.

Boarded off in a corner was a small office inside which a man whom we had seen earlier walking about the marina was sat at a desk with a diary and a dusty, elderly computer. He introduced himself as Dimitri. I asked about boats for sale.

"Yes. What are you looking for?"

"Something in the range thirty-five to forty foot."

"How much?"

"Not too much — the exchange rate — you know..." I pointed downwards.

"Ah..." he smiled, gravely. "We have a very nice Jeanneau 38, but someone is interested. I think he bring money tomorrow. But... Until I have money…" he shrugged then continued. "There is also a Bavaria not quite so good…"

We opted to look at a Gibsea and the nearly sold Jeanneau. The Gibsea was OK but smelt. I opened up the companionway and stared at the engine. A Yanmar. I knew of them, but had not yet 'got intimate' with one. Diesel engines are a mystery to me, but I had with me the *RYA: Noddy's guide to diesel engines* so that was that sorted. A nasty substantial puddle of oily water lay under the engine. You might have expected that sort of thing to have been cleaned up when the owner had gone to the trouble and expense of hauling the boat up out of the water and putting it up for sale. 'Still', I mused, 'I suppose it suggests that nothing has been glossed over — what you see is what you get as they say.' What we saw was a very definitely lived in boat. Shelves full of well-thumbed books — fiction and non-fiction, sailing know-how alongside detective stories. There was a guitar in one corner together with a beginner's guide. The galley had seen plenty of use. There was a musty smell to the boat and mildew on the soft furnishings. Helen did not like it. You had to clamber up on the seating to get around the wheel. It only had one heads (toilet), and the boat smelt.

We looked at the Jeanneau, though it seemed certain that it had gone. Helen wanted to see inside and was moderately pleased with what she saw. We took contact details from Dimitri and left promising to phone up and check on the Jeanneau. What next? Well, we needed to get a phone card so we could get in touch with people without the mobile phone bills heading for the stratosphere.

We had left the car in a seriously rutted track beside the boatyard. There was a small newsstand nearby; a square hut that sold newspapers, tobacco, sweets and soft porn. A Greek man who had stood some distance from his razor when he had last shaved peered from the stygian darkness of a small hatchway in the middle of it all looking like a myopic rat peering out of a hole in a haystack. Most Greeks are cheery, accommodating and friendly. Some are not. Those that serve you from newsstands such as this are quite likely to be of the latter persuasion.

"Telephone card?"

"One euro? Two? Four? Ten?" he barked at me.

I opted for a four-euro card and handed him the change. He withheld the card and tapped the dish just inside his small opening. He wasn't going to take the money from my hand. I had to put it in the dish before I got the card. What did he think I was going to do? Grab hold of his hand, pull him through his impossible small hatchway and make off with his stock of German soft porn?

Armed with a phone card, we were now able to make contact with a broker in Lefkas to see what he had on his books. There was a payphone next to the black hole of Corfu from whence we had bought the card. However, the cars, coaches, taxis, busses, and heavy lorries racing past in Corfu's own version of the Le Mans precluded any attempt at a telephone conversation. We drove to Gouvia and phoned him from the relative seclusion and quiet that the large marina offered. I got the answer phone… "Mr McIntosh is away from his office. You can leave a message or call him on his mobile." I opted for the latter and got through but with such a noisy line that he advised, "I will be back in the office in fifteen minutes. Perhaps phone me on the landline then."

We went for a walk around Gouvia marina to see what was up for sale and saw a notice that pointed the way to a brokerage. We stopped at the office of a small Dutch yacht charter firm where a Danish girl asked us what we wanted.

"Are you the yacht brokers?"

"No, we just charter," and she was about to indicate where she thought the brokers might be when her Dutch boyfriend/husband caught her eye (he was dealing with someone else) and she said, "Hold on, Johan will talk to you." Although he operated a charter company, Johan had some boats for sale. "Some of them are on charter. I will look at the schedules. They will be on sale in September, but maybe some before then; I have one, Jade, she is on sale next week. She is a Bavaria Holiday, thirty-five foot."

"Not really interested in a thirty-five," said Helen.

"We might be," said I.

Johan looked from one of us to the other.

"I have seen Jade on the web. She looks good, but what we are after is a thirty-six to forty-foot boat," I explained.

"One foot is only that much," Johan gestured with his hands.

"I really want two heads. It doesn't happen on a thirty-five," Helen explained. We looked at the details nonetheless. The owners were at Plataria and leaving for Paxos, but would be back at Corfu next week.

"Will you be still here?" Johan asked us.

"Well, we have planned to head for Lefkas. We have some boats to look at there."

"I will get in touch with them. Perhaps they can rendezvous with you somewhere like Plataria… or Mourtos… you know Mourtos?"

"Also known as Sivota?"

"Yes. You have a telephone?"

"Yes, but just for texts. We will get a local mobile. And give you the number."

We talked on about pleasant things like holding tanks and the disposal of poo, and the up and coming regulations regarding the same. I pointed at a huge floating gin palace outside Gouvia.

"That's a big beggar."

"I believe it belongs to Murdoch, Rupert Murdoch, the media…"

"Oh. Do you think I should go over and complain about my Sky rental?"

"It's unlikely he'll be aboard," Johan replied.

"Ah… It was just a joke… a little joke."

"Tiny," Helen added unnecessarily.

When I phoned the Lefkas broker back at his office, I got a clear line and we were able to understand each other reasonably well. He took a brief of what I was after and looked up the boats we had pulled up on the web. He thought that they were still up for sale, but had to contact John Smith of Corfu who collaborated with him at the Corfu end. This was the same John who we had been in touch with and stood up last September. Stephen, the broker, said that he was leaving the next day, but would get his secretary to look up boats that seemed to fit our requirement so we could have some to look at when we arrived in Lefkas during his absence. He said he would text us — promised not to phone on our expensive UK mobiles — when he had some news regarding boats to look at in Corfu.

In Corfu Town, we equipped ourselves with a local pay-as-you-go mobile and changed some traveller's cheques for dosh. The man behind the counter of the bank looked at the traveller's cheques and said, "We have to charge you commission on this — you should do what the man before did." The man in question had come in with a carrier bag full of banknotes in some currency, changed it at the counter, and walked out with the bag full of euros: thousands upon thousands of euros going by the bulkiness of the bag. This led to a conversation about our requirement to get cash over here and our difficulties so far. He pooh-poohed the other banks we had made enquiries at and all their problems. "You can open an account here easy," he told us and then took us to see the manager who presented us with the same problems as we had experienced with other banks. We needed to show evidence of the fact that we were UK taxpayers — UK tax coding and evidence of who we were — passports, P45s etc. In fact, we steered clear of this bank in future dealings as they seemed to charge commission where others did not.

We went into a taverna near the marina that I had visited several years back and mulled over the situation so far while eating delicious squid cooked with herbs and tzaziki.

"I don't much like what we have seen so far," ventured Helen.

"The boats you mean? Early days yet."

"Perhaps we should get the ferry back to Igoumenitsa and head for Lefkas. There seems more choice…"

"Before we bugger off, why don't we phone up John and see what he has to show us?"

"Do you think he will talk to us after we stood him up last year?"

"I should think so — if there is a chance of a commission on a sale."

Regardless of Helen's apprehension, we spoke to John in the afternoon and tentatively arranged to meet him on the morrow to look at *Lullaby*; Helen hated the name. The meeting was timed for about 10.00 a.m. The rendezvous was a bit of a problem as he said he would pick us up from our rooms. We had none. We were phoning him from up in the hills where we hoped we might find cheap rooms in a village that was a bit off the beaten track. However, all we came across were relatively expensive apartments. We asked John for advice.

"There are loads of rooms in Kontokali — the village behind the marina at Gouvia. There is a so-called English pub, the Navigator, up the first road on your left as you leave the marina gates. Next door, there is a shop. They will sort you out."

We headed for the village and found rooms before we came across either the pub or the shop. The rooms took the form of an apartment in the back of a fairly new block in a large plot of land where the owner grew aubergines, cucumbers and onions. Our kitchen door opened on to a lemon tree full of ripe plump lemons. The main road running north from Corfu town along the east coast was also what our rooms looked on to. Ah well you can't have everything. The family who owned the place lived at the far end of the block to us, also facing the road.

That night, I dreamt about money and the impossibility of it all.

John phoned at nine thirty the next day, as arranged, and asked where he could pick us up. We identified a BMW dealer that faced us across the already busy main road. He picked us up a half hour later and took us back to the Corfu boat yard where he unlocked *Lullaby*, a Jeanneau 37. I immediately felt some affinity with the boat, but it was old and there would probably be problems to resolve. The instruments were the original fit and some looked as though they were near the end of their useful life. Most of them were unfamiliar models to me. Unless there were instruction manuals, it might be a struggle to calibrate and use some of them. The engine, a Yanmar, had a peculiar chamber topped in clear plastic where the seal seemed to leak so there was salt water corrosion on the sea cock immediately below. Not good. The chamber was a filter for the raw sea water that was used for cooling the engine. It trapped any intake of weed and other debris. It was a well-known filter but, according to John, there was a direct replacement from an alternative source that was less expensive and less troublesome.

Fendering around the edge of the sugar scoop stern was coming away and there had been a very amateur attempt made to restick it in place. That would have to be renewed or cleaned up and replaced properly. I had seen some boats where the manufacturer's fendering had been augmented by stouter stuff around the lower parts of the scoop. More protection but clumsy looking. Perhaps just avoid reversing into things? Inside there was water damage to varnish below the ports that were just above the waterline. Did they leak? That could be worrying when heeled I supposed. John said they had probably not been closed properly from time to time and said that when he had a Jeanneau of the same type and vintage he had locked them up to prevent people undoing them and setting to sea with them undone without realising it — especially possible in the fore cabin. The floorboards had been screwed down so I did not get a look at the bilges. There was some gel coat crazing in a few places and some tired looking ropes. Helen did not like the size of the saloon table and suggested cutting it down.

We indicated that we were in the boatyard yesterday and had looked at the other Jeanneau. John warned us darkly to be very careful of dealings with Dimitri; indeed, to treat any Greek circumspectly. We said that we were advised that a Greek lawyer was a necessary part of the transaction,

"What for? They are often in cahoots with the brokers — they are often related. They produce certificates that they say are clearances for this or that government regulation, or deregistration, and what do you know? They are written in Greek and for all you know could say 'This man is on the sex offenders register in the UK'!"

"There is something wrong with the Jeanneau you looked at too. Papers, people who have paid for vat exemption then found that is not what they have got…"

Horror story followed horror story… Tales of tears and dark dealings.

Searching Further South

The next day, we left Corfu on the eight o'clock ferry for Igoumenitsa and rendezvoused with Jade and her owners in Mourtos at about eleven o'clock. Jade was a 35 ft Bavaria that was well appointed and well looked after. Her owners, Karel and Nita, or possibly Rita, from Antwerp were very helpful and very accommodating. The boat had two water tanks, one head, no solar or wind power and three large batteries. Access to the steering gear was very good with a wide hatchway and plenty of room to get at the steering gear and all the plumbing that went through that area; exhaust, heater, water, etcetera, etcetera. They ran the fridge whenever they had the engine running, or were linked up to shore power and switched it off the rest of the time. Heating also worked from the engine, or from shore power. The documents he showed me included the log — neatly kept and largely in Flemish. He showed us all the documentation including the document that proved that his son had his permission to use it. Apparently, it is Greek law that you must be able to show that either the owner or someone who has his express permission to use the boat is on board — it could be UK law as well for all I know.

The prop was driven through a sail drive gear box. I had seen them, but had no direct experience of them. The domestic water system was fed from a small sealed pressurised chamber. A pressure switch activated the pump as the act of drawing water off reduced the pressure in the chamber. This is the more normal convention and probably a better arrangement than Tethera where the pump was switched on by micro switches in the taps that continually gave me problems.

We asked about the wintering of his new blue upholstery and soft furnishings — did they go musty and mildewy in the winter? Ours had done in Tethera until we installed a dehumidifier during the winter months — but there we were able to get down and empty the reservoir and check that a power failure had not put the timing out of sync. He shrugged his shoulders in response.

"Johan looks after it for us. He checks all is ventilated, he checks the batteries and will put them on charge to top them up periodically. We pay for the service."

He was paying about 3,000 euros per year for winter storage and care and attention. I wondered if it was antifouled as well by the yard for that price but didn't ask. We told them that we would think about it. The boat was good, but smaller than we had envisaged.

We decided to overnight in Mourtos. It was Saturday. No-one would be at the dealerships that we wanted to contact until the Monday. We found digs and ate at the Blue Coast — a taverna on the waterfront where Angie, the owner, greeted us with warmth recognising us from visits in recent years.

The Sunday dawned cloudy. We could have progressed on down the coast to Preveza and Lefkada, but we had decided to chill today. No driving a right-hand drive car on the wrong side of the road. No driving onto ferries and having Greek ferry hands shout and wave their arms incomprehensibly at you. No clambering onto boats and disagreeing violently about whether the boat suited us or not. No more phoning up UK banks and having to put up with multiple choice menus with your phone card credit reducing in front of your eyes. Can't wait till Monday till it all starts again!

We went down to the harbour as midday approached. A charter fleet that had arrived yesterday were still in. The bars were full. Bags were piled up at the end of the quay. It was obviously changeover day for the flotilla. We shared a beer at the Blue Coast. The wind was chopping the sea up a bit and it was blowing straight into the harbour stressing anchor lines — all the boats were moored stern or bows to the quay so that if their anchor did not have good holding there was a danger that the boat be blown on to the concrete of the quayside. We came back later in the afternoon and the crews were taking the charter boats off the harbour and around the corner to the shelter between two of the islands. There was a fleet of about ten or twelve boats so they had their work cut out. There was a hippie boat, all colours of the rainbow and a serious live-aboard look to it, and a forty-two-foot

Beneteau among a few other non-charter boats. They stayed put. More faith in the anchor holding or was it simply that the crew of the charter fleet had a lot of boats to deal with and wanted to organise things ahead of time in case the weather got worse. In either case, although I had been in there twice, I mentally marked Mourtos as a harbour to be used with caution. An enclosed harbour was being completed north of the town quay. According to Angie at the Blue Coast, it was meant to have been finished already. This, if intended for visiting yachtsmen, would afford a more comfortable overnight stay.

We ate at the Blue Coast in the evening over which enjoyable meal Helen informed me that we were running our budget pretty close.

"What budget is that, dear?"

"Well, I have worked out what we should try to live on out in Greece now we are on a pension."

"Oh dear."

"Well, the journey out here has cost us quite a bit what with toll roads, overnight stops, fuel, ferries…"

"OK. OK. I mean the journey out was going to cost money — we knew that."

"Well we should have come out by plane — it would have been much cheaper."

"We wouldn't have been able to bring all this stuff out with us."

"All the bits and bobs from Tethera? I don't know why you didn't sell them all in a boat jumble. Most of the boats that we have looked at seemed to have all the essentials."

"We haven't looked at many so far."

"We have on the web."

"People tell lies on the web… and, anyway, I am sort of attached to some of the stuff from Tethera."

"You hoard like a squirrel," Helen snorted.

Around Preveza and Lefkada

Refreshed from a relaxed Sunday we set off along the road to Preveza on the Monday morning. We drove to Plateria and were then humming south along a nice wide coast road each side spattered with wild flowers. Yellow broom, Oleander of various white red and pink hues, and thistles, tall and headed in luxurious purple. We overlooked long sandy beaches as we neared the Preveza end of the journey. As we emerged from the Preveza tunnel near midday, we used our pay-as-you-go Greek mobile to telephone the Lefkada broker's office. His secretary, Terri, was in an office which was located in Lefkas marina and she was going to be there until 2.00 p.m. so we were in plenty of time.

First, she tried to sell us Alex, but we told her that Alex was sold in April. We had communication with the owner, Nikos, in the winter during which he dropped his price but finally sold to another buyer before we could get a deal on Tethera. Terri, the secretary, seemed dumbstruck that the boat had gone. She insisted that as far as she was concerned, it was still for sale. We had to prompt her several times to phone and check up so we could progress beyond Alex. I could see Helen was hoping against hope that she really was still on the market. One got the impression that Terri was under the illusion that she was the only broker involved in the sale of Alex.

"Alex is still on our books — we have not been told of any sale — who is this Yiannis Drimo… uh whatever it was?"

"The person who came up when we found Alex on the web and the person Nikos told us to deal with after we had seen the boat."

"Yes, but who is he?" she asked beginning to sound as if she thought we were part of some subterfuge.

"Dunno. Based in Athens according to his emails. His firm is called A2Z Yachts I think."

"Who is A2Z Yachts?" Was the inevitable response.

This was now getting a bit tedious and I indicated that I knew little about them aside from what I had told her. "Why don't you use that computer in front of you and type A2Z Yachts into Google then you would know as much as us." She seemed uninterested in doing anything positive about it, but we were more interested in focussing her on our requirement rather than the double-dealings of brokers and vendors in the pleasure boating industry. We eventually got her around to discussing our wishes and she printed out the particulars of four boats after some confused debate between us all.

The particulars tended to be of boats that were on the big side for our requirement. Two of them were in the marina, but we would not be able to have a viewing until the next day. A third, a 38 ft Bavaria was located in a boatyard elsewhere and we would have to take up contact with a brokerage in Nidri to view it.

We walked out of the office with bundles of paper describing the boats and augmented with our scribbled notes on them.

"We could look at the two in the marina now," Helen suggested.

"I suppose… while we are here. We might be able to eliminate them from our enquiries as it were."

"That reminds me, have you done any more about that detective novel you started."

"No. Look there's G pontoon over there — I wonder why they don't use the Greek alphabet?"

"Why not?"

"Exactly."

"No, I mean, why haven't you done any more on the novel?"

"It's a mystery and it's getting too mysterious. I haven't a clue who dunnit."

"You're supposed to define that. Wow, what a beaut…" We had found the first of the two. It was a large Beneteau Oceanis with a deep green hull with matching green sail covers and bimini. It looked in very good nick and the external appearance suggested that it was probably sumptuously luxurious inside. But what a lot of boat.

"It's too big."

"It's only a forty-four. Four feet over the forty. That's only this much," Helen spread her arms to indicate a smallish four feet.

"Look, a big boat is fine, but it will cost us more."

"It's not that much more."

"I'm not talking about the price of the blasted boat. That's just the beginning. I'm talking about berthing, fuelling, sails, insurance — running costs, the bigger the boat the heavier the wallet that they think you're toting when you want something done or repaired."

"Tightwad."

"Yeah. Not only that, but the size and draft might start to limit the places that we can get into."

"Yeah… anything else?"

"It's French."

"Oh. OK. But you're still a tightwad, so what about this detective novel?" We had started to retrace our steps along G to look for the next boat which was, we had noted, on H.

"Well, it's complicated and my detective has ended up too thick to solve it."

"Nonsense. That sounds like realism. Sharon reckons it's great what you've written so far."

"Yeah and she's the problem." I stopped to admire a wooden gaff-rigged ketch in beautiful contrast to the modern Tupperware boats bobbing up and down in most of the rest of the marina.

"What are you looking at that for? It's not for sale. And we wouldn't have it if it was. Too much maintenance. And what do you mean Sharon is the problem?"

"Huh, have you been reading sailing magazines again? Sharon? She reckons that I have based some of the characters on the family. She says she's worked out which is you and which is Nicky. And it's not true but…"

"But what?"

"Oh, look, here's *Halcyon Days*. Hmm bit of a corny name, but nice boat." The second boat was a Moody and it looked more the ticket to me.

"It's got a centre cockpit with an aft cabin behind it. We agreed that we didn't want a centre cockpit."

"Did we? Why was that then?"

"Well, there's so much to scramble over if you come in stern to — it would make mooring up difficult."

"It's do-able. People do. It's just a matter of sorting out a procedure. Prepping for it properly and doing it, a bit of practice and it'll be fine." But the die was cast — Helen was not struck. We started back along the pontoon.

"Anyway, what's wrong with the name Halcyon Days — sounds nice to me."

"Oh, it's just that it's quite a common name for a boat."

"Unlike Tethera I suppose?"

"Now you come to mention it. Yes."

"What does halcyon mean anyway?"

"Kingfisher. It's Greek for kingfisher."

"Kingfisher days?"

"Yes. Traditionally, sightings of kingfishers were supposed to presage good days to come — good fishing, good weather, that sort of thing — but it has come to mean more a portent of the lazy hazy days of summer. I don't know — something like that anyway."

"If you don't know, why don't you just say that instead of waffling on? Anyway, so what if Sharon has worked out who is based on whom in your pesky novel? What does that matter?"

"Well, it means you're down for an untimely death and Nicky has an unhealthy interest in teenage boys."

Helen took a playful slap at me. It looked playful enough to cause minor injury so I dodged it and kicked over a bucket that a young Dutchman was using to buff up the gleaming white gelcoat of his Bavaria.

"*Aars,*" shouted the Dutchman.

"Jij ook."

"Oh, ik spijt me, ik dacht dat je Engels waren." (Oh, sorry, I thought you were English.)

"I am!"

"God Verdoemd, an Englishman who can speak Dutch."

"Oh, most of us can," I lied, resisting the temptation to confess that I had just exhausted my entire vocabulary of Dutch. "It's just that we are modest about our linguistic skills." With that, I turned on my heels and left before he could try out my claim.

"I'm surprised you can still speak Dutch after all these years." Helen was either impressed, or being sarcastic, so I grunted and refrained from remarking that all I had done was to respond 'you too' to his 'arsehole'. Not much in the way of linguistic skills there then. We returned to Terri and told her, 'Thanks, but no thanks', as regards the two boats that we had just looked at. Then we hit the road for Nidri.

A LIDL on the outskirts of Lefkada seemed to offer us the opportunity to lay in some cheap stores until we discovered that it was closed. Later it transpired that it was a bank holiday in Greece. We resumed our journey. The car hummed along the waterside road, the sea a sparkling Mediterranean blue to our left under a cloudless hot sky. I would have to find a canopy for the car to protect it from the privations of the UV end of the spectrum if we abandoned the car for a boat.

We stopped to look at the possibility of rooms near a small harbour of fishing boats between Lefkas and Nidri where the accommodation would overlook the blue sea. Idyllic but expensive.

Eventually, we found cheap rooms in the village of Vlicho beside a lagoon to the south of Nidri. All sorts of boats, including a couple of schooners, lay along the waterfront. Some were in the very early stages of a frighteningly ambitious project to bring a long extinct boat back to life.

We dumped some of our luggage in the rooms and drove back to the hurly burly of Nidri and the broker who we had to contact to check out the 38-foot Bavaria. We parked the car at the outskirts and walked to the familiar harbourside.

Nidri is a bustling resort in the summer. Yachts are moored along the waterside, along jetties to the south of the main harbour, and over the water in the inaptly named Tranquil Bay. How can it be tranquil with Nidri just across the water? Pebble beaches with sunbeds and parasols extend along the waterline to the north. Loud music emanates from a water sports pontoon where speedboats tow holiday makers around on inflatable bananas, inflatable rings and parascending rigs.

From the town, islands crowded with lush green conifers block the view out to the so-called Inland Sea and the nearby islands of Meganissi and Scorpios. The latter was, at the time, owned by the estate of Aristotle Onassis where he had built a house for Jackie Kennedy/Onassis. It has now been sold to a Russian oligarch. The little island of Meganissi illustrated that the Greeks can do irony (Mega — big, Nissos — island). Along the waterfront immediately in front of the town, various day trip boats were hawking their trade. Particularly eye catching is a boat built vaguely in the style of an old Greek trireme. It was named, of course, Odysseus. Its bearded captain, Gerassimos, was busy taking bookings "Papa Nick's cave, barbeque on the beach, Scorpio and Greek dancing on board," he shouted at us. We smiled. We had been on it a year or two back. The trip was all he promised. We had dived into clear blue waters in the cave, and barbecued on the beach. Heading for home, a large square red sail with a large eye in the centre had been unfurled. It looked down at us as we were plied with brandy and ouzo. The Greek dancing began with the captain leading and urging everyone to join in. He was nothing if not enthusiastic — and pretty athletic too — and I suspect he had taken a little light refreshment himself.

We walked along the waterfront and watched the Meganissi car ferry moving off across the glinting blue, yachts bowing gently in its wake. Across the water from Nidri, yachts lay at anchor in Tranquil Bay with the trees of Geni providing a variegated green back drop.

We had visited IBA at Nidri the previous September when Helen had spurred us into action on finding a boat. We recognised Sarah as we walked into their office and asked her about Sundowner, the 38-foot Bavaria. She fished a double-sided print-out from her files and put it in front of us.

"Yes, we've seen most of the details can we have a look at her?"

"Of course. How about five o'clock this afternoon?"

"Is that the earliest?" asked an impatient Helen.

"I'm afraid so."

We looked through the other boats on their books and then left taking print-outs of the particulars of a couple more. We returned to Vlicho to have a look around and generally spin out the day until our appointment with Sarah and Sundowner.

Sail Ionian, a charter firm that we knew of, seemed to have a presence in Vlicho. Half a dozen of their boats were moored up at the harbourside and another sat at anchor out in the lagoon. Two trailers with their logo on were parked nearby. One was open and showed comprehensive racks of tools and business-like workbenches. I spotted their office and went in for a chat about this and that — a bit of brain picking.

When the subject of *Sundowner* was broached, we were told, "Oh yes, she was one of ours. She is a good buy. She is in good nick. We put her to bed — winterised her — last September so it's all been done properly."

Now, both Terri in Lefkas and the broker in Nidri had told us it was privately owned — one careful owner, carefully and conscientiously maintained, VAT paid, etc. But now, it seemed that she was a charter boat.

Further into the conversation, it turned out that *Sundowner* had been privately owned. Sail Ionian managed and maintained it as part of their charter fleet. The owner got a couple of holidays a year and a little income from the arrangement, and he got his boat maintained. This is a common practice and the standard arrangement for their fleet. Although a charter boat may be seen as having had heavy usage, it will also have been maintained to a standard — the standard of the Sail Ionian boats that we could see seemed pretty high.

"At least any problems will have been put right to keep her earning money," I told Helen.

The balcony of the rooms we had found overlooked the back street through the village. We sat there and looked through the details on Sundowner. She had a holding tank, a plus as far as Helen was concerned, but the boat only had one head (toilet). This was a minus as far as she was concerned. A holding tank, for the uninitiated, holds your poo if you are in a place where it is forbidden, or simply socially unacceptable, to let it go. Then, you can let it go when you are in an area that is suitable. The fish then process it; they get caught by the local fishermen who sell them to the local tavernas, who cook fish suppers for the visiting yotties (yachtsmen and women). What goes around comes around as they say.

"Two heads," I had grumbled when Helen expressed her reservation about there being only one. "What do we want two of the damn things for? One for you and one for me? It seems a bit over the top to me."

"The family will be coming out."

"I expect they will be able to take turns with just the one toilet."

"Yes, but it will be more convenient. Besides, you are always saying holding tanks give problems — having two gives us a spare."

"Or double the problems," I pointed out.

Sundowner

At about four thirty the next day, we made our way to the boatyard and found Sundowner quite easily. The Sail Ionian logo picked her out. She stood on her keel shored up with a mixture of timber and metal props, wooden wedges and oil drums. From the ground, she looked fine apart from a patch of grey primer on the rudder. What was that about?

Sarah arrived, as promised, at five o'clock equipped with the keys to *Sundowner* and a ladder that she had rustled up from somewhere in the yard. We climbed aboard. Some of the running rigging looked a bit sad, but none needed any immediate attention. Some of the timber and plastic was in need of care and attention of some sort, but we were looking at a second-hand boat and this one looked generally pretty tidy — tidier than any we had seen so far.

It had a battened main and a drop bag. This was a plus for me. A lot of the boats we had looked at thus far had the popular alternative of in-mast furling. On the face of it offers a tidy solution and less control lines. However, it is known to jam up which is a bit embarrassing, dangerous even, when you are trying furl it in to reduce sail in a strong blow. I have been told that you should have no problems if it is furled in and out properly, but is everything done properly all of the time? Not in my experience, I have to confess. Besides, the sail has to be cut awfully flat with no roach to speak of, so it is a not such a good shape.

The propeller was mounted on a saildrive gearbox; neither a plus nor a minus, but an unknown as far as I was concerned. An instrument was marked 'GPS', though there was none mentioned on the inventory and I could see no GPS antenna — a mystery.

Helen was sold on it despite the fact it only had one head. We discussed it excitedly as we drove back to the rooms. Helen cooked up a spaghetti bolognese while I telephoned Sarah and made an offer that was quite a lot below the asking price. She said she would put it to the present owners the next day. We opened a bottle of wine with the spaghetti.

"It's a bit premature to celebrate… but —" I told Helen

"Any excuse will do," she finished the sentence off for me.

The following day, I woke early, even by my standards, with lots going on in my head. Unasked questions and the like.

What state would the boats batteries be in after a winter of inactivity? Had someone been charging them from time to time? What state would the holding tank be in? Had that had any attention prior to the boat being put to bed? I needed someone to take me through re-commissioning the engine as it had been 'winterised'. I needed someone to take me through the more obscure bits of the boat. What about the steering gear? I had only had tiller steering before which is elegantly simple compared with a wheel and its gearing, pulleys, belts, whatever. Did this cat's cradle of belts and wheels need routine maintenance? How did I access the steering gear that was in and directly under the wheel pedestal? I needed to check the condition of the anchor chains — and possibly mark them off in fathoms or metres. Why was there water in the engine bay? I had ascertained that it was not salt by tasting it — ugh. I had several things I wanted the surveyor to report on — best write a list!

I am hopeless when it comes to buying a boat, or a car or even a house. I either like it or I don't. If I don't, then I am not interested. If I do, then I am sort of initially blinded by love. I am enthralled by the thought of owning it and, although I ask questions, I invariably come away from the first viewing with more questions unasked than answered.

Where was the outboard for the tender? What about the hole where the sail drive comes through the hull? It's a bloody big hole compared to that of Tethera's prop shaft. Is there anything that we should check there? Again, I am used to the simple traditional propellor shaft — easy to understand. A straight drive shaft projects out from the boat through a tube with suitable seals and lubricated bearings to keep the water out and to enable it to turn with relative ease. No complicated things like gears en route, as it were. I needed to know about the maintenance, and general care and attention of the sail drive. I needed to itemise and thoroughly check the condition of the sails, bimini, main stack pack bag. I had not noticed the lazy jack lines that were mentioned in the specification. I had not really checked out the tender — an inflatable rubber dinghy that had presumably endured the TLC of five years' charter work.

I lay there, staring at the ceiling in the dark, until I could bear it no longer and got up to make lists and action plans. Oh, frabjous day. I got out the iPod that I had loaded up with my CDs and put it onto shuffle. A strange selection came out. Ben Webster and Roy Eldridge were followed by Joe Williams singing, 'Get into the kitchen and shake those pots and pans', then part of Stravinsky's Firebird suite. Then Jane Monheit seductively singing, 'If you were to go away', followed by two or three minutes of the Goons' International Christmas Pudding Plot. What the hell was that doing on my iPod? British "jazzers" Andy Sheppard, and Joe Harriot, vied with the Count, the Duke and the Bird.

Our offer was met with a counter-offer in the morning. I read my list of questions out to Sarah and she provided answers to most and promised to check out the others.

We arranged to go over the boat once more. There were no safety lines and there was no gas alarm fitted — I had remembered that correctly. We found the cockpit cushions that Helen was concerned about. I checked the lazyjack lines. They were gathered in at the mast and seemed fairly new.

Another phone conversation provided further clarifications. The outboard for the tender was in IBA's care. It had been serviced at the end of the last season. We would get it when the deal was done — ditto the documentation for instruments and equipment. I asked Sarah what the procedure would be if we did close the agreement. She told me about the sale agreement, the registration of the boat and the usual tedious necessities. I made an increase on my original offer. She said she would contact the owners and would be back to me later in the day or early tomorrow.

My mobile rang early the next morning. Sarah had an improved figure from the owners. I thought about it then agreed.

"Hells bells and buckets of blood," I shouted to Helen. "We've got a boat. *Sundowner* is ours!"

"Is that it?"

"Pretty much. There are still some questions to be answered and a survey to be done before we finally agree. But the owner has agreed and it is marked as SOLD subject to the normal stuff."

"How long will it take? When is it ours?"

"I don't know. We had better find a surveyor. Then there will be paperwork and money to organise. It will be at least a couple of weeks."

We had a list of surveyors and I set about phoning with not a great deal of luck, but eventually got through to one and asked about the survey and fees but held off committing myself until I had managed to contact some others.

The next day dawned gently enough, but rapidly it became very hot. The poor old Toyota needed a canopy if it was to stand in this all summer.

Peter Norton, the regular at my sister's pub in Suffolk, who had offered help when the idea of buying a boat in Greece was first floated, had supplied lists of telephone numbers for chandlers, doctors, sailmakers, brokers, boatyards and expats that did useful things. This last category listed sobriquets such as "Stainless Steel Phil" (fabricated things in stainless steel), "Second-hand Geoff" (ran an Aladdin's cave of second hand boat bits) and "Stiff Nipples" (don't ask).

We called on Second-hand Geoff to see if he had anything suitable. He produced a tarpaulin that looked as though it might do the trick. But we deferred a decision. Maybe we should get something that was more tailored to the car so that it had a better chance of staying in place in windy conditions. He mentioned, in passing, that the local garage sold an anti-diesel-bug preparation in bulk.

Yacht chandlers sell expensive remedies for the dreaded diesel bug, but it is probably best to buy and use them. The bug is an organism, or rather a collection of them, that will happily live in diesel providing there is a little water in there. Eventually, it — or what it leaves behind as it lives, eats, defecates, reproduces, parties and dies — will clog up the works and your happily chugging diesel engine will not be able to start one day. That can mean getting rid of all of your current fuel, cleaning the tank and fuel system, and changing the filters — the latter, possibly, quite frequently for a while.

Boat designers design boats so that exercises of this sort are difficult — well nigh impossible sometimes. A diesel tank in a boat may well be difficult to access and a real pain to clean. So it's probably best to buy and use a decent anti diesel-bug preparation despite the cost. However, Geoff's information that local garages stock it might indicate that the same consideration could apply to a diesel-engined car in these climes. It would not normally be a problem because a car is usually frequently used and the cycle of diesel through it is comparatively fast. However, our Toyota was going to stand around for weeks at a time and the temperature variations between day and night might encourage water condensation in the tank. I made a mental note to check this out with folks running diesel vehicles locally.

At nine o'clock, we went to see IBA and got their permission to go over the boat once more. We were presented with a contract to sign. I tried to read it, thoroughly, but could feel the mists closing in by the time I had got through the second of the seven pages of mind deadening legal speak.

Insurance would need to be in order by the time we took over the boat. I had been advised by others to "steer clear of Greek insurers — not very keen on paying out on a claim," I was informed. And there was me thinking that was a universal truth for insurance companies world-wide! Sarah said that she had never known any problem with the insurer that they use and there had been claims met satisfactorily. The denigration of Greek insurers might be just a typical expat spat I thought, so I asked her to get a quote.

I made a phone call to the surveyor that I had spoken to earlier and told him thanks but no thanks — this on the rather frivolous grounds that he sounded rather peremptory and brusque. I was hoping to lean on the surveyor for general advice and explanations, so he did not sound quite the ticket. He was the only one of the four surveyors that I had managed to make contact with yesterday. Later, however, another had called back having missed my call. He sounded far more helpful. I arranged to meet him a little after ten o'clock at one of the coffee bars in Lefkas marina.

We arrived at Lefkas marina around ten o'clock and strolled along the waterside in the sun admiring the modern and traditional yachts berthed along the pontoons. We were surrounded by the familiar clatter of rigging and the bustle of crews coming and going or just hanging out. A rigger was going aloft at the mast of a large dark-blue Beneteau with his buddy winching in the halyards that he was attached to as he bounced his way up to the masthead. A couple of boats had genoas unfurling and filling in the light breeze while the crew checked the large sails and the running rigging. Elsewhere, arrivals were loading bags onto a boat. Others, tanned by a week or two in the Mediterranean, were making their departure. Stores, in boxes often marked Heineken, Amstel or Famous Grouse were being put aboard.

We found the bar that had been nominated as a rendezvous easily enough. A sun tanned and fit looking man in his fifties sat at a table with a cup of coffee and some folders in front of him on the table. He looked comfortable in shorts and a blue polo shirt. A largish but neatly trimmed moustache flecked with grey sat on a sun-tanned face. He got up, proffered his hand and asked whether we would like coffee and pretty soon we were sat in the Mediterranean sun sipping coffee.

We heard a bit of his history. He had been the Mediterranean for quite a few years. He was in Spain through the '90s, but has been in the Ionic since around the turn of the century earning his living through yacht delivery and surveys. He apologised for not answering our initial call. "I was called out to look at a collision," he explained.

"Do you operate a boat rescue service as well as surveying?" I asked

"No, but if there is a problem like a collision or a grounding that involves a UK boat, the local port police or the coastguard usually ask a UK surveyor to do the report."

We talked about the survey. What was included and what was not. "The engine? Well, I'll look at it but I won't start it. Running up the engine on dry land doesn't prove much."

"Well it proves it starts I would have thought."

"Well, yes, but it really needs running up to working temperature and putting under load to prove anything out." He went on to explain that the cooling water intake is part of the 'leg', the saildrive mechanism, and that running it up on dry land requires a large tank of water supported under the boat so that the mechanism is immersed in water. There is an easier way, but I didn't interrupt — made a mental note to tackle him at the end then forgot all about it.

"One thing to remember with the sail drive," he continued. "Is that there is a seal where it goes through the hull."

"Well, thank God for that," I could not resist interrupting.

He grinned a 'we've got a smart arse here' sort of a grin and continued. "This seal takes the form of a date-stamped rubber ring that is guaranteed by the manufacturer for seven years."

"Oh, that's all right. The boat is only five years old," I told him.

"Ah, but the warranty is invalidated if the ring is exposed to diesel, oil and the like. It must be kept clean."

"Fat chance of that. Is it worth renewing the seal anyway so that I can start ownership with the seal into a known state?" I asked him.

Jack hesitated sucking his teeth and looking as though he had bad news to break.

"It involves splitting the engine from gearbox, and probably moving the engine forward to lift the gearbox and sail drive out so that you can get the old seal off and replace it. It can be quite an exercise," he proffered.

He was obviously trying to gauge whether I was one of those people for whom dismantling diesel engines and gearboxes and like things were fun, fun, fun. From his face, he had inferred correctly that I wasn't. On that basis, it sounded expensive — complicated. In terms of cost, it would mean a good day of the mechanic's time plus the cost of parts. I put the idea straight on the back burner and changed the subject.

We arranged to meet him for the survey at the boatyard on the following Tuesday. We sauntered off into the town to investigate the possibility of accessing the internet from the boat and like matters. A couple of mobile phone operators offered a modem that would plug into one of the laptop USB ports and enable us link up with the web wherever there was mobile phone coverage.

Base Camp Sivota

We had rented the rooms in Vlicho for a few days, only, and were finding them rather cramped. We had taken them when we were unsure how long we would be in the area. Barring surprises, we were now pretty committed to *Sundowner*, but it looked as though there would be a couple or so weeks before we could complete the deal. We decided to look for rooms with improved space and facilities while we went through the convolutions and paperwork of buying and legitimising Sundowner as a UK registered boat. She was currently Greek flagged. We left Vlicho and headed for nearby Sivota — a place that we were familiar with from years past.

Sivota is a sheltered bay on the south coast of Lefkada that sometimes gets a bit of a cross wind in the late afternoon, but the holding is generally fairly good and it is a popular anchorage.

Tall eucalyptus trees grow at the head of the harbour. Bougainvillea and vines of various sorts sprawl over balconies and trelliswork of the houses and restaurants beside the water. Gardens sport lemon trees, colourful hibiscus, roses and other blooms.

There are tavernas, bars and shops along the waterfront. The bars can be noisy and, because of the number of visiting boats anchoring in close proximity, the water in the harbour is a bit murky. However, if you swim out towards the entrance to the bay you are soon swimming in clear water.

The room that we found was large with cooking facilities, a fridge and a shower. It had a balcony from which we could watch the activity in the harbour, or watch the sun come up. This was to be our home while we tortuously worked our way through the formalities, the survey and the paperwork on the way to ownership. In our spare time, we could read, swim from one of the shingle beaches, or browse the shops, and relax from time-to-time in one of the bars and restaurants. Not a bad place to be while the machinations of buying the boat took place.

We heaved our bags up the few flights of stone steps in the hot sun past a large tree laden with lemons and installed ourselves in the rooms that would be our residence for the next two or three weeks. Having dumped our bags in the corner of the room, we then ransacked them for tea or coffee. I located a kettle and before long we adjourned to our newly acquired balcony with cups of tea in hand, and sat and watched the yotties arriving and mooring up. It looked as though it might be a noisy evening.

I struggled with my mobile to text home the news that we had put a deposit on our 'Bav 38', but there was no mobile signal so we walked up the road that led from Sivota bay to the main road in order to 'refresh' ourselves at the Sunset Taverna. We settled on a table overlooking the lagoon of silvered blue and the boats arriving to moor up for the evening, some choosing to anchor in the relative peace of the middle of the lagoon, others stern-to or bows-to along the harbour sides that ran around the lagoon between stone beaches. The taverna owner arrived as I was sending off the text messages.

"Parakalo?" He enquired.

"Thio mbira parakalo?" I trotted out smugly.

"Sorry?" He said with a puzzled frown.

"Oh, two beers please," I told him. I easily give up on my pathetic attempts to speak Greek — especially if it slows the delivery of a beer. I was looking forward to a large foaming glass of beer, – a large, light cold thirst-quenching beer, a beer so cold that you could write your name in the dewy condensation on the outside of the glass. This may seem a bit of a strange attitude for someone who argues that the best beer in the world is served flat and at armpit temperature, but that is back home and seems somehow inappropriate here in the Mediterranean sun.

"Mythos? Amstel? Heineken?"

"Amstel." I told him — it was the first alphabetically so that would do.

"I prefer Mythos," Helen told me. The taverna owner raised his eyebrows quizzically and looked at me.

"Ah, one Amstel; one Mythos," I corrected.

"Big or small?" he asked. Hell; when was I going to get this beer?

"Megalos."

"I don't want a big one," Helen chipped in.

"Jesus Christ, a chap… I'm going to die of thirst before the drinks arrive at this rate." The taverna owner grinned and raised his eyebrows at me again. "Big Amstel, small Mythos," I told him and added, "in bottles" in case he was going to delay things further by asking me whether I preferred draught or bottled.

"I thought you preferred draught?" Helen asked.

"That's in the UK. Here, by draught beer, they mean lagery stuff in a pressurised keg — bottled beer out of a big tin thing," I explained. "I just didn't want any more delays."

"Hmm, you should have had a small one really."

Oh dear. I had to head that conversation off from its familiar route. I put my mobile phone away and looked around. A cyclist clad in the obligatory black lycra shorts was wheeling his bike in and looking for somewhere to park it.

"There's a bike stand over there," I told him indicating a tree just behind our table. He grinned and wheeled it over to the tree then came over to us, dark stains of sweat blooming out from the armpits of his maroon tee shirt.

"Do you mind if I share your table?" he enquired. The accent suggested French as his native language, but I have been known to be wrong on these things. "I can keep my eye on my bike from here."

"I doubt you will have any problems here," I said.

"Better…'ow you say... safe than sorry. I'm Eric," he told us proffering a sweaty hand.

"Coo. Rather you than me, cycling up and down these hills in this heat. Where have you come from?" Helen asked after we had introduced ourselves to each other. She expected to be told 'Lefkas Town' or somewhere on the mainland nearby.

"Paris," Eric told us and grinned. "But today, Igoumenitsa." Then, he went on to describe how he had cycled down from Paris via Germany, Switzerland, Italy, Croatia, and Albania.

"I thought Albania didn't let outsiders in, or insiders out," I said.

"Ah… Is open nowadays… but is still strange. Nice people though."

"Have you got rooms?" Helen asked him.

"I am looking, but I think I look in Vassiliki."

"Where's your luggage?" Helen asked — always concerned about domestic practicalities.

"Luggage? Ah… there," he said pointing to a small pannier.

"You've come all the way from Paris with just that? You've hardly got a change of clothes."

"I don't need… this change of clothes."

"Oh dear," Helen moved pointedly upwind.

"Is all right," he said noticing Helen moving. "I wash each day. Is simple. Each night I take… ah… la douche."

"Shower."

"Yes, shower, and I wash my clothes while I shower. I hang them in the shower room… or somewhere. In morning, they are dry and ready for put on."

"Ah… Where do you go after Vassiliki?"

"I am going to Ithaca." It turned out that he visited Ithaca quite a few years back with his family. This time he wanted to investigate some of the historical and mythological sites and legends of the ancient island without the distractions that a family holiday imposes. He intended to soak up the peace and beauty of the island for a day or so before heading for Italy and thence Corsica where he was meeting up with his wife… and with his kids if they turned up. His daughter was studying medicine and had got a scholarship to go to Berlin for a year. His son, he told us, was pre-occupied with, "The usual, ah… obsessions of a twenty-year-old!"

His bike was a Peugeot. He had problems with tyres and one or two breakages on the way, but all sorted out with the use of his small tool kit, but then the gearing had broken in Greece. It was a type that I used to call derailleur, or some similar word, when I cycled years ago.

"I tried to mend it, but I needed a new part. Phew, I thought I was going to have to use the high gear for the rest of the trip. That would be, ah, how you say... a challenge here. I look in cycle shops, but when I say or write 'Peugeot' they shake their head or tell me motor car not cycle! I tell them 'Is not a bloody motor car. Is a bloody bike!' but they just shrug." Eric shrugged in a particularly Gallic way to demonstrate.

"So you are still having to go everywhere in high gear. People see a maroon blur and they think: Ah, there goes Eric — le mistral rouge."

He chuckled, "I wish this... but on some of these hills, I will be sweating and standing nearly still. But I... But, suddenly, I see the Peugeot sign in a cycle shop in Lefkas. I am excited and then I think 'what is the chance of them having this particular spare for this especial bike?' and I have the thoughts of the rest of my journey in high gear. But they had the spare, just the one, in the shop."

We concluded the day by driving down twisting roads to Mikros Gialos in the next bay to Sivota. The bay is known as Poros if you are looking at a road map or Ormos Roudas if you are looking at a chart. The route took us past the village of Poros in the hills overlooking the bay. We passed a charcoal burner watching the smoke drifting lazily up from his turf and earth-sealed kiln. Conifers and olive trees were alive with the sound of cicadas. In the bay, the waters were clear blue. We swam under the hot Mediterranean sun from a clean white pebble beach.

Scrumping Lemons

Below the rooms that we rented was a faded yellow bungalow set in a small garden. It was home to an old couple, George and Maria. They both spent a lot of their day sat outside in the shade laughing and chattering to passers by. George was a stoutish, weathered man who more often than not was wearing a waistcoat and a collarless shirt. She was a bag of bones by comparison and dressed always in dark brown and black. Both of them were of the same sort of vintage. They would call me over if they saw me pass and I had to exercise my woefully inadequate Greek.

I came out of the shower, cooled off after the heat of the day, and was looking forward to reading for a while in the shade of the awning over our balcony. I could hear Maria below shouting at someone and occasionally cackling with laughter. The lemon tree, the top of which was at our balcony level, was shaking and the cackling was becoming shrieks of laughter. I peered over the balcony and there was Maria up the tree, right up it, almost balcony level up it, picking lemons and throwing them down to her companion who was trying to catch them and mostly failing. Each failure gave vent to fresh shrieks of laughter from the pair of them and a growing number of bystanders.

How the infirm looking eighty plus year old got up there was a mystery. There was no ladder to be seen. She must have hopped onto the iron balustrade near the tree and swung herself up into the branches — a manoeuvre that would have taxed me. The octogenarian wonder woman was now entertaining the crowds. Her companion could have gone round with the hat. They could have bought lemons from the nearby shop with the proceeds. Lemons that, unlike those they were harvesting, would not have been damaged by being hurled at the hard-as-iron ground.

Undeterred, she shouted at her companion in Greek, "Cop this lot, Anna."

Anna retreated to a safe distance from the tree and Maria, from her position in the upper reaches, shook the tree vigorously causing gales of laughter from herself and all her admirers. It rained lemons, some of them over ripe and exploding on the hard ground.

The girl from the nearby shop came out and yelled at her in Greek "For goodness sake, Mother. Here I am in our shop trying to sell lemons to people and there you are showering them with lemons. Besides which, you should be ashamed of yourself at your age; climbing trees and showing the tourists your pants."

Maria put me in mind of our landlady on Crete a few years back. She was named Kaliroy, was as thin as a stick and bent over with age and arthritis and always dressed entirely in black.

While I was reading one afternoon, a commotion started up outside the room we had rented in Elounda. There was a lot of shouting and yelling going on in the street below. Surely, it was a major row, a riot even, but you could never be quite sure that it wasn't just an ordinary civil conversation — Greek style. I looked out of the window. Sure enough, Kaliroy was involved. She and an equally aged and bent gent were shouting at one another at the gateway to her house, fists were being shaken; the gesticulations were definitely war like.

Seeing me watching, she gave me a grin and pitched yet more vigorously into battle. Eventually, she picked up a shovel that lay by the gate and threatened him with it. It was enough for him. He fled — a geriatric old man crippled with arthritis sort of a headlong flight. She started pursuing him at a similar gait. It was rather like watching runners in slow motion without any of the grace of a natural athlete. The sight of the old boy hobbling down the street as fast as he could pursued by a witch waving a shovel was comical, but her neighbours across the road just looked over and shrugged. "Ah, it's our Kaliroy off on one again."

It turned out that the issue at stake was that she had let her goats eat his grass and he had arrived to register discontent with the situation.

Although Kaliroy appeared to be a rather a ferocious witch of a woman, she was generous too — as Greeks often are. On this occasion,

Johnnie Dangerous and his wife were travelling with us. He had showered prior to going out for something to eat and had sat in front of his room to wait for the rest of us to emerge clean and kitted out for the evening. He was intrigued to see a bunch of branches poking out of the doorway of the outhouse that Kaliroy sometimes disappeared into. His curiosity was roused. He looked inside to find Kaliroy stirring a huge pot over a wood-burning stove. The branches were the fuel for the stove, but rather than chop them into manageable lumps, she had stuck one end of each branch into the cooker and, presumably, as the branches burnt down, she fed them further in! John is of an enquiring disposition, probably a factor in his success as a business man. So he asked her what she was doing. She was cooking spinach and soon, despite his protests — we were shortly going out for a meal — he was sat behind a huge mound of spinach topped with fried eggs.

"You've got to help me out, Rob," he hissed when I appeared to tell him that we were ready to go out and eat. "I just looked into her shed to see what she was up to and she showed me she was cooking spinach and offered me some... and she wasn't taking no for an answer."

"Sounds like you've got yourself to blame," I told him unsympathetically.

"I told her I didn't want any, but she insisted... she put it in front of me and... well... I sort of didn't want to hurt her feelings."

"Ah, well, if you don't want to hurt her feelings you had better eat it all up."

"I don't even like the stuff, but she will be offended if I don't eat it! You like spinach, you have it."

"I'm going out to eat."

"So am I."

"You got yourself into it..." I told him uncharitably.

"A fine friend you've turned out to be."

I had nearly been caught out similarly myself on an earlier occasion, in nearby Aghia Nikolaos, where Helen and I had rooms we didn't particularly like. They were over a bus station but they were cheap. On the evening before our departure, I knocked on the landlady's door with the rent money as I wanted to get away to catch a ferry first thing the following morning. Her husband sat at a table in a string vest. He was a big man and looked like he had just done a hard day's work in an iron foundry! I gave her the money and remarked how nice her cooking smelt — as you do — realising too late that this was probably the wrong thing to say. She was cooking his tea — liver, pan fried in olive oil with onions and herbs.

"You must have some," she told me fetching down another plate.

"No. No. I couldn't," I told her. "We are just going out to eat... with some friends," I added lying.

"Yes. Just a little. I insist. I insist," she said ladling half the content of her massive pan on to the plate. Her husband just glowered at me and was obviously less than happy at the prospect of most of his supper heading my way. I didn't much like the way he was gripping his knife. The body language seemed to say, 'Touch my tea and you're a dead man, Sonny'. On this occasion, I got away without accepting their food and, hopefully, without offending them but it was a close-run thing.

In our experience, this sort of hospitality is quite the norm in Greece. We have visited Symi, a small island north of Rhodes, on more than one occasion. The first time that we stayed there, our landlady always greeted us on our return from a hard day at the beach by ushering us onto her balcony. There, she would sit us down to admire the view over the quaint little harbour pointing out a ferry or fishing boat that had just arrived or was about to depart then she would disappear into the kitchen and come out with steaming coffee and a plate of something to nibble.

We would sit on her veranda drink coffee, nibble and talk for an hour or so. There were few words of Greek, English and Italian that were mutually understood so the conversation was interesting. Pen and paper enabled us to sketch out some things like the family tree — she wanted to know about us, our family back home, and what we did back home. We were similarly informed about her, her family, their life. As usual, there was some surprise when the stilted conversation revealed how many grandchildren we had and that was in the days when it was logistically possible to take each one back a small present when we returned home — long gone now.

If she was out when we got back to the rooms, there was always a plateful of something covered with a lacy doyley — fish or squid her son had caught that day. On one such occasion, there was so much in the dish we didn't go out to eat that evening. On another, we crossed paths with her in the steep narrow streets of the town. She was carrying a bucket covered with a cloth. She proudly lifted one corner to show us snails she had gathered in the hills. Helen was mortified.

"I am not going to eat snails," she hissed as our landlady got out of earshot. "We are going off to eat now. No need to change."

"But it's early. It's barely five o'clock."

"First time I've known you to be a stickler for convention."

"Well, I'll feel uncomfortable if I haven't had a shower. I've got sand in between my bum cheeks."

"Ugh."

Celebration and Moonlight

Returning to the present on the island of Lefkada, we, near-owners of Sundowner, thought it would be nice to celebrate our near-ownership by eating out.

"Let's go up there tonight," I said pointing at a taverna that overlooked the bay from the main road. The cool early evening air was laden with the scent of herbs and pine, and laced with bird calls. "It will be a nice stroll and we've always driven past the place. It has a notice outside that says 'Best moonlight view of Sivota bay'. It's a fullish moon tonight. Perhaps we should try it."

We walked up the steep and winding road that led from the head of the bay up to the main south coast road of Lefkada. The heat that the tarmac road had absorbed during the long hot day was radiated back up at us. The calf-cracking walk and the heat from the tarmac soon had us drenched in sweat and quite seductively alluring to the trillions upon trillions of midges that seemed to have migrated to Sivota from all over Lefkada.

"You certainly know how to show a girl a good time!" panted Helen.

"Do you good. Work up an appetite," I gasped.

"If it doesn't kill me first."

We entered the restaurant sweating like pigs on heat, smelling much that way too I should think. I leaned against the wall mustering enough breath to communicate with the taverna owner — a Cliff Morgan look-alike.

"Ah, English," he enquired understandingly. "You have walked up from Sivota Bay?" He took our incoherent panting as assent. "Next time you want to eat at my restaurant, you phone me. I will send my limousine down for you."

"Thas good of you," I gasped.

"Is nothing. I would like you to live long enough to pay my bill," he explained with a grin.

"Limousine? What sort of limousine?" asked Helen.

"Is that one over there," he said grinning and pointing at a battered old Toyota Space Cruiser.

The food was good. The moonlit view over the lagoon that was Sivota bay was a classic Greek scene. A nearby owl called from time to time. Silver moonlight on a dark blue-black mirror of water mixed with glimmers of light reflected from the tavernas at the water's edge. The charcoal black shapes of the boats at anchor with pinpricks of anchor lights, some pretty unconventional, were just discernible in the middle of the bay.

The walk back down was more fun than the walk up, but a little trickier. Out in the open road the moon lit everything clearly, but the deep black shadows cast by trees concealed potholes and the odd rock or branch in the road. The few drivers that we came across seemed more concerned with dodging the potholes and other obstructions than they were with dodging us.

The next day, we did very little. There was little that we could do to progress the purchase of *Sundowner* for the next few days. I swam from the beach opposite our rooms fairly early in the morning then we idled time away watching boats come and go. During a walk around the area, we saw a massive fish at the harbour entry. It must have been eighteen inches to two feet long — it looked like a rather chunky barracuda, but without the barracuda's mean expression — so nothing like a barracuda really. I thought I would try snorkelling that area later.

I had tried to set up a Greek bank account with the international branch of my UK bank before we left Blighty. I thought it would be useful — fund transfer and all that. Late in the morning, I telephoned my contact at the Piraeus branch of my bank to find out why we had not received the promised documents yet. The conversation was agitated — he was probably frustrated with my poor Greek and his poor English. Eventually, he blurted out, "My manager, she will phone you." However, she never did. In her defence, she may have tried. Our newly acquired Greek mobile phone, on which she was supposed to make contact, had very erratic coverage in Sivota bay. When I phoned again, in the late afternoon, everyone seemed to have gone home. It would be fair to say that I was frustrated with my bank and their current byline of 'The world's local bank.'

We used a local internet facility at odd times during the day with mounting frustration. I was trying to contact the bank and find out whether we had an account in Greece or not. The connection was hopelessly slow. I managed to lock myself out of my email application. Helen couldn't get into the Hotmail account that she had set up and tried to set up a new one which refused her as soon as she tried to log in to it. I set up a Gmail account that seemed to work and mailed a few people with the enlightening information that we might look at this account from time to time, if we don't bollocks it up like we have all the others. Using the internet in the shop cost us five euros for two hours of mounting frustration. Hells bells — did we come to Greece to play with computers?

I swam in the late afternoon, this time from a small beach on the west side of the bay. I swam outside the line of moored fishing boats and tourist yachts at the south end of the harbour and then headed south along a rocky water line overhung with green shrubs and olive trees. It was more interesting than the east side. The water was clearer and the fish more abundant; although, I saw nothing that I had not seen before. Some deep red starfish, and orange fish like small goldfish in the caves and potholes, vast shoals of tiny fish and clouds of bright violet specks made by a shoal of very small fish each with a vivid violet patch that seemed luminescent. Every now and then, the water had a filmy quality and was cold — maybe fresh, cold water run-off from subterranean springs running into the salty seawater of the bay.

We ate in the evening at a taverna on the waterfront. It was one of two or three tavernas that had very a proactive attitude to getting punters in. The first taverna at the entry to the bay had a big waiter who had some sort of early warning punter radar. There would be no one in sight so you would think that you were safe, but then as you walked past, the Russian vine that festooned the front of his taverna would rustle as he leapt out in front of you. He would almost grab your lapels —difficult when my dinner suit was a T-shirt and shorts — and tell you all about the mouthwatering culinary delights he had on offer. Fresh fish from his own fishing boat, lamb and pork dishes baked in the oven, goat, fried zucchini, home-made spinach pie, etc., etc. When he saw that he was not going to drag you into his taverna straight away, he would thrust a card into your hand. I had about six of them by now and told him that if he ever ran short of them, I was building up quite a reserve for him.

At the next taverna, the punter arrester was a Michael Palin look-alike with a hesitant walk and a stiff neck. You could see him focus on a punter like a cat watching a mouse. He leans his body a little forward — straight and slightly canted forward like he was leaning into a bit of a breeze. Then he hesitates as though reconsidering the decision. Then as you thought, 'No, he's not going', he would be off after his prey. To me, he had the air of Michael Palin doing an impression of Norman Wisdom. He caught me and went through the menu: "Fresh fish from my own fishing boat over there, lamb, pork and goat dishes baked in the oven, fried zucchini, home-made spinach pie…" He persuaded us — or else we simply didn't feel like continuing our run of the gauntlet. We had an excellent meal right on the quayside. Right next to a Sailing Holidays charter boat 'Sinope' that was the first boat I had sailed in the Ionic.

The Spartan Warrior

We called in on *Sundowner* quite regularly while we waited for the completion of the deal. Officially, we were not yet allowed to do anything to the boat but we did odds and ends and checked up on things that we realised that we had not thought about during previous visits — how many mooring lines and fenders we had and so forth. As a result, I found myself buying a sponge and cleaning materials from the girl who ran the shop downstairs. I talked to her for some time because she wanted to talk. She was bored.

"What do you do in the winter?" I asked her.

"I go back to Athens with my husband. He works as cook. I get a job."

"You don't stay here then?"

"No! It's a village. Very boring in winter."

"What does the village do during the winter?"

"Sleep most of the time."

I dumped the cleaning materials in the car and then continued on around the bay and, at one of the restaurants near the head of the bay, Michael Palin called me over.

"Hi, Michael," I greeted him.

"Not Michael. Is Dino. Who is this Michael Palin everyone says I look like?"

"Oh, he's a very rich man."

"Oh. Is quite like me then," Dino chuckled.

"Were you busy last night?" I asked him. The bay had been as full as I have seen it.

"Yes, yes. Full. Full, upstairs. Full downstairs. Full, full. What you doing?"

"Oh, just walking around the harbour."

"Always walking around the harbour. Sometime you. Sometime your wife. Why not together? Your wife asleep?"

"No, not this time."

"Why, she not here then — enjoying the Greek sunshine?"

"She is ironing."

"Ironink?" I had to demonstrate pointing to his immaculately creased trousers and creaseless shirt and doing the ironing motion as inexpertly as I do the real thing. "Ah yes. Ironing. Very good. *Poli kala.* Very, ah very…"

"Character forming?" I offered.

"Ah, yes, perhaps that," he said looking puzzled. "What you do now? Back to join in this ironink?"

"No fear. No, I think I will go and find a cold beer."

"Sit, sit. I will get you beer. Mythos? Amstel? Heineken? Small? Large? Draught?"

He sat me out on the front table resisting my efforts to sit inside in the shade. Perhaps, I was meant to make the place look more inhabited and welcoming. He equipped me with a large frosted glass of draft beer.

"*Yammas*… Good health."

"Oh, and you too; how's business this year?" I asked him.

"*Etsi ki etsi,*" he replied rotating his widespread hand backwards and forwards in the universal indication of *so-so.* "Not so good this year."

"Maybe it will pick up next month."

"Maybe."

"What do you do in the winter?" I asked making what Sivotans do in *Himonas* my project for the day. "Stay here?"

"No, no. Not stay here. I go back to my farm in the Peloponnese. Not stay here it's, it's…"

"Boring?" I offered.

"Yes, boring. I am from the Peloponnese. The land of the Spartan warriors."

"So your great, great, great, great, etc., grandfather was a fearsome warrior?"

"Of course."

"And you are a restauranteur?"

"Ah, yes," he grinned.

"Bit of a comedown for a fearsome warrior isn't it?"

"Yes, yes, but better living than fearsome warrior these days."

Vassiliki and Winemaking

The next day dawned as the start of yet another hot day. We checked with the brokers. No progress. Nothing needed our attention. "We'll call you when there is," we were told. We decided to go to Vassiliki for the hell of it.

We had stayed there in September the previous year. We had then arrived late in the day and, as is sometimes the case when arriving late, we had difficulty finding signs for rooms in spite of the fact that the following day we would see them all over the place. We were beginning to panic when we came across a house just outside the town. 'Rent Rooms' it said at the gate. A lady — who turned out to be the landlady — was up on a balcony armed with mop and bucket.

"Dhomatia?"

"*Parakalo?*" she asked leaning over the balcony.

"Rooms. Have you rooms to rent?" I said resorting to English.

"Ah… We are closing… I am cleaning out rooms," she told us, but then a cash register moment struck. It dawned on her that she was turning away money and added, "How long for?"

"Oh, a couple of nights," I said.

She dithered so Helen interjected, "No three… maybe four."

"Ah… Maybe… Just for you… we keep a room open…"

"How much?" I asked.

"Three nights or four?"

"Can we see the rooms?" Helen sensibly wanted to delay the negotiation until we had seen what was on offer.

"Of course. Come up."

We secured a room at a reasonable price overlooking their back garden where an ancient looking wine press stood in the middle of the concrete back yard. They had their own vineyard and olive orchards and pressed their own grapes and olives — probably in the same press — to make their own olive oil and wine.

In the late afternoon, the man of the house would appear with his pick-up full of crates of grapes guarded by gangs of wasps. I helped press the grapes on a couple of evenings during our stay, walking slowly around the press holding the long metal bar that turned on a big screw forcing the pressing plate down onto the grapes — and the wasps. Helen had declined to help because of the wasps. They were everywhere, including in the grape juice.

We had been rewarded when we left with hugs and kisses and a two-litre plastic cola bottle full of a murky brown liquid. "Last year's wine… Country wine… Ready for drinking… Very good… Very good for health," we were told. I doubted the latter. We had driven to the beach beyond the harbour where I unscrewed the bottle top and asked Helen for beaker.

"You're not going to have a drink already? It's not yet 11 o'clock. You're a bloody alcoholic. I should have listened to my mother."

"No. I seriously don't think it's worth lugging this bloody big bottle about," I sniffed the content of the bottle. "Ugh, it smells like something you would clean the kitchen floor with." I cautiously tried a little. It was awful. I tipped the rest into the sea, screwed up the plastic bottle and pressed it into a nearby rubbish bin and we went for a swim.

Now we were back just over half a year later. Perhaps we would call in and say hello to our landlords, but maybe not. With typical Greek generosity, they would probably give us another bottle of wine and there were probably still fish belly up in the harbour — victims of our wine slick of the previous year.

We parked outside the town and walked in through the quaint main street taking advantage of every overhead canopy to keep out of the scorching sun. Helen browsed so I walked along a newish looking jetty and admired a cream painted steel yacht with classic styling and flying the Swiss flag. I spotted a place where the car would be shaded by eucalyptus trees near the pebble beaches beyond the harbour so I returned to the car which was stood in direct sunlight and was hot as an oven inside. Once I had re-parked the car, I decided that it was time for a little light refreshment. I collected Helen from her browsing and steered her towards a harbourside table where we ordered a plate of *kalamari*. When we had fortified ourselves with fried squid sprinkled with herbs and a dewy glass of cold white wine, we strolled along the jetty again looking at the few boats that were moored up, "This retirement, it's very exhausting," I said.

Helen looked at me quizzically, "Hmph. You were the one that was never going to retire."

"I was worried that we didn't have the funds in pension schemes and things to do this."

"Well, we're doing it."

"Yeah, but Greece has joined the Euro. Prices are going up. It's no longer as cheap here as it was. We'll be dipping into our savings to live."

"What else are they for?"

"Yes, but what happens when they run out?"

"We sell the house and buy a cheaper one."

"In Berkshire? There's no such thing as a cheap house in Berkshire. By the time the estate agent and the solicitor have helped themselves to a big dollop of our collateral, we'll find ourselves living in a miserable little hovel with not much change out of the exercise."

"We'll manage. We'll get jobs during the winter."

"Doing what?"

"Stacking shelves in Tesco, cleaning, anything."

I took another long sip from the glass of white wine savouring it and relishing the view of the harbour; the gentle breeze disturbing the leaves of the eucalyptus tree that shaded us from the intensity of the midday sun. "Ahh… I suppose… Another glass of wine?"

Helen looked at me coolly as I poured her a second glass from the small glass jug. "There, aren't you glad you've got me to organise you?" There was no answer to that so I didn't.

We watched *Katerina*, a Bavaria 38, come in and took her lines as she did so. She was crewed by a Jim and Cathy who invited us aboard for a coffee and a chat. It was their boat and they came out on it for a few weeks each year. They use a boatyard at Preveza where it is hauled out between times. We spoke of autohelm, web access, mosquito nets, how to get weather information, and cabbages and kings. Jim advised on the mobile connections that were available for web access, but I was aware that he was still at work and operating on a less restricted budget than I. He also advised on the different websites for weather forecasts. He favoured a site called Freemeteo, but he told us that the Greek site Poseidon was used by a lot of yotties.

We went on to swim from the pebble beach south of the ferry port. The water was clear and cool and my goggles' strap broke.

Sivota bay was pretty full by the time we got back and yet more boats were piling in looking for space. The sailing flotilla and bareboat charter operators turn boats around once a week. Departing holiday makers bring their boats in the night before, party the night away then get up early to be coached to the airport. The operators clean, prepare and possibly repair the boats. They have about four hours before the coaches return with the next set of holiday makers

Two charter firms were turning around in Sivota at that time. A large luxury coach was just pulling out as we arrived. The boats had fresh new crews of holiday makers scrambling over them and checking the local bars out. With a week or two of relaxed sailing in front of them, they were clearly and understandably excited. But one of the 'turned around' boats had a new crew who appeared to be neither fresh nor excited. He was asleep — completely crashed out — in the cockpit of one of the charter boats. We found out later that he and his bride, who was asleep in the boat's cabin, were married on the Saturday night in the UK. The wedding carried on until the small hours. They were both scooped up after about an hour's sleep and driven to Gatwick for the flight to Preveza. So they were now recovering.

We watched a Dutch flagged boat try to force its way into the smallest of gaps between the sleeping groom's boat and a small motor launch. He was jolted awake. The Dutchman asked him to free off his lines so that they could squeeze in. Helen's sympathies lay with the hung-over pair, "Look at that lot there. I've a good mind to go and tell them to anchor in the bay."

I looked anxiously at the Italians dozing and reading on their balconies to each side of us. "You're not going to shout at them from here?"

"I've a good mind to."

"Hell. You're not at the Mad Stad — Reading Football Club's Madjeski Stadium — shouting at the referee. We are sharing the balcony with holiday makers who have come for a relaxing holiday, not a demonstration of British football hooliganism!"

"Well, there's not room for that boat. That poor man was asleep. He fell onto the floor of the cockpit when they came in so fiercely."

"We're in the Med, dear. That's how they moor here. Some boats are quite happy to attempt a six-foot gap when their boat has twelve-foot beam. It's called Italian parking for some reason."

Around Lefkas Town

We had a rendezvous with the surveyor in the boatyard at ten thirty on Monday morning. He arrived shortly after eleven o'clock. He apologised and said that he had been called out to a boat which had got stuck in some shallows.

"Heavens, the last time we met you had just been called out," Helen exclaimed. "It sounds dangerous round here."

"No, no," he laughed. "First two for ages. It's fairly safe sailing round here."

"Well, what did you find when you got there?" she prompted.

"Extensive damage. Two ribs gone. It will need the mast out and rebuild."

"Where was it? How did it happen?" I asked.

"Lefkas channel — puzzlingly enough."

"It's a bouyed and dredged channel isn't it? He must have been trying hard."

"Not only that, it's silt, rather than rock — though there are rocks in places outside the main channel."

"And he managed to find one?"

"Yes. And he did the same thing last year. Now he has had two insurance claims for damage due to the same type of accident."

"So it's him who's responsible my ever-increasing insurance premiums?"

Jack started looking at the boat. I asked him about the rudder repair and drew his attention to the fact that the engine bay was flooded.

"The repair looks sound enough," he told us. "It looks as though the blade has got nicked and the repair looks good. Ask the vendors about the damage but, whatever incident caused it, the damage seems to have been minor so I doubt if it has stressed the stock and bearings. I will look at it in a bit more closely later."

I then pulled away to Lefkas town where I wanted to check out the possibilities for web access from the laptop whilst on the boat.

We quickly found a couple of internet service providers that seemed to provide the service we wanted — both at exactly the same price. The proprietor of the shop that we ended up using was a tallish man with crinkly black hair, flecked with grey and a serious face above a bushy but neat moustache. He was under siege behind his counter by a scrummage of customers waving their arms and shouting for his attention and disputing and occasionally paying bills. Queuing is not something that occurs naturally to the Greeks so we joined the scrum. When we finally got the attention we required, he gave us a brochure. It was written in Greek, but he underlined the deal that he reckoned would suit us best and that part of it seemed pretty self explicit.

We sat at one of the desks and scrutinised what he had pointed out to us. The deal seemed similar to that offered by the other ISP, but with the added inducement of unlimited upload and download until October — if we signed up before the end of the month.

"This suits us — where do we sign?"

"Two problems, sir: you need a Greek bank account and a Greek tax number."

"What on earth do we need that for?"

"You have to. To buy certain things, you have to have a Greek tax number and you need a Greek bank account for automatic pay for the service every month."

"OK, OK. How do we do it?"

"Well you go to the tax office next to a bar called the Kalma — do you know it — the Kalma?"

"No."

"Everybody knows the Kalma."

"Not me. Where is it?"

"Near the bridge."

"The swing bridge where the boats come through?"

"No the little bridge at the far end of the harbour."

"Uh, OK."

"OK, go to the tax office next to it and ask for a tax number."

"As easy as that?"

"Of course."

"Do they need anything?"

"Proof that you are you… I think your passport..."

"Are they open at the moment?"

"No. Closed. You go tomorrow morning."

Helpfully, he had written the Greek for "tax number" (or I think he had) on the brochure that we had picked up and tried to understand.

We walked into Lefkas and located the building so we would know where it was the following day. It was at the foot of the pedestrianised (except for motorists that thought different) street that was full of bars, shops and restaurants.

A lot of the shops seemed to be closing down for the afternoon siesta. We called in at a chandlery where the staff were clearly shutting up shop. The proprietor was moving the pavement stock back into the shop and glaring at us impatiently as we browsed. There was another chandlery further up the street. We walked to it avoiding the cars and mopeds that were pretending to be pedestrians. A young girl was serving behind the counter… well, not so much serving as talking on her mobile and avoiding eye contact with anyone who looked as if they might interrupt her conversation. We browsed while the girl talked and the proprietor pulled down blinds at the windows and wrapped a tarpaulin awning around his pavement display.

We walked up side streets where a lot of the houses had a fairly conventional foundation and ground floor, but the upper floor was built from wood to offer some resilience to the movement caused by earth tremors. The wood is clad with corrugated metal usually colourfully painted. We found a café up one of the narrow stone paved side streets and had spinach pie and *tzaziki* for lunch before returning to *Sundowner*.

Back at *Sundowner*, Jack had a couple of items of cheerless news to impart.

"All the batteries except the VHF battery are flat as pancakes," he told us. "And one of the seacocks is jammed open."

"Anything else?"

"Only minor stuff really. You could do with aligning the forward navigation lights a bit better. The wind speed instrument is showing wind speeds that appear to be low. I couldn't get the GPS to work. I'll have the report typed up and with you next week."

We drove into Lefkas the next day primarily to see if we could get this damn Greek tax number. We parked near the marina and walked towards the office, but a shop got my attention first.

It was a bit of a shambles of a shop that occupied a peculiar triangular room of a building that was built along the building line of two converging streets. It was triangular because it was where the streets converged at an angle. It was what was left over when all the sensible square bits of the building had been taken up as shops and offices.

The building was pretty run down; the triangular room, even more so. But it sold car stuff — leopard skin seat covers, sporty steering wheels and maybe, possibly, car covers?

I was concerned about the amount of UV the car was likely to get if we left it parked in the open for the rest of the summer. A standard square tarpaulin could be the answer and should be comparatively cheap. However, wind can tease at an apparently securely wrapped car and with my abilities at wrapping up parcels of this sort it might not be long before I return to find the car partially undressed with a tarpaulin sail flapping untidily in the wind. We probably need something a bit more tailored to the shape of the car.

We entered a dusty room crammed with stock of all sorts of shapes and sizes. A very rickety looking desk was covered in oddments of paper. Derelict junk occupied a fair bit of the available space. Squeezed in behind the desk was a large youth; large in every way — tall, broad, thick, rotund. He had a round face and a beard that straggled unevenly around the lower part of his face. He was busy on the telephone and sweating profusely in the heat, but looked up at me.

"*Nee?*"

In almost faultless English, I explained that I was looking for a car cover for a Toyota Avensis. He stood up looked puzzled and sat down again and shrugged his shoulders. We tried again. He picked up a car seat cover and looking at me enquiringly.

"*Nee?*"

"Ochi."

He put it down and picked up something else.

"*Nee?*" he enquired again.

"Ochi."

The charade was repeated a number of times until I saw some bundles on a shelf above his desk and, looking closely, saw the legend 'car cover'. I pointed and jumped up and down with great excitement. He looked where I was pointing, and an iridescent light of comprehension lit up his round sweating face. It was at this point that things became dangerous.

He tried but, even with his reach, could not get a grip on the bag and so hitching up his trousers that tended to head south every now and then, he put one massive foot on the ancient wooden swivel chair behind his desk and stepped up on to it. With both feet on it he began to rotate like a pirouetting ballet dancer in slow motion — but with little of the grace. He transferred one foot to the desk. It slipped on all the loose paper but just about held off further rotation. The desk creaked and bent alarmingly as he put all his weight on it. I selfishly withdrew from the immediate locale. I am no lightweight, but his weight landing on me might mean a serious visit to hospital or even the morgue. He grabbed hold of the shelf containing the bundle. Bits of plaster fell on and around his desk as the shelf all but came off the wall. However, precarious as the exercise was, he was able to collect the bundle and bring it down to me beaming all over his face.

The list of cars that this bundle was designed for included one of the smaller Toyotas. I pointed this out to him. The price was 170 euros; a bit stiff for a car cover. He looked up at the shelf and, despite my protestations, "Don't do it. It doesn't matter. I was only asking. Not going to buy," the Greek answer to Edmund Hillary started the ascent of the north face of his shop again. He had the bit between his teeth now. Wiping his dusty, sweaty hands on his dusty, sweaty T-shirt he set off a second time and this time handed me down two bundles. As before, the Avensis did not feature on the list of cars.

He looked puzzled now and phoned a friend. The number "*epta*" (7) was mentioned once or twice. This, I noticed, was the number on the one remaining bundle up on the shelf. He fetched it down. It had no mention of any type of Toyota in the list of cars for which it was tailor made and it was marked at 120 euros. It was the cheapest so far, but still a bit steep compared to Second-hand Geoff's tarpaulins. The dimensions printed on the package seemed to be about right.

"It doesn't say Avensis," I pointed out. The youth frowned.

"Is OK," he told me.

I felt guilty after all his mountaineering in the heat, but I wasn't about to buy a cover that might not fit at a price that didn't fit either. I muttered something about going off to measure the car and left for the tax office.

The Greek Tax Number

I had checked up with Sarah the previous day when the question of a Greek tax number was raised.

"Yes, you cannot buy certain things in Greece without one," she told us.

"What things?"

"Mobile phones, white goods."

"Why?"

"I don't know. It's the rules! But don't worry. Getting a Greek tax number is normal. I've got one."

"Yeah, but you work here so presumably pay Greek tax. I don't want to."

"You won't have to. It seems to be just a way of registering that you are all above board. A regular citizen drawing a salary, or a pension, and paying tax somewhere. A lot of expats have them. Folks with holiday homes need a tax number if they want to buy a fridge or a cooker. I know a number of yacht owners have them too."

The reassurance was OK, but I still felt apprehensive about it all as we nervously entered the building to which we had been directed.

"Are you sure we've come to the right place?" asked Helen.

"It must be the right one," I muttered to Helen looking at a number of official-looking notices that were fixed to the wall each side of the main entry.

"Can you tell what they say?" She asked me.

"Well, they have a government office air about them…"

"So that's a 'No' then?"

"Ahh… Yes… But that says Dhimos," I said pointing to a collection of Greek characters, 'as in 'democracy'…"

She yielded to my irrefutable proof that this was the tax office and we climbed the stone stairway to the second floor. We had been told the third floor but the Greeks, or at least some of them, call the ground floor the first floor. On what appeared to be the third floor, there were several doors to choose from and plenty of notices to read… If you were Greek.

"Can you read these notices?"

"Ahh… No, but let's try this door."

I apologised to the couple inside who seemed so interested in each other that I doubt they noticed the intrusion. We hit upon what appeared to be the correct place on the third try. The door opened into a lobby with offices off it behind glass screens.

A man sat behind a glass screen just inside the door. I showed him my bit of paper with Greek writing on it and said, "Tax number," very loudly and slowly hoping that the Greek writing that the Vodafone rep had written on his brochure did not say, "Give this hopeless English prat the run-around" or something worse. The man behind the counter read the writing and motioned to a couple of counters where about half a dozen people stood waiting and a youth was filling out a form.

We went over to the counter and stood and waited. Behind the counter, a couple of middle-aged women sat behind terminals talking and studiously avoiding eye contact with any of the punters on the customer side of the glass screen. Some of the people in what we perceived to be a straggly sort of queue moved away and stood somewhere else for a change of scene and others went through office doors and stood talking to officials. So it wasn't a queue, just a collection of people who happened to have drifted into a straggly sort of a line.

A wiry Greek, smoking a cheroot in flagrant disregard of the fading 'No Smoking' notices on the glass screens, arrived and appeared to be helping the youth with his form. I interrupted and said "Tax number," once again and waved my battered brochure with the writing on it at him. He looked at it and looked at me suspiciously then held his hand out and said, "Passport." I gave him Helen's and my passports. He looked at them, turned them over in his hands and opened them then looked at me and said, "Two?" incredulously.

"Yes. Two. Two tax numbers."

"Two," he repeated, laughing as if it were all a bit of a joke and turned to a bystander who had been watching it all with a bemused expression and repeated "Two!" and some more words including "*Anglika*" (English) and they both enjoyed the joke immensely. Then he waved the passports at me and said, "I make copy," and disappeared somewhere. He appeared about four minutes later with the copies and some forms only to engage someone else in conversation then disappear again. This time, he re-appeared behind a glass screen at the far side of the lobby and shouted, "English. Here."

We ambled over. "This is Nikos," our new friend said pointing at a sleepy looking youth sat at a desk sucking a pencil, "He will help you."

With Nikos' help we completed the form with all sorts of information; mother's name, father's name, mother's maiden name, country of origin, town of birth, date of birth, inside leg measurement, etc., etc. We were then instructed to return to the original counter and the wiry Greek appeared again from nowhere — like a white rabbit out of a conjuror's hat. He brusquely took our paperwork from us, marched into the office and thrust it at one of the two women sat behind computers who had been determinedly avoiding eye contact with possible customers. She continued to sit behind the computer and asked us questions across her crowded office in broken English.

We were outside the door of the office. The woman at the desk indicated that we should come to the counter and talk to her through a sort of cashier's window. She continued to sit behind her computer, so the conversation was difficult as it was carried out in stilted English across the conversations and comments in Greek of the other people in her office. Eventually, I disregarded what I took to be a 'Staff only' notice on the door and went in and sat beside her — after all, the 'No smoking' notices were being blatantly disregarded. The conversation was still tortuous but, eventually, with the help of another lady who appeared on the scene, it transpired that to complete the form we needed the name and tax number of a resident who would vouch for us. Here we had a problem.

"Do we have to bring this person to the office?"

"*Ochi*... Of course not."

"Does the person have to sign the document?"

"*Nee...* Of course. Just put name and tax number here." She put a pencil cross in a space on one of the two forms. We took the forms and promised them that we would be back on the morrow.

We returned to Lefkas the following day determined to get the tax number, a local bank account, and the wireless internet issues resolved. Sarah had obligingly written her details and tax number on both forms. At the tax office, we found the room that we had visited yesterday occupied by a woman whom we had not seen before. She was wearing the stern unyielding countenance of a civil servant who had just had her morning cup of tea and rich tea biscuit interrupted by visitors — us. We submitted our completed forms and stood back apprehensively, wondering what omission she was going to come up with. What further condition would have to be met. The woman checked it through, expressionlessly drew in her breath, then paused to add drama to her pronouncement as though she was about to announce which contestant had to leave the jungle or X-factor. Eventually, she told us to return at midday the following day.

We had two hours to kill so we wandered along the waterfront in the sunshine and found an internet café at the harbour front. We settled ourselves there with a coffee and a PC apiece. I composed an email home to bring them up-to-date with the painfully gained progress so far. Helen had composed an epic email and had saved it to the memory stick last night. She now proceeded to paste it into an email she composed on her email account and fed in the email addresses she had assembled in a text file. She then spent some time embellishing the email, but found to her disgust that for some reason she could only send off to half a dozen addresses at once. It took her several sessions to get her mail off to everyone she wanted to. She quite obviously has more friends than I.

It was back to business on the Monday. We attempted to communicate with the manager of our account in Piraeus. A tortuous exercise not helped by the fact that our mobile phone coverage in Sivota Bay was minimal and erratic. The calls frequently dropped out in the middle of a conversation. One of the points that the manageress wished to get over to me was that the Greek cheque book did not serve the same purpose as the cheque book from a UK bank. "You cannot pay bills with cheques in Greece," she told me. I never fathomed what the purpose of a Greek cheque book was for if it wasn't writing cheques. She also said that she could not forward the card and code to me. I had to go to Piraeus to collect it! This message had now taken a week to get across and had cost me God knows what in phone cards and pay-as-you-go telephone calls. The conversation went on for some time as she told me what could and could not be done. I eventually came to the conclusion that opening a Greek account with this particular bank was not worth the aggravation it seemed to be causing.

A Greek Bank Account

We were pleasantly surprised to find our tax certificates awaiting us back at the tax office, so it was straight to a local bank in Lefkas to open a bank account having worked out that bank-to-bank transfers would be cheaper than using ATMs to draw money from our UK account. Whether this bank was going to prove a wise choice was in the lap of the gods, but our experience with changing money and other transactions in the past was that this particular bank seemed to be more accommodating than many of the other banks — probably a shaky bit of logic.

We found the bank near an intersection in Lefkas where the pedestrian precinct emerged at a junction where traffic priority was unclear. The technique for pedestrians who wanted to cross was to wait until the road was blocked by interlocked traffic. This happened reasonably frequently and was accompanied by a shindig of shouting and car horns. As traffic movement hit zero, and the sound level maxed out, it became relatively safe to pick one's way across the junction squeezing between the interlocked cars, taxis, lorries, pick-ups and buses. Safely across, we walked through the large heavy green-painted doors of the bank into an oasis of air-conditioning and quiet.

There was a sort of a queue but, at the same time, the lady sat at a counter marked 'Exchange' seemed to have time on her hands.

"We want to open a bank account," I told her.

"Not me — him," she replied indicating a man in an office who was sat at a desk at the other end of the building. He was having an animated conversation on the phone accompanied with a lot of gesticulation. He wore an open-necked shirt from which peered quite a lot of curling black hair. I thought at first that he was a janitor or something because all the rest of the staff were neatly suited and booted, but he sported about 48-hours' worth of stubble and an exceeding lively head of hair due mainly to the fact that he was continually running his free hand through it. He raised his eyebrows enquiringly at me while continuing his conversation on the phone — quite obviously a master of multi-tasking.

"We want to open a bank account."

He turned his attention to the phone conversation and spoke rapidly in Greek and then he spoke again to us.

"I need some things from you first."

"What things?"

I could just about hear a voice demanding his attention on the phone. He responded to it by folding over a page of paper, holding it down and writing on it all with the same hand — the one that was not holding the telephone receiver — a neat trick I thought. He spoke rapidly into the telephone in Greek, and then turned his attention to me, "A tax number from Greece for one thing."

"I have it." I triumphantly pushed the four bits of paper (two for Helen and two for me) at him.

"Four tax number?"

"No two. One for me and one for my wife."

"Ah, joint account."

And then he was back to his phone conversation for a minute or so rifling through our four bits of paper while writing again on the folded over page in response to the voice in his ear. Eventually, he muttered in English, "And your passports."

"I have them," Helen produced and pushed the passports at him.

Some more phone conversation interspersed with examination of our passports. "What sort of account? Do you want cheque book?"

"I shouldn't think so, but we would like a card to be able to withdraw from an ATM."

He pulled a partly filled-in form from a heap of paper next to him, read it with a puzzled expression on his face then turned it over and started writing notes on the back. After more conversation on the phone, he put the thing down. He turned his full attention back to us and played his trump card.

"You need to be okayed by Greek citizen with tax code and address."

We gave him Sarah's details. These appeared to puzzle him so he handed the whole sorry mess over to the girl sat next to him. She asked some more questions, asked us to sign a couple of bits of paper and disappeared into some sort of inner sanctum with the various bits of paper.

"She is going to give us them back?" hissed Helen.

"I don't know. I hardly care. I'm losing the will to live."

"But she's got our passports and those flipping tax certificates that it has taken so much of our life to get."

Eventually, she returned with all our bits of paper. The inner sanctum had contained a scanner or a copier. She handed back our bits of paper placing them in an untidy pile in front of us and slapping a withdrawal book on top pointing out the account number and explaining the various other codes on the first page.

"Your card. Not here yet. Tomorrow, you pick them up."

Out in the sunshine, again, we picked our way down the main street where greengrocers and fruit shops had extended their territory over the pavement. Stalls with crates of burly looking oranges, red apples, shiny purple aubergines, courgettes, carrots, dandelion leaves — yes dandelion leaves — and spinach prevented progress along the pavement. Cars and motorbikes were parked and double parked between these so that we had to dice with the traffic on the road.

"Well, we've got a bank account — no problem — OK we are short on the card but, hey, that's to be expected. I didn't even think we would get an account in one visit," I told Helen in one of the short intervals where we were able to walk side-by-side along the street. "Let's get to the phone shop while our luck's in. They say good things happen in threes, don't they?"

"That's bad things."

"Just things?"

"No. Definitely bad things."

'Could we have three successes in one day?' I wondered, as we entered the mobile phone shop. The same man was still in siege behind the counter surrounded by customers and displays of mobile phones and accessories.

After waiting patiently for a while, and not appearing to move any further towards him, we tried the ploy that seemed to be the standard approach. We shouted at him regardless of whether he was serving other customers or on the phone, or frequently both. Our dialogue with him was interleaved with what sounded like arguments with other customers and conversations with the telephone that was permanently stuck to his ear. When he appeared to be talking to me, it was difficult to know whether it was me that he was addressing or the telephone or another customer who had just barged in front of me. It would have helped had I more than the flimsiest grasp of Greek.

At the start of each snatch of conversation, he would address me in Greek in the vain hope that I had mastered the language since the last time he spoke to me — a minute or so ago. He only resorted to English when it became apparent, I had not got a grip on Greek as yet. A pantomime with the treasured bits of paper that had our Greek tax numbers written on them ensued; this time, interleaved with other people's bits of paper that had Helen hissing at me to keep hold of our bits of paper for fear that our passports would be switched with somebody's phone bill that they were querying.

Once again, the passports and the Greek documents that proved — well, whatever they proved — were copied and mixed with more paperwork that he produced, filled out and got me to sign. Finally, it appeared that we had a contract but with the slight disadvantage that we had no device to plug into the laptop in order to link up to the net. He had run out of the things.

"I ordered yesterday. We will have by tomorrow I am 99% certain, but I will phone and let you know."

As we left the shop, uncertain as to whether we had won or lost that round, our Greek mobile came to life with a text message:

'Get the batteries to us and we will check them. Sarah.'

"Two 140 AH batteries manhandled down that ladder. No bloody thank you," I told Helen.

"Well, you had better reply then."

"Ah, let's get back home first."

"Our room in Sivota you mean?"

"Of course. I didn't mean I was heading back to Blighty — though, it's tempting right now."

"Victor bloody Meldrew," she retorted, referring to the character that epitomised the archetypal grumpy old man in the TV series, *One Foot in the Grave*.

We returned to the car and thence to Sivota where, just below our room, a battle-scarred flotilla lead boat was trying for an impossibly small space between two fishing boats that had similarly seen better days. I took the boats' lines while Helen disappeared into our room.

"Who's the Tigers supporter then?" Among the many pennants that were flying from the boat was a Leicester Tigers flag.

"Ah, that's our hostie."

The lead boat in a flotilla typically boasted a crew of three: the flotilla leader, an engineer and a hostess. The flotilla leader sets the destination for the day, briefs the flotilla each morning on where they are going, the course to steer, landmarks to look out for and hazards to avoid. The engineer is there to sort out boat problems in the flotilla as and when they occur. The hostess comes aboard each boat at each new overnight stop to brief the crew of the boat on where there are showers, shops, and shenanigans — and, of course, tavernas.

In some flotillas, the lead boats are festooned with flags identifying the nationalities of the crew members, bars or tavernas they favour, their predilections (such as the Tigers flag) and anything else they can lay their hands on. It enables the flotilla to pick them out as they hurtle by. Having got the flotilla away from the previous night's destination, and thus being the last to leave, they steam off to be first at the next port of call ready to 'park' the boats of the flotilla as they arrive. "Just parking attendants that's what we are," one of them had drawled at me in an antipodean accent.

Boatyards

I slept soundly and woke at about five o'clock on the morning that the surveyor had promised that his written report would be available. The sky was getting light. Pinpricks of light from the far shore were mixed with the riding lights of some of the boats that lay at anchor in the bay. There was a fairly loose interpretation of what constituted an anchor light. It is supposed to be a still (not flashing) white light, displayed so it is visible from all around the boat. It is normally located at the top of a mast as that is the location where it will be visible all round. There is an argument that lights, at something more like eye level, make more sense than one forty feet in the air where it possibly mixes with stars and hillside or otherwise high shore lights.

One boat had a flashing anchor light; two others had their steaming lights lit halfway up the mast and not visible aft. I suppose a white light is a white light. The absence of other navigation lights means that it must be an anchor light, except for the fact that it is not visible all round. One boat had correctly raised the round black shape during daylight and had a solar powered white light dangling from it. Again, it was a lone white light and probably served as an anchor light, but the problem with that arrangement, besides the question of all-round visibility was that the charge acquired during the hours of sunlight was now running low and the light was pretty dim. It had just about made it through the night.

Three quarters of an hour later, the water in the bay was a mirror. The sky had lightened further and heralded the arrival of the Mediterranean sun that was presently behind the hills across the bay. The waters of the bay were split between the black reflection of the olive-covered hillsides and the burnished silver of the lightening sky. A haze of ripples cut into both as did the reflections of boats at anchor, stately and still, save for the odd pennant shifting gently in the lightly moving morning air. Ah, well, today we have to sort out the batteries and perhaps do a bit of research on winter storage for the boat. We breakfasted as soon as Helen was up then got into the car and hit the road.

There was no news from the surveyor regarding the completion of his written report, which he had promised for today, so we phoned him as we drove through Nidri.

"Should be finished about lunchtime," he told us confidently.

We continued on along the coast road towards Lefkas Town with the twinkling blue water of the gulf between Lefkada and the mainland on our right. One or two sailing boats were heading north for the Lefkas canal that leads to Lefkas town and the swingbridge that opens on each hour to the open waters up the Greek coast to Paxos and Corfu. Some were headed south to the flat waters of the Inland Sea and the islands of Meganissi, Kalamos, Kastos, Ithaca, Keffalonia and others.

The road traffic was slow, but it was a pleasant drive until we were in the hustle and bustle of Lefkas town. We worked our way through the traffic in the town then over the swing bridge that joins Lefkada island to the mainland.

The swing bridge is a small car ferry that spans the water when stuck across it with both ramps down. Traffic can drive across it to cross the water. Once an hour, a hooter is sounded, the ramps are raised and the ferry is swung alongside the shore leaving enough space for boats to pass through in both directions. Why a ferry rather than a purpose-built swing bridge? I was told that the fact it is a ferry means that Lefkada is by definition an island and thus gets some concession from central government.

We buzzed along the coast past the Venetian fort that overlooks the sea to the north. A bridge over 'Cleopatra's Canal' marks the entry to the village of Aghios Nikolaos from Lefkas. The canal is, I was told, where Cleopatra hid her warships from the enemy prior to the battle of Aktio where the forces of Octavian, encamped in Preveza, defeated those of Antony and Cleopatra based across the water at Actium (Aktio). They must have been small warships. Viewed from the road, the canal looks for all the world like a small UK inland waterway.

We noted a petrol station with very cheap diesel at Aghia Nicholaos before turning left to the airport and Aktio which faces the busy town of Preveza across the entry to the Gulf of Amvrakikos. Aktio itself seemed rather out on a limb. There were no shops within walking distance. There was a bus stop out on the main road about twenty minutes' walk away. In theory, this would get you to Preveza in one direction and Lefkas in the other, but the buses were not very frequent. However, for the moment, we had a car so we checked out all three boatyards along the waterside facing Preveza.

There was quite a choice of places to winter the boats in and around Lefkas and Preveza. There was the marina at Lefkas and yard across the harbour from the town. Elsewhere on the island of Lefkada, there were yards between Vlicho and Nidri as well as yards and marinas around Aktio and Preveza. They varied quite a bit. The hard standing could be on Spartan concrete in one and hard ground among oleander trees and wild mint and other herbs in another. It was not unusual to come across cows or donkeys and goats browsing the grass in the yard. In one, the cows were a bone of contention. There was a running battle between the yard owner and the farmer, "Keep your cows out of my yard."

"No. My family has always grazed cows here. My grandfather did, and his great grandfather and as far back as records go…"

The yard owner kept dogs to keep the cows away from the yard. The farmer laid poison for the dogs.

We ended up at Aktio Marina, one of the boatyards facing Preveza on the Aktio shoreline. The owner, Gianni, was dressed in shorts and a yellow T-shirt. His long grey hair was tied back and a greying beard framed what seemed to be a permanent smile. In spite of the fact that we were not yet the owners, we jumped the gun and told him that we had a 38-foot Bavaria to bring in either in September or October. He explained the rates: 180 euros a month for hard standing for the first 7 months then 90 euros per month for any months over that in the rest of the year. The lift out and pressure wash at the end of the season and the lift back at the start of the next was 330 euros.

While Sundowner was in the yard we could live aboard while we prepared her for the winter or re-commissioned her in the spring. Alternatively, he had some rooms that could be rented. The boat would have access to water and electricity, and we to showers and washing machines. If we stayed on the boat in the yard it was two euros per day for the water and electricity and showers. The two washing machines were metered and we were to note down meter readings in a book when we used them.

He also offered a daily run into Preveza so if you didn't have a car you could do some shopping. The car left about ten o'clock in the morning and returned about midday. If all you wanted was bread and milk, you could order it and they would pick it up for you. The yard was more isolated than the yards at Preveza, Lefkas, Nidri and Vlicho. However, a fifteen-minute walk would get you to a bus stop for the Preveza or Lefkas bus that ran four or five times a day.

We paid 150 euros to secure our place. It was more expensive than the traditional boatyards, such as the one that Sundowner was presently in, but less expensive than some of the others that we had considered. Gianni also seemed to have a "can do" attitude that was lacking in some of the yards and marinas that we had investigated. The steel props around each boat in the yard were attached to a frame of rolled steel joists on the ground and cross braced to the frame to support the boat in a much more secure looking manner than the assortment of oil drums and baulks of timber that we usually encountered in yards in the UK and Greece.

We stopped at the village of Aghia Nicholaos on the way back and filled up with cheap diesel from the garage that seemed to offer the cheapest in the area then made our way back to Lefkas town. We drove along the waterfront where yachts lined the quayside and, at the end of the town quay, parked in a plot of stony ground between the town and the marina wincing as the aging Toyota hobbled the cobbles and stirred up clouds of hot dust.

Our first port of call was the mobile phone shop. "Sorry — modem is not here today. Tomorrow for sure," he told us repeating word for word what he had told us yesterday. I took the laptop back to the car while Helen waited in the shade. I had brought the laptop along as I intended to plug in the modem and run it up in the shop so if it wasn't as 'plug and play' as he claimed, he could get it up and running for me before I signed on the dotted line.

As I got back to the car, Helen hailed me from down the street. She had noticed a little tailor's shop along the street.

"I'm going to see if I can get my handbag repaired," she said as she dived into the back of the car and burrowed among plastic bags, holdalls, tins and tosh to retrieve the bag. She had bought it, a little black knitted number, in Greece a couple or so years back. It was her lightweight version for holiday essentials only — she used it to 'decant' the bare essentials from her workaday bag that normally contained everything including the kitchen sink and was thus a bit heavy to tote about if she was 'travelling light'. One end of the carrying strap had come loose in Corfu.

We took it into the little shop. The single deserted room had a desk to one side faced by a couple of black vinyl covered seats that had sagged under the stress of years of parked bums. At the back of the small room were racks of trousers, skirts and jackets that were either waiting for repair or had been repaired. Pushed into the racks in the corner, so it was almost overhung with garments, was an old Singer sewing machine just like the one that my mother used to spend a lot of time preventing us from repairing sails on many years ago. It looked as though it had seen years of service.

The room was empty, but a door behind the desk was slightly ajar and you could see through into a living room. I went to the door and gently shouted "Hello". It should have been "*Yassoo,*" but there you go. There was some movement and then a pause like someone had stirred then gone back to sleep. We waited for what seemed to be a minute then a chair scraped back and there were a few shuffling steps. A frail and pale old man appeared. He was thin, emaciated even. Helen showed him the bag and indicated what needed doing and we tried to converse with him.

We told each other it was hot (*zestig*). He said something about the traffic and how busy it was these days (I think). He selected some black thread from a cardboard box of all sorts of tailor's bits and bobs beside the machine, and proceeded to thread up the machine in a measured manner that suggested that we would be a while in his shop. No matter, but I thought I would go and try to locate the post office while Helen was waiting.

I strolled around the local streets and, by the time I returned, Helen was trying to pay for the repair, but he was having none of it. He had repaired the broken end neatly and effectively and, furthermore, he had deemed it necessary to reinforce the intact end. He refused to take any money for the repair. We felt inadequate as we said thank you very much in a jumble of English and bad Greek.

Jack phoned up late afternoon when we were back in Sivota. The long-awaited report was now ready. We collected it the next day but there were no surprises. The batteries seemed to be the only immediate expense we had on our hands.

The modem (dongle) that would get me internet access on my laptop finally arrived in the shop on the Saturday. I once again took in the laptop to prove it out. It "plugged and played" successfully apart from the fact that we were unable to pick up a signal.

"The circuit may take an hour to start," the shopkeeper explained.

"So we have to wait an hour to prove it in the shop?"

"Maybe… But even then, it may not work in the shop. The signal is weak — sometimes none."

"I would have thought that you would have some means of demonstrating it."

"The signal is weak — sometimes none," the shopkeeper re-iterated.

"How do we know it will pick up the signal where there is better coverage?"

"It will... If it doesn't bring it back."

"And wait another week for a replacement."

"*Nee* — Yes."

"Oh great…" Helen ushered me out of the shop.

I plugged the dongle into one of the laptop USB ports when we got back to our room in Sivota. It successfully picked up a network, but it was slow... oh so slow. Helen used the internet café in frustration with the slowness of our device, but the connection at the internet café was no better.

I was up early on the Sunday and took the laptop and modem up to the Full Moon taverna that overlooks Sivota bay. I set up the laptop on one of the tables as the sun rose above the hills. I had previously used the Greek mobile here and found there to be a relatively good signal and, as both mobile and modem were on the same network, I anticipated a better internet connection for the laptop. It worked, but was not a terrific lot faster. The popup that announced the connection on the laptop told me that I had a '2G' connection. The modem was 3G compatible according to the bumf. I had been told that the network in Lefkada was in the process of being upgraded to 3G through the year. The upgrade had obviously not yet reached this part, if indeed it had reached any part, of Lefkada.

I rattled off an email to Andreas, my pontoon buddy in Gosport and advisor on things Greek:

'Hi Andy

Thanks for your advice on the use of the word "scata". It puts a whole new meaning on "We plough the fields and scatter". I now understand the derivation of the word scatological but I didn't realise the use of the word had quite the impact you describe. I will follow your advice and will be careful in my use of it. As you so rightly observe, I don't want to be involved in stand-up fist fights at my stage of life. For the same reason I won't use the term mallaka or mollocker or however you spell it. I didn't realise the meaning when I used it last. I thought it was a friendly greeting. I thought the chap looked surprised. Now you have defined it for me I shan't use it again, unless the Greek that I'm addressing really is a football referee.

All the best

Captain Pugwash'.

As it was a Sunday, and there was not going to be any progress on any part of the Sundowner front, we decided to go for a spin. We headed west along the main Nidri to Vassiliki road and took a left turn at Kondarena. The road surface turned from tarmac to concrete road and took us between fields where we saw the occasional dark, black donkey sheltering in the dark black shadow of a tree, safe from the glare of the midday sun.

The road eventually opened up into a bay with a shingle beach and, set back from the waterfront, a small taverna and bar. We stopped and had a plate of small fish (*gavros*) and some roasted vegetables (*briam*) then walked along the stone road that led east out of the bay. We found a small unpopulated bay about a ten-minute walk away and so fetched the car with our gear in it and swam in the bay for the afternoon. The road was not bad, but was the worst that we had taken our ageing Toyota on thus far. The car was covered in dust and the grisly remains of insects from the UK, France, Italy and Greece all glued on by their own blood and baked in the sun. I would not get away without washing it for long.

Once the weekend had finished, I got on to Sarah again. She told me that she was still trying to get in touch with the current owners of Sundowner. She phoned back later in the day and told us that the owners were going to be in Sivota on their new boat on Wednesday night and she was going to pick them up on Thursday morning. We were to pack our passports and follow her car so that we could both sign contracts and have them witnessed by some legal beagle in Vlicho. So we had a couple of days before the next step in the process.

In fact, we pretty much made almost daily visits to Sarah with requests and questions all of which she bore with patience and good nature. At one stage, she produced the manuals that we were to inherit. The good news was that every bit of equipment that seemed to require documents had them. The bad news was that some of them were in Italian. No matter — I would have to shake myself out of my current torpor and get to grips with the language!

Solar Panels and an email Home

While we were living in Sivota waiting for the successful completion of our purchase of the boat, Peter — our adviser on cruising the Ionic and whom we had not yet met — texted us to let us know that he was on board his boat, Ventus A, and was coming in to Sivota.

We took their lines when they came in and, once they were shipshape and secure, repaired to the Taverna Delphini which was Peter's favoured watering hole in this bay. He and Annie asked how everything was going so we brought them up-to-date.

"A Sail Ionian boat?" Peter asked drawing deeply from his beer and wiping white froth from his white beard. "They always seem to be in good nick. Are you happy with it?"

"Yes. It seems just the job. But there are a few things I want to do."

"There will be. Do like everyone else. Make a list and watch it grow."

"Oh, I have started."

"What's top of it?"

"Probably solar panels to keep the batteries topped up."

"What sort are you going to have?"

"Don't know at the moment. I see all sorts: moveable arrays that you tie on to whatever is convenient, flexible arrays that can be stuck to the deck and will apparently stand up to you dancing all over them. But I rather favour the conventional panels on some sort of stern gantry over the cockpit."

"Ah, well, Ad is the bloke to go to for the panels. He is a Dutch guy with a marine electronics place in Lefkas. You will need a frame to mount it on. Stainless... that is Phil did an 'A frame' for us so they could be mounted above the cockpit and he did a bloody good job of it... but he is in demand."

"So book early?"

"Yes, and keep reminding him. He gets all sorts call in on him with small repairs or emergencies. Second-hand Geoff wanted something made up and Phil told him that he was a bit tied up at the time, so Geoff said it didn't matter, it wasn't urgent and expected to have to wait about a month or two — in the end it was more years than months!"

We finally exchanged contracts with the previous owners of Sundowner on a very hot Thursday in July. This was done in the presence of some sort of official in offices above what appeared to be a school in Vlicho. Signatures were countersigned and stamped. Sundowner was still not technically ours, but we were scheduled to take possession in a few days so we felt that we could surely now be permitted to carry out some work on her — such as the awful job of rubbing down and renewing the antifouling. Responses to our request to do so had been cautiously ambivalent, so we took them as a yes and booked a launch date. We celebrated that evening and did some work the next day in what was turning out to be an exceptionally hot July. At the end of the day, after I had showered off the sweat and grime from the day in the boatyard, I sent a long email home:

'We have all but bought the boat, Sundowner, a 38 ft Bavaria. The money is winging its way lethargically between my account and that of the current owner whom I met for the first time today. I have insured the boat — though as yet, I have no proof of that and have to fill in a form that they will send either to our address in the UK, or to Aktio boatyard in Preveza or else a post office in Nidri (I forget what I told them — so that should work like clockwork). I have registered the boat on the SSR (UK Small Ships Register) — though as yet I have slender proof of that. I have completed the first stage in getting an up to date vhf licence for the boat — I have applied for a login at the site that will enable me to fill in forms online after which they will send me something in the post that will probably be sent to my UK address or one of the other places previously mentioned. So that's that pretty well sorted. Later this week I have to present myself at the offices of the Lefkas port police complete with my passport, my late father's profession, my late mother's maiden name, and my inside leg measurement. All this to get a "Dekpa" which is a 6-page A3 book that apparently must be presented to and stamped by the port police once a month or so.

Sundowner is scheduled for launch next Wednesday. This is going to be a bit of a thrill as in this boatyard they do a sledge launch. It is exactly the way they launched boats in ancient Greece except the power was then probably provided by slaves and donkeys. Today they have a tractor'.

Paperwork, Paperwork

A phone call from Sarah, who was competently leading us through the tortuous paper chase of the transfer, informed us that there was more paperwork that we had to complete after the exchange of contracts. "Could you meet me at the IBA office in Nidri at nine thirty on Friday?"

"What for?"

"It's to register the transfer of ownership. Remember, I told you when we exchanged contracts?"

"Ah, yes," I lied. "What does it involve? What do you need us to bring?"

Sarah patiently explained that she was going to take us to a local office and they would endorse four bits of paper that declared that the boat was de-registered from the current ownership. These bits of paper then had to go to someone in Corfu, who looked after this sort of thing for IBA, so he could de-register the current ownership and register Helen and myself instead. Eventually, we would get one of the bits of paper back to add to the tome of ships papers that we were accumulating. The other three bits would presumably be shared between the previous owners, any other interested parties and some grey metal government department filing cabinet.

"I don't know what commission IBA gets on the sale, but they do seem to earn it," I told Helen as I put the phone down. Thus, it was that on the morning of Friday July 4th we got up early, checked the state of the batteries that were being charged up on Sundowner (not too promising) and then met Sarah in Nidri. She took us to an office that overlooked the waterfront.

We were ushered into a small first floor office. Three uniformed port police sat behind paper-littered desks with small stands of rubber stamps and other office impedimenta scattered about them. Leaning against a wall and talking to one of the uniformed desk wallahs was an un-uniformed man — undercover man no doubt.

"*Oriste?*" The uniformed man at the desk nearest the door sprang to life. Sarah explained that she wanted these forms endorsed so she could send them off to the person who deals with that sort of thing for IBA. He raised his eyebrows and held out his hand for the forms. He examined them one by one, read each carefully and satisfied himself that they were indeed all exactly the same form.

He turned them over and established that each one was completely blank on the other side. This turned out to be a very good thing too. The form was covered in printing, writing and, if I remember correctly, endorsing stamps leaving him no room for all the work that he had to do. He signalled that he would have to put his endorsement on the reverse. Sarah signalled 'whatever' and he put the plan into action.

First, he took a big square endorsing stamp and pressed it onto the pad of endorsing ink firmly, deliberately, and several times over. Satisfied that he had extracted sufficient ink from the emaciated pad, he made the first imprint at the top right of the reverse of the first form. This two-inch or so square took the form of a form (oh dear) and he had to fill in a couple of places with ball-point pen and initial each entry. He then took a smaller rectangular stamp. This was pressed on the ink pad a few times before the imprint was stamped near the first. Finally, he took a round stamp. This looked pretty official with some sort of crest or coat of arms incorporated into the design — much in demand on the black market no doubt. This again was pressed on the ink pad a few times before the imprint was stamped artfully overlapping both the previous stamps in a sort of government department sort of a way. Finally, he endorsed the stamps by adding what appeared to be a florid signature, the date, his mother's maiden name, his father's professional status, and his inside leg measurement across the whole mess.

"That's one of the four done," I thought to myself and surreptitiously looked at my watch. Five minutes so far. We could be out of here in half an hour. He repeated the three-stamp trick with as far as I could tell — although my vision was misting up a bit by now — the same three stamps, signatures, and written in information. He added it slowly and deliberately on the already endorsed form and positioned below the first cluster. There was no acceleration, no sign of him getting into his stride. I suppose the slow deliberation; the reading and re-reading signalled the importance of the task he was undertaking.

It was all as exciting as watching paint drying without all the thrills and spills of paint actually drying. I examined the room in great detail as he heroically ploughed through his Herculean task. The desks practically filled the room. The next room was empty apart from a lone tall grey steel filing cabinet with a green chart of the South Ionic taped to the front. Published by a well-known charter firm, the chart was to be seen everywhere — tavernas, shops, government offices, the lot. There were a couple of near vacant rooms on the same floor. A twin fluorescent strip was mounted on the ceiling. It was fed electricity by a cable that emerged from the wall just below the ceiling in one corner of the room. The cable run was loosely tacked to the ceiling with a couple of cable clips and painted firmly into place. A very old cast iron radiator stood at one wall. An air conditioning unit was mounted on the wall above our head. Neither were working indicating that the temperature was just right I suppose. A door opened on to a balcony overlooking shimmering blue water. I stared out of it looking forward to when we were one of the white-sailed boats that were scattered about the glistening blue sea bathed in the Mediterranean sun. I lost myself in a sort of reverie as I gazed at the mix of sprawling conifers and pencil thin cyprus that contrasted with silver green olive trees shimmering in the slight breeze on the green slopes of the shore opposite the harbour.

"You would think that they would spread themselves about a bit rather than cram themselves all in the one room," whispered Helen having spotted the unoccupied rooms across the passageway.

"Perhaps they like each other's company," I whispered back.

She shushed me then giggled, "Or their body odour."

Our man seemed to specialise in paper clips and endorsing stamps. A rack held about twenty different stamps and an old tobacco tin was overflowing with paperclips. The man seated opposite was obviously the chap to go to if you wanted to post something and be as frugal as possible with postage and packing. I watched him take a thick sheaf of A4 papers and fold them double in order that they could be accommodated in an A5 envelope. They didn't fit very well. He took them out and peered inside the envelope to see if there was anything obstructing their insertion. He folded the sheaf firmly in two and hit it several times with his fist. He tried to limit the fanout that 30 pages of A4 show when bent double. He put a heavy looking book on top of the folded sheaf and pressed down. I think he was contemplating sitting on it, but probably thought that was hardly a dignified action for a uniformed officer. He tried them in the envelope again. The envelope was beginning to show signs of strain. He was getting closer to his target but the fanout effect looked like defeating him. I was considering pointing to the crisp pile of A4 envelopes in a tray on his desk but thought better of it. They were probably for important things like fetching spinach pie and cakes from the local bakery.

The whole process must have taken an hour at the end of which we got loads of paper with things written on them in Greek.

"Do we owe you anything?" I asked.

Rubber stamp man scratched his head and reached out for a large ancient calculator. He started pressing buttons. It appeared to be a lengthy calculation and my heart sank. To my mind, each button pressed meant an increase in cost. Eventually he looked up at me, drew in a deep breath and told us, "Three euros."

Three euros for an hour or so of his time. I reached into my pocket, produced the three euros, gathered up the paperwork, thanked him profusely and walked into the fresh air outside

Outside, we said goodbye and thank-you to Sarah and crossed the road to George's chandlery for antifouling and insults. Then we went on to the Lefkas equivalent of B&Q for wire brush, abrasive paper and like things and finally to the Lefkas pedestrianised street for knock down prices on crocs, a couple of pairs of XL shorts (I must do something about that), a couple of new fenders, some rope and a gas detector. Returning back through Nidri, we stopped at a shop that sold fresh fish, frozen chicken and cigarettes — a strange mix of merchandise for that was all it sold. Here we bought a couple of fish that looked like a pair of mackerel with face transplants. Then back to Sivota to get the fish into the fridge.

Preparing for the Launch

We revisited the boat in the cool of the evening to recheck the batteries. They were not very promising to say the least. I had disconnected the 55-ampere-hour engine start battery and it had dropped back to about 5.5 V overnight. I swapped the charger from the first to the second domestic battery. The first domestic was charged to about 12 V, not very good, but it was a large capacity battery and a feeble little charger so it would probably take some charging to get it fully charged.

There was more water in the bilges, but not too much. I had mopped it dry the day before, but water seemed to be draining into the bilges from other parts of the boat. It must have been a spill when the engine was drained and the cooling system was recharged with inhibitor and water at the end of last season, but there may have been rainwater getting in through the winter. In the forecabin, we discovered a windscoop for the hatch so that was a bonus. Rigging the thing was to provide us with hours of entertainment in the season to come!

The sun was already making its presence felt when we got to the boatyard early on Saturday morning.

We dripped sweat as we manhandled the genoa out of the forehatch on to the foredeck. It was neatly folded to start with. By the time we had finished struggling with it, it wasn't. It was like wrestling with a half-ton jellyfish. The mainsail was just the same. We had to manhandle it through the saloon, up the companionway and then try to spread it on the deck, tack at the mast, clew ready to be attached to the outhaul at the boom end. Then I had to get a box to stand on in order to comfortably feed the mast runners for the mainsail into the track. It was too high up the mast for me to reach when I was stood on the deck, and the mainsail was heavy to lift to get the runners into the track entry point, and it was hot.

"Why have we bought a 38-footer? Everything is bigger and heavier," I moaned.

"Yes, 38 foot against 28 foot, it will be. You're just making a meal of it because you still favour Tethera."

"Well, it was easier to rig. I could do with one hand what is now taking me two hands to wrestle into place and sweat is getting into my eyes."

"You poor thing."

"Well, it is hot."

"That's what we come to Greece for isn't it — the sun, the heat."

"Well right now I would settle for rigging my nice little Tethera in a steady Portsmouth drizzle."

"Last time I remember you doing that in the rain, you were cursing like a drunken sailor."

"It's all right for you downstairs."

Helen was sorting out storage and other things below, out of the glare of the sun, between popping 'upstairs', to make encouraging remarks.

"Why don't we put up the bimini so we can get a bit of shade in the cockpit?" She asked brightly.

"It's over there," I muttered.

Sundowner's bimini is a roughly square cloth cover with pockets that the tubular stainless-steel struts of the collapsible support structure can be zipped into. Once fitted, it can be deployed by opening up the supports or folded away by closing them down to give you shade as and when you need it.

As Helen wrestled with the bimini, she began to see my point of view just a little.

"It's not fitting on properly."

"That's because you are trying to put it on the wrong way round — back to front," I told her.

"Ok, you try smarty pants."

"Well, look, we'll both do it."

What sounded like a good idea was not straightforward. Normally quite a good partnership, we seemed to have differing ideas about what went where. Between us, we managed some really interesting configurations considering that there are only a limited number of ways that a square bit of cloth can be laid out. It is not a heavy bit of cloth, but it has to be stretched across the support structure which is moderately high in order that there is standing room beneath it in the cockpit so we were stretching up and screwing our eyes shut against the glare of the sun and the ingress of sweat.

The cloths, yarn and plastic zips used are all subject to UV degradation especially in the Mediterranean sun. After five years' usage, there were some repairs and some areas that were suspect. So stretching it over the support struts (tubular stainless steel) was done with a certain amount of caution at first to avoid stressing any weaknesses. However, in the hot sun, pretty soon sweat was dripping into our eyes as we struggled to zip the bimini into place and caution was soon thrown to the winds.

Having tried upside down, back to front, arse about face and face about arse, we finally got it right. One of the zips was pretty suspect and broke as we struggled to zip the pocket over the supporting strut. We managed to hold it in place and seize up the broken part of the zip by sewing it up with whipping twine. It could now be deployed with ease.

A sledge launch was being prepared as we completed the rigging of the bimini. We watched fascinated. In the UK, I only had experience of being craned in and out of the water

I clambered down on to the yard and wandered over to watch them align the sledge with the stern of the boat. There was a lot of shouting and a lot of laughter — what I imagine was the usual banter that you get from men working in a man's environment but, frustratingly, I understood little of it.

The yard hands removed iron tie bars that held the runners together at the front of the sledge. They moved it forward under the boat keeping the runners aligned using brute force and big lumps of wood.

Once the sledge was in place, the tie bars were reinstalled, and supports on the sledge were raised on each side to support the boat. Then the whole charabanc was pushed and pulled along the track that they had laid out down to the water's edge.

The ramp at the water's edge looked like a rail track made of wood. It lay with one end on the shore but most of it floating in the water. Sledge and boat were manoeuvred onto the track then given one final push to slide it all out along the track that sank as it took the weight of the boat. The boat, sledge and track all parted company as the boat reached its flotation point. Clever stuff. The only notable failure was the engine of the newly launched boat. It did not start. The boat drifted out and the owner shouted to the men in the yard that there was a problem with the engine. "No problem," shouted the ever-cheery charge hand. "We come help." Two of them leapt into the yard launch. That too refused to start. The owner steered the drifting boat clear of other moored yachts, dropped anchor and disappeared below to kick the bejasus out of his engine.

Back at the ranch, Helen had a message from 'little H' — our granddaughter, Hollie, who had slipped into the role of our UK liaison officer! A letter had arrived from MCA (Maritime and Coastguard Agency in the UK) saying that as our online application for the registration of Sundowner on the SSR was 'incomplete', they had cancelled it and returned the money. No explanation of why it was incomplete — not a hint as to what information we had failed to give them or got wrong. I tried to get in touch via the laptop. I could not access the web and the messages that were displayed on the laptop seemed to suggest that we had blown up the phone dongle — disaster.

Ships Documents

The following morning, I was torn between progressing the preparation of the boat for launch and remedying the SSR situation. In the end, the SSR registration won.

"I thought we were going straight down to the boat?" Helen asked as she emerged on to the balcony where I was fiddling with the laptop — a cold half cup of coffee beside me. She stretched and yawned. "Nice morning though — which is more than I can say for that coffee — it looks disgusting."

"I want to sort out this SSR thing."

"Oh, phone them Monday. You'll just get frustrated and the laptop will probably end up in the harbour."

"No, it won't. It's working; it's just slow — very slow."

"Is it really necessary?"

"Vital. Besides, we still have to get this Dekpa thing and we probably need the SSR certificate for that. At the very least, I want a contact point — an email address or a phone number that gets me to the person I want first time without having to sit through two hours of menu selections and piped music."

"I doubt if there is any such number."

I had two attempts before I progressed through the registration forms on the internet. A notice informed me that I had applied successfully, but another little popup listed a number of things that it claimed that I had not done. One of the things was change of ownership. I was sure that it was just a question of selecting an option and I was equally sure that I had selected the correct one. Maybe the slow link had caused some part of this tenuous procedure to time out.

"Ballcocks and laptops."

"Failed again?" enquired Helen.

"I don't know. It seems to be telling me my application is incomplete — again. I don't know whether I should re-attempt or whether that would just confuse the situation further."

"Well, if you've followed the same procedure and it is telling you it is incomplete again, there is something that you are doing wrong — consistently!"

"Ta," I grumbled but I aborted and started again. The initial pages seemed to suggest I was right, but on the third attempt the application went right through as it had done before. I noted down contact details that were available at the end of the procedure and gave the laptop to Helen. I had had my fill of the thing. Helen emailed them with a plea to confirm whether the application had been successful, and if not why not.

When we eventually got to the boat that day, we achieved quite a lot. The winter rains had brought with them fine brown gritty dust (from the Sahara Desert I was told). Helen hosed the boat down to get rid of most of that. I checked the batteries again. There now seemed to be a reasonable voltage across the terminals of the domestic batteries. I put the engine start battery on charge again. I rigged the genoa attaching the sheets, running the sail up the track of the forestay extrusion and furling it up. Helen got the interior of the boat in some sort of order and asked me to sort out my gear around the navigation station. We took excess stuff off the boat. I had bought some kit from Tethera that was now duplicated by the kit we inherited with the boat. I fixed my hand-held vhf next to the epirb that was part of the boats kit. The licence for the latter would expire in October next.

Back on the deck of the boat, the heat in the sun was searing.

"Let's deploy the bimini," I suggested (we had folded it back on its frame the previous day). "It will provide a bit of shade in the cockpit."

Once we had done that, Helen set about wrestling with the problem of dirty seat covers. We took off the cockpit cushions and one of the internal seat covers, to try and do something with them at the digs. Most of the cover zips had corroded and were jammed in the closed position. But as we left, we were pleased to see that she was starting to look like a boat ready to take to the water.

I awoke at five o'clock in the morning with the recommissioning of the engine on my mind. It was dark, so I quietly made a cup of coffee, picked up a notepad and pencil (to make lists of jobs) and went to sit on our balcony overlooking Sivota bay. I savoured the coffee and the slight lift that strong black sugarless coffee gives. I started on my list of things to buy and do before the launch.

I had been sat on the balcony for less than ten minutes when a large fishing boat started up at the north (inshore) end of the bay. I put down the pencil and paper and watched as, minutes later, it was on its way cutting a silver V through the flat black water in the pre-dawn light and gently rocking the boats at anchor. Only about one third of them sported anchor lights. The engine made a nice throaty dependable thrum-thrum-thrum like the purring of a giant contented cat. A smaller fishing boat left the south end of the harbour as I poured my second cup of coffee. I abandoned the lists and simply watched the community waking up. Three more smaller fishing boats left in the next hour. I was on my third cup of coffee. It was time to get moving.

At the boatyard, I knocked on Maria's door and entered her office. She looked up from her desk.

"Good morning. Can I help you?" she greeted me effusively.

"Yes, I want to book a launch for Sundowner."

"It is complete then? You are the new owner of Sundowner?"

"I will be by Wednesday which is when I would like to launch her."

Maria came out from behind her desk smiling and shook my hand vigorously. "Well, congratulations," she said enthusiastically. "You are the new proud owner of Sundowner. You must be pleased." She then returned to her desk and shuffled through some files. 'Oh good' I thought, 'straight down to the business of booking the launch,' but no. She held up a piece of paper and said, "The first thing is to pay for the launch. No cash, no splash."

"Hang on. I was told that it was all paid for. No yard fees to come."

"I have no record of that. I have not been paid. Who told you this?"

"The agents who are handling the sale. IBA. I will go and see them."

"No, I have to call them anyway to confirm that you are ah... you know... the new owner."

I emerged from the office into the bright hot sunlight.

"All OK?" Helen greeted me at the boat.

"Yeah, yeah," but my tone of voice gave me away.

"What's wrong."

"Oh, nothing. It's just that Maria wants to charge us for the launch."

"How much? We seem to be spending money like water at the moment."

"I don't know. I told her that IBA have told us there is no bill to pay."

"I don't remember them saying that."

"I do."

"When? When did they say that?"

"Dunno. Can't place the conversation, but I am sure that we have been told."

"I'll ring them," said Helen.

"Maria said she was going to check it out with them. And anyway, I'll do it if there is telephoning to do. In fact, I'll call in to the office and beard them in their den."

I had IBA recommission the engine as they had decommissioned (winterised) it at the end of the previous season. I watched what needed doing and picked up on what had been done to winterise the engine and why. Although there are numerous articles on this topic, there also seemed quite a spread of opinion on the ways of going about it — what was necessary and what wasn't. Among other things, we noticed when running the recommisioned engine up at the end of it all, that there was a button with a projecting pin missing from the gear shift/throttle control lever. Neither the surveyor nor I had noticed this. I could still set the engine into neutral by sticking a screwdriver in the hole left by the pin of the button and pressing it in as I moved the control arm through the upright neutral position. 'I should be able to get hold of a replacement', I thought to myself, but in fact one of my smaller screwdrivers remained tied to the control by a short length of light line and did the job for the whole of the first season.

The audible engine alarm did not work and investigation showed that I needed a new 12 V buzzer. The sea cock for the holding tank outlet was freed off by unbolting the handle and using a large spanner to apply some brute force to the square end on which the handle was normally bolted.

In the middle of all this, Maria made one of her rare appearances in the yard and came over to see us.

"All OK. All paid for. Wednesday you want to launch? Is midday OK?"

So that was that. The date was set. I felt excited, but remembered the often quoted saying: "There are two best days of boat ownership. The day you buy it and the day you sell it. Buying it is the second-best day."

Antifouling

The various bits and pieces we had bought since agreeing the purchase of Sundowner was running us short of money. I traipsed off to the bank at Lefkas at lunchtime to see if we had successfully transferred some funds from the UK as yet, and whether we could get hold of some dosh. However, the bank was suffering from a power outage and nothing was working so I came away empty handed. On the way back, I decided to finish preparing the boat for antifouling so we spent the hot afternoon rubbing down. What a messy job. Blue antifouling dust in our hair eyes, noses mouths, everywhere. We should have been wearing protective clothing but face masks steamed up and the heat precluded wearing any more than was absolutely necessary to avoid upsetting onlookers.

"We've got to get back to our rooms and get cleaned up," I told Helen at the end of the day.

"Christ, the landlady will have a fit if we turn up like this. You're bright blue. She'll worry that we'll turn her furniture blue."

"Never mind the landlady — the car upholstery will be blue by the time we get there. Look, there is a shower block around here somewhere." We armed ourselves with towels and shampoo and stumbled across the yard to look for it. We asked a Greek where the shower block was. He was sitting in the shade of his boat sipping from a small beer bottle. He looked up at us as we approached.

"Is that antifouling on you? You are meant to put it on the boat you know. It is not nice for you to wear." He paused then added, "But I think that neither of you will not suffer from barnacles this year," and burst into paroxysms of laughter at his witticism.

"Yes, yes we know. That's why we want to wash. The shower block…"

"The showers… That building there," He said pointing to a shed of building blocks and corrugated iron and ominously added, "Good luck."

116

"Why? Is there no hot water?"

"Hot no... water no... Well, only little."

"A little is better than none at all," I told him as I thanked him and we stumped on toward the tin shed. He watched us shaking his head and returned to his beer. He was quite correct. The pathetic dribble of cold water only moved the blue dust about a bit to make patterns on our bodies.

In Sivota, we drove along the narrow back lane that led to our rooms and Helen remarked that it was handy that the landlady had allocated a reserved car parking space for us right next to the room.

"We should be able to sneak in without her noticing. We can wait in the car if she's around and sneak in when she's not looking." Then she shrieked, "Look. Hell. Some bugger has parked in our space. What are we going to do?"

"We'll just have to park in the car park at the head of the bay."

"Can't we find something nearer?"

"Well, we'll try, but not much chance at this time of day."

There wasn't. We drove a tortuous route back to the car park but there was no spare slot elsewhere. We parked and gathered up our kit and walked the gauntlet back to the room suffering several remarks along the lines of, 'Well, you should have a barnacle-free season'.

'Ha, bloody, ha'.

Our neighbour, Maria, caught us climbing up the stone steps with sweat running rivulets down our faces and shrieked with laughter yelling for George and anyone else within earshot to come and have a look. We scuttled into the rooms and scrubbed each other with carbolic and a scrubbing brush.

"How do I look?" Helen asked emerging scrubbed raw from the shower.

"Well, with the blue highlights in your hair, you look like one of Margaret Thatcher's blue-rinse bandits."

We received notice that the money for Sundowner had reached the previous owner's bank during the course of the evening so, the following day, we collected the stuff that IBA at Nidri were holding until the money was paid — outstanding documents, the outboard motor for the tender and a few other bits and pieces. In view of our failure to withdraw funds the previous day, we returned to the bank. Our money had come in and their electricity was on so were able to withdraw some funds, but there was no sign of a bank card as yet.

As we had built up a list of bits and pieces that we needed we took our new-found wealth to the shops. One of the bits was a 12-volt buzzer for the engine alarms. The alarm indicators for low oil pressure, alternator output, etc., consisted of a line of four indicator lamps at the foot of the wheel pedestal. They were dim enough that when lit they were scarcely visible in the Mediterranean sun and they were well away from a normal line of sight so, as the visual alarm was so weak, it was essential to replace the failed audible alarm with a working one. Neither of the two chandlers in the high street had one so I went in a nearby electrical shop and tried to explain what I wanted with little hope of success. The shopkeeper foraged around some wooden drawers that seemed to contain an assortment of electrical junk and produced a brown cardboard box with the legend ALRM 12 V written on it in untidy blue biro.

"Can you open it?"

"Of course," he said as he produced a dangerous looking knife.

"That's a bit big for cutting through sellotape," hissed Helen.

"Yes," I agreed. "It looks like the sort of thing you'd use to kill and gut wild boar, but I suppose he's got about six miles of sticky tape to slice through."

Helen rummaged around in her bag and produced her nail scissors and offered them to him. "It would be easier with these," she told him.

"No, no. Is OK," he said affronted by the suggestion that he should use part of a feminine manicure set instead of his alpha male hunting knife. 'Ah, very Greek,' I thought.

Eventually, he pulled a small dubious looking lump of plastic and metal with a couple of wires poking out of it from the carnage of brown paper and sticky tape. I looked at it doubtfully. "Does it work?"

"Of course."

"Can we try it?"

"No. I have no 12 volts."

"You must have a battery."

"No battery."

"What if I get it to the boat and it doesn't work?"

"Bring it back. I give you money back if not work."

Back at the boat, I tried it across the 12V battery. Nothing. There had been no indication of polarity but the leads were coloured red and black and, following the normal convention, I had connected red to positive. Just for the hell of it, I tried it the other way round. It worked, so I fitted it. It did not fit where the Volvo buzzer fitted — for a start, it was square and the Volvo buzzer was round. I found a space beneath the instrument panel and bound it in place with sticky tape thinking that I would come back and make a decent job of it later — I never did...

Antifouling is horrid stuff even though some of the more toxic components that used to be part of the mix are now banned. The afternoon saw us putting antifouling on the boat and once again getting the paint over ourselves as well. We tried not to because apart from the toxicity of the stuff, its price was such that applying it anywhere else than on the boats underwater surfaces was a gross waste of money.

The Launch

Wednesday was launch day. We were down at yard at eight thirty in the morning. All went well. I was on the ground with antifouling as they moved the sledge in and moved out props. The boatyard owner came to see us and congratulate us again on our new boat. Helen was up in cockpit while it all happened. The men were using long timbers as levers to steer the sledge this way or that as a little bit of winching edged it under the boat. It was a delicate operation performed with large blunt tools. Huge baulks of timber used as levers to steer the sledge under the boat so that it missed the props that were still in place holding the boat up. Pig fat and olive oil was liberally brushed over all bearing surfaces. They took out a prop here and there when it seemed to be in the way and hammered a replacement in a slightly different position so that the sledge could continue on its way.

Eventually, there she was; Sundowner supported entirely by the sledge. I set to with the remnants of the anti-fouling filling in the patches that had previously been obscured by the props while trying to keep clear of the yard hands who were doing a job of work and who were wielding big baulks of timber. Having completed that I wandered off to have a pee and came back to find Helen isolated in the boat — the ladder was removed when the stern prop (an oil drum with bits of wood and wedges on it) had been removed. I asked if I could get aboard: "Of course." They retrieved the ladder that they had removed, I climbed up and they took it away again.

They then started moving the whole shebang over the track of timbers. This time it was being pulled by a steel hawser wound in on a winch that was mounted on the front of the tractor. The tractor was positioned at the waterfront beside the track down which Sundowner was being pulled so the pull was becoming more offset from the desired direction of travel as Sundowner got closer to the water's edge so they were having to counter the offset with their big baulks of timber. Soon they had us poised on the shoreline, and they all disappeared.

"Have they gone off for their dinner or something?" Helen enquired worriedly.

"Dunno."

"They are not going to leave us up here, are they?"

"Ready?" a voice from below shouted. I looked down and a grinning face looked up at me. "Ready?" he repeated.

"Yes, I think so."

"Hokey dokes then," and we were off. Sledge and boat gathered way down the ramp and within seconds we floated gracefully off. The engine started first time and we continued in reverse in a gentle curve, waving goodbye to the waving, laughing and shouting yard hands. I slipped her into neutral and, as she lost way, into forward to arrest our reverse motion. Sundowner hesitated and the wind started to move the bow away then she started to move gently ahead and the steering became precise. We took our time to find a nice spot on the lagoon to drop anchor. Everything worked. *Yippee.* A few minutes later Peter and Annie Norton steamed past in Ventus A. We waved and he came over to congratulate us on a successful launch — as though we had anything much to do with it. He was off to catch up with Second-hand Geoff. They had arranged to have a meal in a nearby taverna with him this evening. We also planned to call in on Second-hand Geoff later to buy a tarpaulin and some line to shield the car from the Mediterranean sunshine for the next three months — having drawn a blank at finding a suitable sized tailor made one.

Yippee — we had done it. Years ago, we had promised ourselves that one year we would buy a suitable camper, Dormobile, or similar and head for Greece and simply bum around and see how long it took us to get bored with it. Now we were doing it and, even better, in a sailing boat.

We went ashore to see what Second-hand Geoff had on offer and to drive into Nidri to buy an adaptor for the dinghy pump. Without a suitable adaptor, we could not inflate Sundowner's tender. Rowing it in its half-inflated state was difficult. You knew where you wanted to go, but it was difficult to communicate that to the dinghy.

Back on board, in the late afternoon, we ran the engine for about an hour to put a bit of charge in the batteries and then switched it off. The boat swung quietly at anchor. The village of Vlicho looked pretty from the lake with the steep slope sparsely wooded with silvery green olive trees, tall slim Cyprus, and other shrubs brought into sharp relief in the early evening sun. Swallows skimmed over the water and perched on the boats rail chit-chitting to each other. We sat in the cockpit to eat our first meal on board. A bright flash of emerald blue and the "kri" of their call as a pair of kingfishers swooped along the near shore. Halcyon days indeed.

We woke afloat in the bay early the next morning with the rest of the summer in front of us. We took coffee in the cockpit and discussed plans. There were none — why would there be? We had been so obsessed with bargaining, buying and preparing the boat we had not really thought beyond the launch. It was a cloudless windless blue-skied day in the bay. Idly we went over the places we knew and those we knew of. Peter and Annie chanced by and were invited aboard for coffee and to look at our acquisition.

"What are you planning to do now you have your boat?"

"We've just been talking about that very thing. We have no firm plans."

"We're off to Port Atheni. There's a nice little bay you can tuck into. Why don't you come?" Adding, as an extra inducement, "It is Greek dancing night at Captain Jimmy's."

"I don't really want to spend the evening Greek dancing," I moaned after they departed.

"Why ever not?"

"I don't know. I think it's all that enthusiasm. I can't take a lot of enthusiasm."

"You just don't like dancing. You used to though. You seemed quite happy to dance with me when we met."

"Ah, well. We were both on our best behaviour then."

"So that's it is it? Now we're over courting what I've got is the real you — unpacked?"

"Guess so."

"I think I preferred you all wrapped up in the courting packaging."

As midday approached and zephyrs of wind started to darken patches of water in the lagoon, we pulled up the anchor and motor sailed through fluky winds out past Nidri to Scorpio — a private island bought from the Greek government by shipping magnate, Aristotle Onassis. After his death, it continued to be scrupulously maintained but was eventually sold. It is now owned, or at least leased depending upon which rumour you subscribe to, by the daughter of a Russian oligarch. It has neatly trimmed lawns, a pristine harbour, and one or two houses are visible through trees and palms. Verdant vegetation and trees conceal much but cultivated vines and olive trees are visible at various points around the island and the livestock of a farm can be heard. There are bathing areas with changing rooms, one specifically built in a small cove for Jackie Onassis. Strategically placed blue buggeroff notices used to forbid landing. But there was one point where they seem to tolerate day trip boats pulling in to let day trippers swim on the island. Anyone going ashore was detected on a security system and soon met by a man in a van or a car with a degree in shouting. The Russians have now bouyed off all approaches to the island and security men in fast RIBs will not tolerate you even approaching any of the beaches or harbours.

We cut the motor once we had passed the harbour and emerged into clearer air at the north-east end of the island. Sundowner leaned into the water and picked up speed. We continued on in the direction of mainland Greece to the east, sailing nowhere in particular, sailing just for the sheer enjoyment. Coursing through the water exhilarated by the first sail in the boat that had been a twinkle in our eyes a year ago, but had just taken us a month to find and buy. There was not a terrific lot of wind, but Sundowner sailed well. Her helm was light and responsive. After a while, we changed course to return to a bay we knew on the island of Meganissi where the waters were clear and green leafy branches overhung the rocky shoreline. We dropped anchor for a swim.

I put on face mask and snorkel and went looking for octopuses in the warm water — not to catch and eat — they just fascinate me. Sometimes I spend ages looking without success. I know they are there laughing up their eight sleeves at my feeble efforts to find them, but I cannot see them. This time a scatter of white stones and shells caught my attention. I looked at the surrounding area but, just as I was about to move on, I discerned eyes peering out from a shallow hole in the sea floor. Eyes with a slitted iris — like a goat. The eyes were staring from behind the pale pink underside of a tentacle lined with white suckers. Once I had spotted the octopus, he seemed quite conspicuous, I wondered why I did not see him straight away. It looked as though he was trying to mask his face with one of his tentacles, but I suppose the tentacle was positioned ready to strike at a crab, or some other sandwich on legs that happened to chance by.

My presence did not seem to trouble him. As I watched, he eased himself out of his hidey hole and, spreading his tentacles, seemed to half glide half walk across the sea bottom toward a patch of weed. In movement, they are intriguing — like a cartoon that has come to life. They change colour and skin texture to provide chameleon-like adaptive camouflage. Now, as he moved into the weed, his colour darkened and white flecks appeared that melted him into the background of weed. Sometimes they morph from an octopus-shaped octopus into something that can slip into the safety of a narrow fissure that really should not be able to accommodate much more than a cigarette paper. I used a stick that I had picked up to move the weeds to one side and he seemed to inflate his bulbous body and his skin became warty expressing anger or fear maybe. I played with him for a little until sick and tired of my attentions he squirted me with ink and jetted off trailing his eight tentacles and leaving curly wisps of black ink hanging in the water.

I remember the first time I had come in contact with the tentacles. It was sat in a taverna in an October dusk watching a light in the sea close inshore. Intrigued, I went over to investigate. It turned out to be a taverna owner catching octopus with the aid of an underwater torch. He emerged from the sea as I stood watching. He wore his torch on his head in the manner of a coalminer and had a sort of netting bag slung around his waist with two or three octopi inside wriggling to get out. Frequently, a tentacle or two would emerge from the top of the bag reaching up his stomach towards his chest and the octopus would begin to emerge and attempt to crawl up him. He would bundle the escaper unceremoniously back into the bag. The taverna owner's son appeared and took them from him.

"You should be doing this. I have a taverna to run."

"I can."

"You're not good at it. You don't seem to want to put your hand inside dark holes."

"No, I don't. I never know what might be in the cave."

"Arghhh. No good. You're no good."

"I can't say as I blame him," I interjected. "Can't say as I would put my hand in a cave to be grabbed by an octopus."

"It's not octopus that worries me…" the youth butted in.

"Huh. Octopus. They're no problem. They're small," his father retorted.

"Yeah, but those tentacles and the suckers," I interjected.

"Huh. Here… Hold this one," he said holding one of the escapees out to me. I looked at the proffered cephalopod hesitantly then took it gingerly. Two of his tentacles wrapped around my arm. As I peeled them off it was like pulling sticky tape off my arm.

To return to the present… later in the afternoon, we pulled away from our bay on Meganissi and made our way to nearby Port Atheni where we followed Peter's instructions and found Ventus A moored in a bay within the larger bay that led into Port Atheni. He was in the company of two fishing boats. They waved us in, "Drop anchor about where you are and bring a line ashore. I'll come and fetch it." Peter was already in the water and swam out towards us as we moved the boat slowly astern towards the shore. We passed Peter the line and he swam it ashore while we paid it out. He tied it around a rickety looking jetty and we prepared ourselves for an evening of eating, drinking and Greek dancing.

Kingfishers made their appearance again. There was a flash of bright blue so quick that I almost missed it. I stared into the dense foliage of the branches overhanging the shoreline and made out the classic kingfisher shape and pose — a stubby but elegant bird with its powerful beak and colourful emerald and chestnut plumage. It was joined by another within a minute. I had long associated them with inland waterways, canals, freshwater rivers and streams but here they were happily frequenting the saltwater environment. I had thought of them as shy and retiring too, frequenting tranquil stretches of water and requiring patience on the part of the twitcher to spot them but the first one I saw in Greece was in Rhodes harbour happily perched on the taut mooring line of a fishing boat staring into the water below, untroubled by the tourists and locals on the quayside and the bustle of a busy harbour.

That evening, Peter asked me how the boat was faring. "Found any snags yet?"

"Hmm, I feel that the anemometer under estimates wind speed and the log over estimates boat speed. There is over a knot difference between the GPS and the ship's log so it computes a really dubious boat speed reading with an inaccurate apparent windspeed reading and comes up with nonsense for actual windspeed."

"Ah, you'll get used to it."

"But there's more. The least significant digit of the echo sounder reading only has three of its seven segments. So what appears to be 7 could also be 0, 3, 8 or 9. What appears to be 1 could be 4. The number 2 is the top horizontal and the top right-hand vertical segments and 5 is indicated by the top horizontal and the bottom right hand vertical segments, but that may also be a 6."

"Come on, you grumbling old beggar. You'll get used to it. Time for another beer."

The Leaky Tender

Some days after having 'checked all the boxes' as regards ship's papers and other formalities, we found ourselves back in Vlicho at anchor with a rising wind blowing along the length of the lagoon. We had good holding so the wind was not a problem, but we wanted to get ashore and see whether we could get a suitable adapter for the dinghy inflator as the pump outlet did not match up with the valves on the dinghy. We had made several sorties to several chandlers and now had a bag full of bits of plastic nozzles that were all almost exactly the wrong size. We couldn't cart the tender around the various chandlers, but we described the make and model and the man behind the counter would stump up something, swear blind it was the missing link that we had been seeking, take a couple of euros off us and donate another useless bit of plastic to the collection.

"I thought you had mended that leak," said Helen dismally watching me — half in the dinghy and half in the sugar scoop stern of Sundowner and struggling to put a bit of air in the thing.

"Well, so did I. I stuck a patch over the only leak I could find."

"Well, either your patch has come off or there is another leak somewhere."

"Ah, your speciality subject — the bleeding obvious."

"You are chancing your luck with your backside stuck up in the air like it is," Helen countered. "You are just begging to be kicked into the water."

The lack of a suitable adapter to couple the pump to the valves on the tender meant that inflating her was a matter of keeping the hose end pressed firmly on the dinghy valve in question while pumping furiously. In some situations, this was nearly impossible. On this occasion, I was kneeling in the sugar scoop stern with one hand clamping the end of the pump hose to a dinghy valve and attempting to operate the pump bellows with alternately my other hand or a foot. The tender was bobbing about totally out of sync with the boat which was swinging fairly vigorously in the gusting wind.

"Why don't I pump the pump while you hold the tube onto the valve?" Helen suggested. Following her suggestion, we secured the tender at the stern and attempted to inflate with Helen on the sugar scoop stern trying to pump at my command and myself lying in the tender, holding the end of the hose as hard as I could against the valve inlet. We could, I suppose, have attempted to bring the tender up over the rail and onto Sundowner's foredeck and pumped it there. However, Helen was against the idea. She was convinced that a gust would get under the tender at the crucial point of lifting it aboard and would take us hanging on to the tender and parasailing over water sports beach of Nidri.

After a quarter hour of furious pumping and spat out expletives, I said that we had probably got enough air in the tender.

"It doesn't look any different to me," grumbled Helen.

"It'll do. The hose keeps slipping off the valve. Once we get ashore, we can haul it up on the side and give it some more air. It will be much easier with it on dry land."

"Do you suppose the dinghy is safe in this weather?"

"Safe as houses."

I got into the tender and Helen passed me the outboard. I fitted it into place on the transom and pulled the cord. It came to life immediately.

"It does seem to be a reliable little outboard."

"Shh," grunted Helen. "Don't tempt fate."

"Stop being stuperitious and get aboard."

"It's so bloody awkward getting into this thing," she grumbled as I hamfistedly helped her aboard.

"Ah, it'll come as the season progresses," I said encouragingly. "I used to dance about from one tender to another when I was doing it regularly."

"That'll be all of 40, 45 years ago when you were young and supple. I don't see you doing much dancing these days."

Undaunted, we set off in our under-inflated dinghy. Pretty soon, the tender was slinkying over the small waves that the blow was setting up but, rather than bouncing vigorously over the waves, it tended to follow the contours of the waves closely and moved through the sea more like a supermarket shopping bag floating half in and half on the water. The steerage — a bit of a knack at the best of times — was very hit and miss but I was managing a fairly straight course when the outboard stuttered, faltered, faded and stopped. A few pulls on the starter cord convinced me that, whatever the cause, I wasn't about to get it started. Besides, the weather was taking us along the lagoon away from the quayside that I had been aiming at.

"I told you not to tempt fate. What are we going to do now?" moaned Helen.

"Row," I said unpicking the webbing buckle that secured the oars in the bottom of the tender.

"You can't use those they're broken," Helen shouted above the increasingly windy weather.

We had recently used one of the oars for fending off a stray dinghy — an entirely inappropriate activity for a metal oar with a plastic blade that had been made rather brittle by several seasons of Ionian UV. The blade had snapped off leaving us with a pair of oars that was actually an oar and a bit.

"Only one of them is," I shouted back.

"We'll just go round in circles!"

"I'll just have pull ten times as fast with the stump as I do with the oar that's whole."

"Stupid."

"There's no alternative. We'll be out past Nidri if we do nothing."

I pulled at great speed with the very much reduced oar while completing a stroke for every ten or so with the other. We managed a sort of crabwise progress in a direction that was not too much off the direction we wanted to go. But it was exhausting. It was like rowing a giant jelly fish — one that really didn't want to go where you wanted it to go and hardly helped at all by the oar-and-a-stump propulsion technique that drove us in all sorts of directions but the required one.

"Uh, we don't seem to be heading towards the quay."

"I'm doing my best — it's difficult," I grunted.

"But we are not heading in the direction that we need to go in."

"Yeah — I'm just getting a bit of practice in."

"It will be handy to get ashore before the shops close."

The weather seemed to abate at one point, but that was just because we were in the lee of a massive floating gin palace sitting rather more sedately at anchor than Sundowner had been. The owner sat in the stern sheltered from the weather by the wheelhouse and a large blue awning. He looked up from his book and his pink gin and gave us a wave then returned to his book for a fraction of a second before he did a double take looking up again at the half-drowned twosome on what must have looked as much like a carpet floating on the water as a dinghy. He took in the asymmetric rowing technique with one oar whizzing around so that it was almost a blur and the other taking the occasional pensive dip in the water. He burst out laughing.

"He's bloody laughing at us," I shouted to Helen.

"So would I be if I was where he is," Helen shouted back encouragingly.

He turned and shouted below.

"Oh, now, he is getting his mates up on deck for a laugh."

Sure enough, a couple more men appeared from below and he gesticulated in our direction.

"Oh, God, I hope he's not got a video camera," Helen groaned. "The last sighting my grandchildren will have of their grandma will be a video posted on YouTube of me disappearing to the east apparently abducted by a deranged oarsman."

We were being swept away from the gin palace but there was activity going on and pretty soon a large RIB sporting a very large outboard motor was hurtling towards us. Far from pointing at us and saying, "Want a laugh? Look at those two prats." The owner had been directing two of his crew to come to our rescue.

We were towed back to the gin palace. He asked what we were trying to do and we explained that we were trying to get ashore in Vlicho and he directed his crew to get us there. We thanked him profusely as we departed, but he waved away the thanks, "No, I had to get you out of the way. You were spoiling the view."

At the quay side that we were originally aiming for, I tied our dinghy up by the jetty and thanked the young men who had brought us in. Scrambling stiffly and awkwardly from the tender I noticed a couple of the regular Sail Ionian staff.

"My, you are arriving in style today."

"Yeah well... The engine stalled so we were attempting to row across and one of the oars is busted and we were not getting very far."

"Going round in circles?" said Chip, the taller of the two trying to restrain his laughter.

"That sort of thing."

"Yeah, we saw you," The other said then exploded in laughter.

"The little Honda I inherited with Sundowner. It doesn't start — any tips?" Not for the first and certainly not for the last time, I leant on the goodwill of the charter firm that was in charge of Sundowner until we took it over a week or so ago.

"Hmm, they're usually pretty reliable and I know for a fact that it was serviced, winterised and stored properly."

"Ah, so there's nothing you can suggest?"

"Here, let me look at it," Chip stepped easily on to the tender that I had so awkwardly crawled out of a minute or so before. He leant over undid the clamps from the transom, hefted the motor up and walked back along the undulating tender stepped onto the quayside and carried it to their maintenance trailer.

"See, I used to hop on and off boats like that," I told Helen.

"Well, you certainly can't now," she told me primly.

I walked over to the maintenance trailer and watched the engine being fixed to a bracket. The Sail Ionian engineer checked the fuel tap and the air bleed in the tank filler cap and took the start cord in his hand.

"That's the advantage of these air cooled 4-strokes you don't have to put them in a water tank to start them ashore," he gave the cord a vigorous pull, then another and the engine roared into life. "But the disadvantage is that they're flipping noisy," he added as he gave it some throttle. He revved it a few times and then let it run for half a minute, revved it some more then pressed the cut-out button.

"Well it seems OK..." He said.

"Ahh, yes."

"So it's a bit of a mystery."

"Yes... I suppose... Well... Ahh you switched the fuel on?"

"Yes," he said turning it off. "But there; it's off now."

"But you switched it on to start it?" I asked sheepishly.

A look of understanding dawned, "You mean..."

"Yes, I'm afraid so. I forgot to switch it on. That's why it ran out of fuel then wouldn't start. I'm sorry..."

"Hah," the look of understanding changed into a grin. "No probs. It happens. Here let me put the outboard back on your tender."

"No, really... I'll do it... After putting you to all this needless—"

"Nah, come on, mate. The way you're going today both you and the motor will end up in the drink."

Second-hand Geoff's emporium was a shop selling second hand boat spares that has some of the attributes of a maritime museum. A couple of Seagull outboards, a windsurf board, assorted aluminium and wooden spars and some sort of partially dismantled gearbox stood outside the door. "I haven't seen a Seagull since... I don't know... my schooldays," I said to Helen in a sort of hushed tone of reverence. Once inside, and once our eyes had become accustomed to the stygian gloom within, we found Geoff sat at his desk to the left of the door. A table bearing a huge pile of second-hand charts occupied the space to the right of the door.

In front of us, a long rack extended down the centre of the long narrow room. Blocks, shackles, fairleads, rope clutches, winches and windlasses of every size, age and material that you could envisage lay on the table top, the shelf above it and the floor below it. Brass, jostled with bright stainless steel, wooden blocks vied with Bakelite and metal blocks, clutches, cleats and other contrivances. Along each side of the room, similar shelving was stacked with electronics, compasses, vhf radios, binoculars, anchors, cookers and god knows what else. Above us, spars were fed through frames that hung down from the ceiling.

"Coo, some of these charts are a bit old," I said as an opening gambit.

"A bit old. They're all bloody old." Retorted Geoff. "They're collector's items. That's what they are."

I brandished our broken oar at him.

"Selling or buying?" he enquired. "Because you'll get bugger all for that."

"Ah, no, I want a replacement. Would you have an oar just like this one…"

"Well, I could saw the end off a good one I suppose…"

"No, I mean like this one but not broken."

"I don't sell oars singly, but I think I have a pair that will do you." Geoff disappeared into the gloom and came back with a pair that looked pretty much like a direct replacement and after some haggling, we had a decent pair of oars once more. He failed us on the adapter front but gave us one or two suggestions — chandlers that might have them. We had tried most of them already, but there were a couple of possibilities. We discussed it as we wandered back to our half deflated tender.

"We could unwrap the car and go into Nidri," Helen suggested.

"What for?"

"To get an adapter from that place that Geoff suggested."

"Nidri on a day like this?" As I spoke, a lorry full of the spoil from some building site emphasised my point droning past in the direction of Nidri leaving swirling dust behind it. "I'll hoick the tender onto the quay and one of us can hold the nozzle onto the valve as the other pumps."

"We will need to sort it sometime," Helen countered.

"Yeah, yeah, let's find a nice bay and go for a swim today."

"When are we going to get this adapter then?"

"Avrio." (The Greek word for tomorrow has the same connotations as the Spanish, 'Mañana' does).

Helen offered little resistance to the idea so we headed off to Meganissi. We found a sheltered bay, anchored and spent the rest of the afternoon swimming, reading and listening to the shrill clatter of cicadas. In the evening, we ate in the cockpit with a darkening sun dropping behind the peaks of Lefkada.

I woke the next day at six o'clock. I quietly made myself a cup of coffee and sat in the cockpit drinking it. Flat, calm water mirrored the images of other boats in the bay. The lights of Spartochori were still on, bright jewels in the soft morning light.

Spartochori

Spartochori is a village that overlooks a bay on Meganissi. It is a steep climb from the bay (Spilia) up into the village, but it is well worth the effort. Small well-kept gardens sport vivid bursts of bougainvillea or grapevines tumbling over arbours and pergolas. In the late summer ripe red pomegranates hang from trees. In one garden I spotted a tree of kiwi fruit. Colourful roses scramble up walls. White paint picks out the outline of flagstones on narrow streets and the walls of a lot of the houses are freshly painted bright white or mellow yellow. There is a delightful church, and a number of viewpoints that look down on Spilia bay and across to Scorpio and beyond. There is a taverna where they play Greek music and an old lady dressed in black sometimes dances with a table balanced on her head. It is said that Aristotle Onassis, keen to keep the old traditions alive, was a major benefactor to the island of Meganissi. If that were the case, he should be turning in his grave because the view as you approach Spilia bay from the sea is now besmirched by an ugly hotel complex that looks like a line of huge double decker busses parked on the hillside. It dwarfs the white village buildings of Spartochori that once peered, unsullied, over a steep slope clad with dark green conifers into the blue waters of Spilia. On an earlier visit, I had asked a taverna owner, "How did they get permission for that terrible hotel complex?"

"Money," he had replied darkly "Money… it talks. But never mind. You can't see it from my taverna can you?"

As I sat, thinking and drinking, a small fishing boat puttered away from the harbour its engine clear to hear over the quiet still water. Then I heard the gentle creak of an oar being pulled against a wooden rowlock. An old man was manoeuvring a small fishing boat around the boats moored in the bay. He would pull on one or both oars then let the boat glide while he used a sort of glass bottomed bucket to peer down into the water. He had a trident ready to hand. He might not touch the oars again until his boat had either glided to a halt or he needed to correct his course to prevent him bumping into a boat or another obstacle such as a jetty. His progress was slow measured relaxed. What was he looking for, I wondered? Octopus? Fish?

I had seen local fisherman use a spear or a trident to catch fish from a quayside. The trident is a three-pronged fork sometimes with cruel-looking barbs that is mounted on the end of a long wood or metal pole. When they fished from the quayside, they had a line attached to the trident so that once they had thrown it, they could retrieve it — hopefully, with a nice fat fish impaled on the fork. Early one morning, I had seen a fish bleeding on the quayside. Further along, there was another. Curiously, I had followed the line of fish and saw a young man standing stock still with the trident held still prongs just above the surface of the water; suddenly, with an economic, but powerful movement, he propelled the trident down into the water then retrieved it with the line, pulled yet another fish off the trident and dropped it on the concrete quay later returning along the quayside with a plastic supermarket bag to pick up the fish that he had caught.

The man in the boat manoeuvred his way around Sundowner and, seeing me watching from the cockpit, he gave me a grin and a wave as he headed away from the jetty along the shoreline. He paused from time to time and peered into the water beneath his boat. Now and then he stabbed his trident down to the sea bottom and came up with a sea cucumber or similar. Disappointing; I was expecting to see an octopus.

Bartering for Batteries

I started the engine when Helen had emerged from below and it seemed not too antisocial an hour to do so. The domestic batteries were flat and needed charging up. We had renewed the engine-start battery before we launched the boat as it simply did not hold charge. The domestic batteries had not seemed as bad so we had nursed them along, but they too were not really up to the job. Today, we decided that we would try to resolve the domestic battery problem. I measured up the existing batteries and the additional space that might allow for some variation in battery size.

We sailed off discussing whether to pay chandlers prices at Nidri or get back to Vlicho and unwrap the car again and look for an agricultural shop that we had been told about in Vonitsa. We opted for the latter, put the boat on the jetty at Vlicho and unwrapped the car.

We stopped at the bank in Nidri to withdraw some cash and then drove on to Lefkas and over the swingbridge to mainland Greece past Cleopatra's canal, through Aghia Nicholaos and into the agricultural mainland. We passed blue lakes, wet marsh lands and fields of crops. Distant blue grey mountains made a backdrop to the verdant countryside. We took about twenty minutes to get to Vonitsa. A great big, bright green, brand spanking new John Deere tractor easily identified our shop as we approached the town.

The shop was a modern concrete cube with a concrete forecourt some of which was occupied by the big green tractor. A central entrance door had a large display window to either side and inside you could see an unholy mess of agricultural and horticultural, implements, spare parts, and general detritus mainly arranged seemingly where they had been dropped on the floor.

The room was bare of furnishing but a sectioned-off glass fronted office occupied the far-left corner. Steel shelves of spare parts, lubricants and other mysterious liquids and potions were visible at the back over the top of the heaps of dusty horticultural impedimenta that occupied most of the shop floor. To the right, a half-finished flight of stairs led up to a mezzanine floor that promised more of the same. The equipment on show ranged from the brand new to the returned, broken, or defunct. Brand new displays of Husquana chainsaws, strimmers, and protective gear stood alongside heaps of mechanical detritus, shackles, bolts, broken drive shafts and couplings and some unfathomable metal contrivances that it would take more than one man to lift — or certainly more than one of me!

An old man stood by the door smoking a very strong cigarette. He grinned and greeted me as I walked up and followed me into the shop. No one else about. He must be the proprietor I supposed.

He took the cigarette out of his mouth and coughed, "Parakalo?"

"Er batteries — do you have batteries?"

"Uh?"

"BAT-ER-RI?"

"Uh?" He shook his head. A few more grunted exchanges and I did a mime of me writing something on paper. He beckoned me into the office in the corner and seated himself behind a desk that was simply groaning under the weight of catalogues, samples, paper, empty coffee cups and two ashtrays overflowing with cigarette butts underneath a 'NO SMOKING' sign. On the desk was a photograph of him holding a small child — his grandaughter he informed me proudly before offering me some scraps of paper and a pencil. I drew a box shape with two studs labelled '+' and '-' and then added '12 V DC' for good measure then showed it to him.

"Ah. Batterie. dhodeka volt."

He rose from the desk and took me up to the mezzanine floor and showed me batteries, lots of them. I got my ruler out and measured them. I cracked my head several times against a low concrete beam that ran across the ceiling. Each time he muttered something that might have been 'mind the beam' in Greek. We found a 120 AH battery that would fit the space in the boat. Not the 140 AH of the lame battery, but it would do. "*Poso kani?*" (how much) I asked.

"*Ah. Poso kani,*" he said thoughtfully putting more accent on the "i" than I had. He went down the stairs and I followed him clouting my head once again for good measure before I left the mezzanine. He repeated 'mind the beam' in Greek. We went into his office in the corner and he offered me one of his pungent cigarettes.

Behind his desk was shelving full of technical books, catalogues, pamphlets, manuals and dust. He took an armful, dumped them on the desk and started riffling through them one after the other. He looked quite lost and I wondered whether he was the janitor rather than the proprietor. I watched him delve deeper and deeper into the piles of catalogues and price lists. Eventually, he looked up at me, shrugged and foraged under the paper for the telephone which he unearthed by the simple expedient of finding the flex and pulling it until the phone emerged from the piles of paper. He located the handset using the same technique then dialled a number and had a short conversation before replacing the handset.

He looked at me again before motioning me to sit down. 'Was the price going to be that much of a shock?' I wondered.

"Micro," he grunted at me. Small? The price? No… He grunted a few more words of Greek and it gradually dawned on me what he was saying was wait a small time.

Meanwhile, he turned his attention to a man and two boys who had turned up in a pick-up that had seen plenty of use. They had entered the shop carrying a battered metal something-or-other. The shopkeeper, janitor, or whatever he was returned to his party trick of riffling through catalogues until he got to a picture that resembled the metal gizmo. His new customer looked at it and scratched his head. His two sons wandered off bored by now and played with the various makes of chain saw that lay around the place.

His new customer looked at the picture that he was being proffered, took the catalogue, turned it around in his hands and did a lot of shrugging and grunting. The shopkeeper dug up some more pictures. Eventually, the customer gave up on the pictures and picked his way among the tractor parts, cans of oil and like things to a small display stand that supported three large prop shafts with universal couplings.

One of the end couplings looked a bit like the gizmo that he had brought into the shop. A conversation ensued of which I understood very little.

"There, that's what I want — a bloody coupling."

"The whole thing?"

"No just the bloody coupling off the end."

"You've got to take the whole shaft."

"I don't want the whole bloody shaft. I can't afford the whole bloody shaft…"

Or something of the sort.

By now, a younger man had pulled up in a shining new pickup and strode into the shop. He spoke rapidly to the shopkeeper-cum-janitor establishing which battery it was that I was interested in I supposed. He then set off up the stairs. I followed him up. He wordlessly inspected the battery that I had selected then went back down. I followed him cracking my head on the beam once again. Down in the office he picked up a catalogue — right one first time — and turned to the price lists in the back.

"Hundred and forty euro," he told me after fussing around with a calculator.

"I want two and I want a better price than that."

"Better for you or me?" he grinned.

"For me of course."

He shrugged and fiddled with the calculator a bit more before offering me 122 euros.

"I'll take two for 220."

"Uh?"

"Two. *Thio.*"

"No two. Only one."

"I want two."

"Second one Thursday."

"Exactly the same type and size?"

"Of course."

"So I buy one now and the other next week?"

"Yes, you can."

"And you are certain that you will have one next week."

"Of course."

"Ok. Ok, if you're certain. We have to have two, exactly the same," I turned to Helen. I was anxious that we would get the pair I didn't want to buy an ill-matched pair.

"Well, just tell him that you'll have them both when you see them both."

"We will have both batteries when you have the second in stock." I told him, "*Endaksi*?" (OK)

"OK. But if someone comes in and wants him, I sell him, then you only have one battery next week!"

"But if you can't get the second battery, we only have one. We need two. Identical."

"We have battery next Thursday."

"Supposing it's out of stock."

"Not out of stock. We have next week," he looked at me and sighed. "But if we don't have you bring old battery back and we give you money back. *Endaksi*?

He motioned to the shopkeeper-cum-janitor who went back to the mezzanine floor and lugged the battery down the stairs. Thank God I didn't have to do that. My head could not have taken many more collisions with the concrete beam without sustaining permanent brain damage and the battery was very heavy. "Did we get a deal?" Helen asked as we left.

"Yes, it was cheaper. Quite a lot cheaper."

He was as good as his word. He phoned my mobile to tell us the battery was in on the Wednesday night and he had it waiting for us when we turned up the following day.

Horrid Heads

Sami on Keffalonia is a working town. The port offers ferry connections to the Greek mainland and a number of other islands. The town is not to everyone's taste but it has water on tap at the quayside, a visiting fuel lorry and a fair range of shops. Sailing into the port from the sea, Sami is backed by green clad hills that drop away to a gently sloping plain to the west. The site of the ancient town of Sami is located in the hills — hidden in trees. Local archeological sites, a monastery, beaches and caves attract visitors to the place and in summer it is bustling with a range of tavernas along the front that offer plenty of choice if you eat ashore.

We sailed Sundowner into Sami to pick up supplies and take our first visitors on board — our granddaughter, Hollie, and her boyfriend, Stu. We were in Sami, located about midway along the east coast of the island, and they were arriving at the airport on the south coast. Our car was in Lefkada so they seemed to have a choice of using a bus or a taxi. Using the bus to get from the airport to Sami requires a changeover, and probably a lot of waiting about, at Argostoli — the island's capital. A speedier option is to take the taxi but, on making enquiries, we found that hiring a car for the day was about the same cost as the taxi fare so this is what we did. It enabled us to meet our first visitors at the airport — great excitement all round — and pick up stores at the more competitive supermarkets away from the harbour front. The flight was delayed so we had plenty of time to stock up at a LIDL and make other necessary visits to shops and a bank in Argostoli before reaching the airport near Lassi. There was, as I say, great excitement all round with Helen describing the many attractions of this beautiful island. I felt a bit of a heel when I had to point out that the weather was looking like getting uncharacteristically nasty. "It's possible that we may have to sit it out to-morrow — stay in Sami."

"Oh, surely not," said Helen looking at the blue cloudless sky.

"I will check the forecast in the morning of course."

"It just doesn't matter g'ma," Hollie said. "We're on holiday. It will be great to have a look around." It was uncharted territory for Hollie and Stu and I felt too that there are far worse places to be stormbound than Keffalonia.

Although it was fairly wild the next day, the forecast storm did not arrive and more benign weather had settled in by the evening. The following morning, we set sail under clear blue skies on clear blue water. Starting early and motorsailing north in the light headwind we made good time up the channel between Keffalonia and the island of Ithaca — the kingdom of Odysseus in Greek mythology.

At the north end of the channel, the wind was freshening and we were able to cut the engine and romp eastwards Meganissi. We anchored in a bay for lunch and a swim and then sailed on to anchor in one of the many bays at the north of the island. A couple of bright blue kingfishers watched us drop anchor. Once the anchor was down, they shot across the small bay to find a new perch on overhanging branches. Well perhaps they were not watching us so much as looking for their supper, but Hollie felt it was a personal welcome to Greece.

I awoke early the next day. Sundowner was moving gently on her anchor. The early signs were good for our guests. The weather was indeed looking more benign, but there was an indication that we had a problem to deal with first. I made myself a cup of coffee as quietly as I could and crept up into the cockpit stepping carefully over the creaky bottom step of the companionway. I settled down to savour the pleasantly acerbic taste of black instant coffee and watch the day coming to life.

The eastern sky was streaked with pearly pink. The water around the boat was as flat as glass and shone in the distance with pink and silver. To the north a small fishing boat cut a silver Vee through the water on the other side of the bay. The larger fishing boat that we had anchored near was being prepared for departure by a husband and wife team who had arrived noisily on a single moped while I was making my cup of coffee below. As I finished my first cup, they dropped their mooring lines and waved as they departed with the gentle rhythmic thud of the diesel breaking into the quiet of the morning. The kingfishers were back — iridescent blue flashes across the bay that found vantage spots on branches overhanging the water. By my third cup of coffee, noises below meant folks were stirring. There was the noise of pumping and a guttering sound and a whiff from the holding tank breather that probably announced a certain problem — the holding tank was full, or blocked, or something. I went below and tapped quietly on the door of the heads.

"Yes?" a theatrical whisper from the other side of the door.

"What are you doing in there?"

"What the hell do you think I'm doing in here?" Helen hissed.

"Well, don't pump any more."

"Why?"

"I think we have a problem."

"Oh shit!"

"Yes, that's about the long and the short of it."

"Well, what are you going to do about it?"

"Nothing until we are out at sea."

"What are the others going to do?"

"They will have to use the taverna down the road."

We motored out of our idyllic little bay in Meganissi and made for the wide-open spaces to dump the dump so to speak. You find somewhere well out from bays harbours and open a seacock and it all drops out — in theory. If this fails, then a popular remedy is to stick a bung in the breather tube and pump to pressurise the tank then let it go. There are stories about of this remedy backfiring, the tank exploding and the heads, and further beyond if you have left the door open, getting covered in the stuff.

We sailed the boat to a likely looking spot miles away from the shore, bays, harbours, and other boats. We plugged the breather, shut the seacock and pumped. Pumped until a fizzing sound came from the cupboard in which the holding tank is housed — uh oh. I opened the cupboard door and there it is. The inspection hatch is seeping smelly liquid under pressure.

"Ah. An inspection hatch," I hear you say, "The answer to your problems." Not so I'm afraid. The top of the holding tank is jammed so close to the underside of the deck above it that you can only just get the cover off and you certainly cannot see in or poke anything useful into the hole. The cover is a very substantial plastic plug of about six inches diameter with a screw thread and a large plastic "O" ring effecting the seal. It is screwed down tight so that if what is inside is fizzing out past that, then there is a lot of pressure in there. I released the seacock beneath the tank listening for the rush of the tank emptying. Nothing.

"Well, what do we do now?" Helen demanded.

"I'll try and poke something up the seacock outlet from the outside. See if I can get it far enough up to jiggle things about and shift it."

"That sounds pretty desperate. Why don't we just call IBA."

"They'll charge us money."

"You tightwad. What are you going to use to poke up the pipe then?"

"The hose."

"What? The hose that we use to put drinking water into the boats tanks with?"

"That hose," I confirmed.

"You can't use that," Exclaimed Hollie. "It's unhygienic."

"It'll be all right. I will chop a bit off the end and use that."

"How are you going to poke it up there from here?" The outlet from the seacock is a little below the waterline roughly under the heads.

"Well, I am going to get into the water, swim around to the seacock and just poke it up," I shrugged.

"It will come out all over you, Pops," Hollie looked worried — not to mention disgusted.

"Yeah, what are you going to do about that?" Helen demanded.

"When it comes, I'll keep my mouth shut and swim away from it — fast."

"Yeah, you'll probably break Ian Thorpe's time for the 100 metres," chuckled Stu.

"Ugh!" was Hollie's only contribution.

In the end, it didn't work. I was quite relieved really. I was treading water beside the boat and trying to push the hose up the outlet. It was difficult. There were too many bends in the pipe between the tank and the seacock to force the pipe up very far. This was compounded by the fact that there was nothing to grab hold of, so the harder I pushed, the further I floated from the boat. I had fiddled about with the hose and other likely bits of equipment, wriggling them about up the outlet expecting all the while to hear a demented gurgle and then get deluged by what we normally like to leave behind and forget about. All to no avail. Nothing happened apart from a chat with a passing Yottie curious to see what was going on. Why we were sat in the middle of the open sea doing nothing, but with one person in the water.

"Are you all right?"

"Yes, fine thank you," I shouted back treading water by the offending outlet expecting it to choose that moment to explode into action and cover me with scata so that I looked like the old tar baby and smelt like nothing on earth. Fortunately, it didn't happen.

"What are you doing?"

"We're practising man overboard," shouted Stu.

"You don't seem to be getting him back on board," shouted the yottie.

"That's because we've forgotten how to do it," chuckled Stu.

"Oh, my husband will tell you," Shouted the yottie's wife. "He's a Yachtmaster you know. Just qualified." The Yachtmaster looked a bit embarrassed by his overbearing wife.

Stu assured them he was only joking and fobbed them off with some other excuse — checking the antifouling I shouldn't wonder. So they departed with a final check as to whether I was OK and wishing me goodbye. "And you can yachtmaster off," I muttered uncharitably as I clambered back on board and dried off.

"Any more bright ideas, or do I call IBA?" Helen wondered.

"I'll do it," I grumbled and Helen passed me the boat's mobile phone with an 'I told you so' look on her face.

I picked my way through the menu of spoken options and eventually got through to Lucy. I explained the nature of the problem and she put me through to Kelvin.

"Where are you?"

I gave him my position.

When we rendezvoused with the man from IBA, he went through the motions (an inadvertent pun I assure you) doing everything that I had already gone through with just the same level of success. Eventually, he sent for the big guns. Kelvin arrived and considered the problem.

The final solution was a form of keyhole surgery. The three-inch pipe that took the waste from the holding tank to the seacock had a right-angle bend. We made a small hole in this elbow with a length of stainless-steel rigging. Once through the pipe, the inserted wire was jiggled up and down and eventually disturbed the blockage at the bottom of the tank. With a great woosh, it fell out down the pipe and out into the sea. What a relief, but what a mess.

The keyhole of course leaked so, although it was a relief to have overcome the immediate problem there was a significant amount of foul-smelling liquid spreading itself thinly, stinkingly and widely down the inside of the locker and under the floorboards. Where, we wondered, did the unpleasant stuff end up? 'In the bilges' was the answer, but via a very tortuous route. So there was a great deal of flushing through to be done with disinfectant and detergent until everything was sweet(ish) smelling and, we felt, clean again.

We came to the conclusion that the blockage had been there when we took over the boat. We had assumed that because the outlet was in the open position when we had first met the boat — propped up in the yard — that the tank was empty. However, when we freed the outlet off by jiggling the wire about a large quantity of white stuff was ejected before the brown stuff appeared suggesting, to the experts in these things, a mature 'calcified' blockage.

The pipe was tightly bandaged with duct tape and we were left with a reel of the stuff to use if the repair started weeping. We moved off to Sivota — a sheltered bay on the island of Lefkada — getting a bit of a sail en route. We dropped anchor in the bay as the sun set.

I later discussed the problem with Danny, a local chandler, who had become my adviser on many things. How best to avoid a repeat of the problem; how best to put a permanent solution in place of the temporary lash up that we had. On leaving, I apologised for the scatological nature of the afternoon's topic. "No problem," he said. "Toilet talk is one of your yotties favourite topics."

He recalled how he had got caught out in a storm off Spain on his way out to the Med and, while screaming down big rollers, managed to roll his boat completely inverting it then completing the full 360 degrees ending upright but battered. When he eventually limped into a Spanish port a yottie took his lines.

"The boat was in a state," Danny explained. "The rigging and spars were twisted and bent. It was obvious I had come in with major problems. I had a young child and a hysterical wife on board. The bugger who took my lines ignores all this and asks what sort of toilet I have and, when I told him, he said that he had one of those too and wanted to know how I got around such-and-such a problem. He was quite offended when I told him to go forth and multiply."

"A full three sixty," I said. "Christ, I've heard of it happening. It's quite a hazard for these high-tech boats they race around the world when they're going for it with fierce following winds and seas in the wilder parts of the world..."

"Well, that was what was happening... Surfing down big rollers with the wind up our tail... You hit high speeds, it can be exhilarating but you have to be on the ball, a loss of concentration, an out of place twitch of the rudder at those speeds and you're suddenly beam on to the weather and over you go!"

"Exhilarating?" I exclaimed gathering up my bits and pieces and change. "Frightening I should think with the wife and child on board."

"Ah," he winked at me as I left the chandlery. "The worst thing was that it completely spoiled the Sunday roast."

The Optimistic Log and the Emu

Our second batch of visitors in the first season were our two daughters, Sharon and Nicola. They were flying into Corfu. Helen used the car to meet them off the Corfu/Igoumenitsa ferry which gave me a few hours to try and resolve an electrical fault. Having done that, I sat reading in the cockpit under the shade of the bimini, but the peace was short lived. Whoops and shrieks announced their arrival as they clattered on to Sundowner.

"Hey, Dad, the boat, it's terrific. I bet you're pleased."

"It's OK," I said grudgingly.

"He's still grieving Tethera," Helen informed them.

"Tethera... Really Dad?"

"Yes, it was a fine boat, Tethera."

"Dad, you can't be serious. This is much nicer; much roomier, and not so old. I bet it's faster."

I grinned, "Yes, it is that."

We had a good week. Sharon was familiar with the islands from a fortnight we had sailed there with Sailing Holidays a couple of years back, but it was Nicky's first taste of sailing the Ionic and she was stunned by the boat (in comparison to Tethera roomy and speedy so she kept reminding me) and the islands. They competed to see who could get the most speed out of the boat leaving 12.7 knots in the visitor's book as a challenge to their younger brother, David, who was due the following week.

"12.7 knots, Dad. That's much faster than Tethera going downhill with a gale behind her."

"Downhill? On water?"

"Well, if she could! 12.7 knots — all down to the skill of the helmsman — or woman, in my case. David won't beat that."

"Ah, the log is a bit optimistic. This boat won't do 12 knots. Seven knots more like."

"Shut up, Dad. It's accurate."

"How do you know?"

"I'm a woman. I know stuff. You men just don't understand."

"Huh, I knew it was a mistake inviting you both on board. I'm seriously outnumbered."

However, one thing neither of them could really get their heads around was the name Heikell. Rod Heikell's pilots for Greek waters, particularly the Ionian Sea, are seen by many visiting yachtsmen as the 'Bible' for these parts. We had an old dog-eared copy on board. The information on approaches, moorings, bays, harbours, and hazards is interspersed with notes on history and local points of interest. Sharon or Nicky often referred to the pilot when we were planning what island we were going to visit next, where we might anchor for lunch, where we could stay overnight.

"Dad, where's that book?"

"What book?"

"The one by Hinckle, or Heineken."

"Ah, Rod Heikell, the pilot."

"I didn't know he was a pilot."

"No, it's the book that's a pilot."

"How can a book be a pilot?"

"Ah, never mind."

The poor man got all kinds of sobriquets and in the end having been transformed to Rod Heineken and then to Rod Hull and then "You know, the one with the emu"[1]. He finally became the Emu and when there was doubt about anything, the cry 'Consult the Emu' was heard.

It was on this trip we found ourselves in Mourtos on the mainland. We arrived late afternoon and a bit of a blow seemed imminent. The blackest of black clouds was headed our way from the open sea. The water front taverna owners were winding down and securing their transparent windshields and ushering people inside. Moored stern to the

---

[1] Rod Hull was a ventriloquist and his dummy, the Emu, were infamous for an attack on chat show host Michael Parkinson where they jointly wrestled Parkinson to the floor.

harbour with the main anchor and chain securing the bow of the boat we seemed to be secure and certainly the initial blasts had little effect. Three owners took their boats off the quayside obviously having decided that they would be safer riding out the storm on the water or anchored in the lee of one of the nearby islands.

"Let's get into the shelter of one of the tavernas. We can watch from there." By now, we had a full-blown storm with rain and then hail adding to the trials and tribulations of the new arrivals. However, with Helen having made a dash for the shelter of a taverna, the storm intensified, and our anchor started to drag.

"See, if you can tighten the anchor chain a little." I shouted at Sharon, but it had no effect. I had put extra fendering at the stern and now transferred some from the starboard to the port side of the boat. I was going to lay the boat alongside, there was just space to do so, the boat wanted to do it and, in this weather, I was not going to argue with it.

Helen returned and a couple from another boat had seen our predicament and helped me to ease the boat alongside and adjust fendering so that the boat was well buffered from the harsh concrete of the harbour wall. The anchor caught as we had the boat almost alongside. I shouted at Sharon who had by now clambered off the boat and was helping ease it alongside, "Can you get up on the bow and pay out all the anchor chain so it's slack and laying on the bottom?"

She looked up at the bow. We were to a small extent sheltered being on the lee side of the boat. Up on the bow seemed awfully exposed, "Why do we want to do that, Dad? It's bloody wet up there."

"In case someone wants to come alongside. We don't want him tangling with the chain," I looked at her. She was as I was wet through. Her hair was plastered flat to her head and as I looked a large dewdrop of rain hung from her nose. "I'll do it," I said. "You'll be wanting to do something with your hair before we go to the taverna."

"Ha ha, very funny; I'll do it. No problem. Can't get any wetter," she grinned. "What will we do if another boat comes alongside? Surely, they will be right on top of the chain. We won't be able to get it up."

"Just let it out till it hangs straight down so we are sure that it's lying on the bottom. We will worry about retrieving it when this lot is over. It will blow out soon enough."

With Sundowner secure and snug, we thanked our helpers before Helen and Sharon dashed for the shelter of a taverna. I took a last look at the mooring before following them.

"Where's Nicola?" I was asked when I arrived sopping wet at the taverna.

"Isn't she with you?"

Helen made a show of looking under the table, "No."

"She's probably in her cabin. She went for a lie down before the storm started," said Sharon.

"You must be joking. She can't have slept through this lot — boat being battered by wind and rain, us leaping on and off, the windlass rattling chain in then out again."

"Want a bet?"

I checked and sure enough there she was. It must be said that she was having problems with her back. Complicated problems that would eventually lead to an operation but, for the moment, the doctor had prescribed her pain killers that contained a liberal dosage of morphine — so she was on cloud nine, quite possibly having a better time than us.

Back to Corfu

The girls were catching their flight home from Corfu and David, one of our sons, was arriving there on the inbound plane from Gatwick. We came in to the Naok Yacht Club located under the Venetian ramparts of the old fortress of Corfu town. The club steward shouted us across to a berth in front of the club house as we arrived. He held up a lazy line which we immediately caught in our prop. The engine stopped with a thump and Sharon, who was on the helm, gave an anguished shout.

"I think I've broken your boat, Dad."

"Just stalled the engine… I hope. Let's get moored up then we can look at it."

We threw a stern line to the steward who handed us another lazy line and we were soon securely moored.

"You have wrapped the lazy line around your prop," the steward told us unnecessarily.

"You handed us the wrong line," I countered.

"No, you wrap the line; have you got dive gear?"

"No."

"I will get my diving gear and unwrap," he told us.

"Is that all part of the service?"

"No," he looked at us measuring how much he could take us for. "Normally a hundred euro… but…" and he studied my face, "I could do for less."

"I'll have a look first."

He shrugged and walked away. In fact, a face mask and snorkel did the trick. It was a minor wrap due to the fact the engine was just ticking over when it happened and the engine stalled as soon as the lazy line caught the propeller.

We were next to a large dark blue Beneteau owned by a Brit who clambered off to lend a hand as we arrived. I spoke to him once we were sorted and the girls had gone off to explore.

"First time I have been in here. Seems a nice enough spot."

"Ahh, there's a bit of a swell from the ferries from time to time but it is fine."

"Been here long?"

"It's my base. Winter in Gouvia. Launch round Easter and come straight here."

"Easter's a big deal in most of Greece. What's it like in Corfu?"

"Mad, mate. They chuck pots out of top floor windows to smash in the street below. Make them specially for the event. Quite elaborate some of them are too."

"Oh, an extension of the plate smashing?"

"Yeah, but more dangerous if you're in the street below at the time!" he said with a grin.

"There's a big expat community here I hear."

"Yeah. There's even a cricket club for chrissakes."

From the yacht club, it was a bit of a climb into the town but well worth it. The Ionian University faculty of music is housed in a large white monolithic building that overlooks the yacht club and the wooded island opposite. Wandering past you can hear a singer, or an instrumentalist practising scales and arpeggios adding a dream-like quality to the walk up through the stone passages. In the fortress, you cross high above a canal before emerging into the squares of Kolla and Enosios beyond which are the fascinating streets of Corfu — narrow and buried between traditional Greek buildings intermingled with elements of Venetian, French and British architecture. There are shops selling gold, wild honey, baklava and fig cakes in the alleyways. The new town has a cosmopolitan flavour. Stalls on the narrow pavements outside grocery shops are piled high with big red tomatoes, glossy purple aubergines, olives, oranges, grapes, and apples.

With the girls homeward bound and David on board, we headed south and planned a two-day trip back to Lefkas. The first night was spent in Gaios, the capital of the little island of Paxos. Gaios is a picturesque village built around a port that is protected by the two small islands of Aghios Nikalaos and Panagia. The following day was a longish sail with the following wind and sea causing that uncomfortable rolling gait that you tend to get with a bit of a sea and the weather up your tail. Helen doesn't like longish trips and never came on any of our cross-channel excursions in Tethera for that reason. She put on a CD of late fifties, early sixties pop. What was rather spooky was that David, who was born in the late sixties, knew all the words, which was more than I did.

"Didn't you listen to pop music in your teens, Dad?"

"Well, jazz was more what I was interested in, but I listened to some of this stuff. You couldn't avoid it. In fact, I had a friend whose brother used to do the 'doo-wah-diddy-diddy' bits on some of the records."

"Doo-wah-diddy-diddy?"

"Well, you know inane phrases someone else sings between the bits that the main singer sings."

"He was a backing singer?"

"I suppose."

A song came on that I recognised.

"Christ, this one used to get right on my tits," I said.

"Why's that? It was OK," Helen interjected.

"Oh, when I worked in Leicester, I had a colleague from Chesterfield who sung it all the time, badly and in a Derby accent."

"What's wrong with a Derby accent?"

"Nothing, I suppose. I think it's the lyrics that got to me. They are so stupid."

"No, they're not."

"Yes, they are, especially when you hear them sung badly all day."

"What's wrong with them?"

"What? 'I beg your pardon — I didn't promise you a rose garden'? What sort of idiot goes around promising folks rose gardens?" I asked them. "Here, I really fancy you. Would you like a rose garden?"

"What? Didn't you ever promise Mum a rose garden," David said in mock horror.

The silly song about the rose garden finished and Helen Shapiro started walking back to happiness.

"I used to quite like her," I admitted.

"Why's that?"

"Oh, she had a nice fruity voice. She didn't go about promising people rose gardens. And she did her own 'doo-wah-diddy-diddy' bits."

"She doesn't sing 'doo-wah-diddy-diddy'."

"Well, 'whoop-ah-oh-yay-yay-yay' then".

"Yeah and I bet NUBS were furious."

"NUBS?"

"National Union of Backing Singers."

"National Union of Backing Singers? You're kidding me. There's no such thing... surely?"

"Yeah, there is too. All two of them."

We made the bridge at Lefkas late in the afternoon which brought the entire debate about the artistic merits of pop music to a welcome close. Once through the bridge, we made for the town quay and moored stern to the quay so we could re-stock with stores from the shops in Lefkas. We decided to stay overnight.

We were woken from a deep sleep at about three o'clock in the morning by a cacophony of sound. It sounded like we were about to be the victims of an aggravated burglary. Helen and I were sleeping in the forepeak. I scrambled out of my bunk in a panic.

"What the hell is that?" Helen had blurted out in some alarm.

"Sounds like someone is laying chain right on top of us," but as the sentence came tumbling out, I thought 'no it's our windlass'. In the forepeak, we were separated from the chain locker and the windlass by thinnish panelling. I isolated the windlass at the main control panel and the sound stopped. A bleary Helen peered out of the forepeak.

"What was it?"

"It's raining outside. You know that new windlass switch that I put in the cockpit earlier this season? I think the rain has got into it and shorted it out."

A modification I had made soon after launching the boat was to put a switch to control the windlass in the cockpit so that the windlass could be operated from either the bow or the stern. This would help me to moor stern-to a harbourside with ease when on my own on the boat. I pulled on some trousers and went out for a look. At the bow, the anchor chain was as rigid as a solid rod of steel. I manually eased it off a touch and, as I was out there and wet anyway, I checked the fendering and mooring lines. It was still tipping it down and the people were still boogying noisily at the Peoples' Cafe. I looked at the console on which I had installed the switch. Nothing much seemed amiss. The cockpit switch was isolated — it could wait until morning. We were near a comprehensively stocked chandler if a new switch or sealant or something was needed.

The following morning, I replaced the switch and ensured that it was sealed against water ingress with silicon. As soon as that was done, we motored down the Lefkas canal and set our sails in the freshening breeze that greeted us as we emerged from the canal into the open water between Lefkas and the mainland Greece. It was the first time for David and he was tickled pink by the trip along the canal and the entry into the Inland Sea. The Inland Sea is defined by the Emu as an area off the mainland that is bound by islands such as Lefkada and Keffalonia to the west and the Greek Mainland to the east. The outer islands seem to shelter area from the worst of the winds that sweep down the Ionic from the Balkans so the sea is relatively flat. We got a good strong late afternoon breeze and David, who had spotted his sisters' entry in the visitor's book was able to trump their 12.7 knots with 12.8 (about 7 really!).

The First Season Ends

I woke quite early on a Wednesday in the middle of September. We had planned to pack the boat up and head home in late September, so I would have to contact the boatyard and arrange a time and date for the lift out. The year had been a great start to our retirement. An adventure really — at least by our standards. We had found a boat — not without a few difficulties along the way — and while we were not exactly exploring new waters, we now had time for a more leisurely exploration that our previous two-week holidays in the Ionic had not really allowed us time to do.

It had been a hot summer, even by Greek standards. Fitting the boat out and antifouling the hull had been carried out in intense heat in June. July was even hotter but at least we were on the water then. We could anchor in a bay and providing there was some breeze we would benefit from a cooling waft of air in the shade of the bimini. We had also bought a curtain of a sort of woven black and green plastic hessian from a hardware shop in Lefkas which we tied in place where extra protection from the sun was needed.

I drank my first cup of coffee watching the sky lighten pearl pink to the east and listening to the crowing of a couple of cockerels. August had been hot too — no hotter than July — but it had also been crowded. Half of Italy seemed to be in the Ionian Sea and pretty much all of Greece was on holiday too. The flotillas of English and Dutch were fully subscribed as the holiday season was at its peak. It was a time to avoid the popular bays and go exploring further afield. That's certainly what we would do more of next year — probably.

The warmth and light of the sun heralded another perfect day. The days in September were shortening but the balmy warmth of the month was much appreciated after the intense heat of July and August. We had observed that many of the Brits disappeared off home for August and some were now returning for the relative quiet and cool of September and maybe October before they finally packed their boats away for the winter.

It was a calm relaxing start to the day. It was the sort of morning to string out and savour. The sort of day when you could sit in the cockpit and let your mind wander over things prompted sometimes by something going on ashore or in a nearby boat. We had to get ashore at some point to get some stores aboard but no hurry. No stirring from below. I was still on my own. A second cup of coffee perhaps and fire up the laptop and have a peek at what the weather forecasters had to say. According to the last forecast that I had checked there was a bit of a breeze due in the afternoon, but nothing too much. I put the laptop up in the cockpit and switched it on while the kettle was coming to the boil in the galley. Helen emerged just as I was listening to the happy gurgle of the hot water that I was pouring onto instant coffee. She returned my morning greet and added, "What's it like out there?"

"Idyllic," I said dreamily.

"Weather?"

"Just going to look it up," I poured water onto her teabag and took my coffee up into the cockpit. The laptop told me it was installing updates so it would be some time before I got any sense out of that. I left it to its own devices for a while and sucked at my coffee ruminatively.

By the time I made my third cup of coffee, the "chip-chip" of swallows announced their first forage for food. I know I know, too much coffee is bad for blood pressure. But, I mean, blood pressure? I was seated in the comfortable cockpit of a boat moored in the middle of a lagoon whose waters mirrored the bluing sky above. I was watching yet another perfect dawn break over the Ionian Sea and its islands. It was probably the best cure for blood pressure that man could devise.

The island was coming to life as the laptop resumed normal service and Helen arrived in the cockpit. The odd distant shouted Greek greeting or rattle of a car along the opposite shore echoed across the water. I looked at the shapes and shades of green on the slopes above the village. Slim dark Cyprus erect and unmoving like sentries, olives with the wind shimmying their light silver-grey foliage about and all manner of shapes and greens between. They were all standing out with the extra relief that the low early morning sun provides on that hillside some mornings.

"I will probably ring up Aktio to-day. Book a date for lift-out. Any thoughts?"

"It's so nice now. Let's make it the end of the month."

"Blimey, I thought you would be dying to get back to the family by now."

"Well, some of them have been out to see us and it's nice now. It's quietened down a lot and it's cooler."

We agreed that I would try and arrange a liftout in the last week of the month and we would start making lists. All boat owners have lists and they are organic. They grow. They outstrip even the most Herculean efforts that the owners may make to shorten them. There are different lists — things going home, things staying on the boat, things to do to the things staying on the boat, things to buy in the UK. You even have ultra-nerdy lists of lists if you are not careful.

A replacement for the tender went on the 'things to buy in the UK list'. Cheaper in the UK than in Greece, see. Our present tender had survived five seasons of charter work and one season of us. It was now distinctly showing its age. The webbing that the plastic seat slotted into to provide something like the traditional thwart (to sit on and row) had given way and the replacement seat that we inherited was an inflatable PVC sausage that was difficult to secure in place. Tags with fixing eyelets at each end had torn out. The seat was useless and the tender was leaky and degraded by six seasons use, abuse and Mediterranean UV.

The cockpit table was another casualty.

It never ceases to amaze me when inappropriate materials are used in equipment and devices that are specifically intended for use in a marine environment. If the equipment in question were dirt cheap then you might expect it, but none of it ever is.

"I don't believe it," I told Helen.

"Oh, what now Victor?" Helen, rather uncharitably, has Victor Meldrew down as my alter ego.

"They've used bloody mild steel for the screws in this table."

"Well what else would they use — plasticine?"

"I would expect stainless steel or maybe brass."

"They're probably expensive."

"Oh, yes, the manufacturer has saved the smallest fraction of a penny on a handful of very small screws — but doubtless that's brought a blissful smile to their chief accountant's face.

The cockpit table was made out of wood, or, to be more exact, something that passed for wood when it was brand new. The bulk of the table was the sort of wood that comprises a heart of fibrous stuff sandwiched between thin — almost veneers of wood. God knows what sort of tree they got that from. The fibre was visible where the edges and corners of the "veneer" had come unstuck and were starting to curl away. The damp that was now getting in from time to time was causing the fibre to swell so that it was bursting out of the fractured seams — like cotton bolls ripened and bursting at harvest time.

"Never mind. With my woodworking skills I should be able to make a duplicate," I told Helen. She groaned, and I knew what she meant. Since when had I been endowed with woodworking skills?

The holding tank was to be listed too. This went on the 'Things to be thought about during the long winter nights in the UK' list. It was still giving us some trouble from time to time. God knows what we would do about it. The sails, sail cover and bimini all needed repairs here and there and Helen wanted to re-cover the cockpit cushions. Perhaps we would see what Waypoint (local riggers and sailmakers) would charge us for cleaning, overhaul and storage of sails and sailcovers.

The lists also detail what has got to be taken off the boat and what is left with the boat and anything special to do with either. And then there are measurements to be made where I am intending to make something up at home. And there are sheets, towels etc., that are going to be left aboard but sealed up against damp and mildew for the winter. And the engines to winterise (oil changes, filter changes, air intake and exhaust to be opened up sprayed with inhibiting oil, swabs stuffed in every orifice). Unless I make lists, something will get forgotten. In fact, I often forget things in spite of these elaborate lists. In truth I frequently lose the lists — and then where am I without my lists? Bewildered — that's where.

Helen went below to get one of the Greek school exercise books that we had always used for notes and diaries — even in our backpacking days. I watched a small battered Fiat that had been parked on a patch of waste ground pull out in front of a gleaming BMW 4WD causing it to slow to the leisurely pace of the Fiat. The Fiat could have waited to pull out. There was nothing following the BMW, but the Bema driver took it all in his stride waiting patiently for a chance to pull out and resume his headlong pace.

'A bit different to the home counties,' I mused recalling a driving instructor whose normal response to a harrying blast on the horn from a pissed off driver was to lean out of his car window and shout at the passing car, "What's up mate? Never seen a bad driver before?"

I have long held that cars should have two horns: a 'do excuse me,' and a 'bloody watch it' horn. I recalled one incident when pulling up at traffic lights behind a mini full of youngsters. After a short interval, the light for the 'filter' lane that we were in went green while the lights for 'straight ahead' and 'right' remained resolutely red. I waited a few seconds then gave them a gentle pip on the hooter. It was meant to come out as, "Excuse me, I've done exactly the same myself on previous occasions, but you don't seem to have noticed that the lights have changed." But, of course, it came out as "PRAAAAAATTTTTT!!!" There was a revving, grating of gears and a squealing of tyres as the driver hurried away from the scene of her embarrassment. Fists were stuck out of windows with one or two fingers pointing skywards.

I also thought back to an early holiday on Crete where we discovered that the locals, when overtaking, gave a quick pip-pip to warn the car he was passing. The overtakee, far from getting irritated as you appear obliged to do if you're driving a BMW in the UK, would respond by temporarily abandoning his meandering from side to side of the road and drive straight and close to the kerb. The two exchanged cheery waves as the overtaking took place and the overtaken would revert to his happy meandering once the manoeuvre was complete. A far more civilised and relaxed approach.

Lift Out at Aktio and the Diesel Bug

Lift-out went without a hitch. We arrived at the Aktio slipway which ran between two concrete jetties equipped with a rail to tie up to and rope fendering all round. The lifter was not a crane nor the hoist that I had been used to in the UK. At Aktio, they used a modern version of the sledge that we had been launched from at the start of the season but instead of the sledge of timber, concrete and metal, Gianni, the yard owner, had a long carriage on wheels with hydraulic hoses snaking from a control panel on the tractor unit to various hydraulic rams which raised pads to support the boat, extended arms that stuck out from the trailer and extended the link between tractor and carriage.

Two of the yard hands held the boat alongside with a rope to pull and a long boat hook to push so that they could square the boat up to align with the approaching carriage. The tractor unit pushed the carriage down the slipway. Once it was squarely under the boat the driver started operating the hydraulics pulling and pushing levers from the small forest of them in the tractor cockpit. Hydraulic pistons operated large pads that were raised to support the boat then the whole lot was towed up the slipway and stood in the yard for a jet wash.

Once the jet wash was complete, the tractor unit roared into life again and pushing the trailer unit, threaded sledge and boat through the yard to its storage berth. Here it was carefully pushed into place so the keel could be lowered onto a couple of wooden pads on the central beam of the metal cradle that the boat was to be supported in. A central stand-alone stern support went in first then two supports hinged onto the cradle were swung into place either side of the stern so that end pads rested on the hull. The pair were cross braced with chains which were tightened with bottle screws and the sledge could start to be withdrawn. Other supports were swung into place and braced as the sledge was moved out. Then there it was — our home for the next week or so while we winterised our boat, made our way through lists, sealed sheets and clothes and the like into black plastic sacks for winter storage on the boat.

Living on the boat in the yard is pretty primitive. You are out of the water so the heads are not in use. If you want a pee in the night, you have to clamber out of the boat battling with the mosquito net that seems determined to wrap you up while you endeavour to leave it in place then stumble across the crowded boatyard rousing the dogs into a barking frenzy and getting consumed alive by mosquitos. Either that or use a bucket on the boat and slop out in the morning. The yard is reclaimed marsh land and is surrounded by marshes. You hear the toads most of the day and feel the mosquitos all of the time. It's not so bad when you are in the boat but when you descend to ground level, especially in the grass, the mozzies attack in their hundreds. This autumn seemed to yield a breed of super mozzies. They were as big as mice and take half a pint of blood at a strike... well all right, I exaggerate a bit, but they were big and if you swiped one of them off your leg it left a big gob of blood in place.

But it's not all bad. The boat can be coupled into a water supply and a mains supply that is there quite a lot of the time. The environment has its charms too. It is in beautiful countryside. There are boats of all sorts to look at and folks of all nationalities coming and going. There is the sight of Preveza across glinting blue water, mountains and the Gulf of Amvrakikos. The owner of the yard is charming and helpful. I have rarely seen Gianni without a smile on his face.

I had decided to take the sails to Waypoint for overhaul and winter storage and had dropped the Genoa on to the deck. There was sailcloth all over the deck and domestic disharmony in the air.

"Pull it straight and fold it over," I shouted to Helen who was at the other end of the heap of sailcloth. "No no, not like that. Get those creases out first."

"I wish you took as much care over your trousers when you drop them," She grumbled. "They just hit the bedroom floor and get kicked into a corner."

"It's an expensive bit of kit this sail. Besides, you've got to fold it moderately neatly. It won't fit in the sailbag otherwise."

"I don't know why you just don't leave them rigged — other boats do," she indicated several that still had the sails furled on the boom and the forestay.

"Yes, and they may come back next year to find them in tatters or gnawed at by rodents or nested in by wasps or birds. Anyway, they are expensive. It's good to clean them up check them over and store them off the boat for the winter."

"You didn't with Tethera."

"Ah, well, that was in the marina. There was always the prospect of sailing it in the winter."

"Yeah, I suppose that was important considering how many times you took it out in the winter — like never…"

A job I was not looking forward to was preparing the engine for winter. It wouldn't be so bad if the boat designer had taken the trials and tribulations of the owner into account when putting the blasted boat together. If you think working on a car engine is difficult, try working on a boat engine. However, determined to keep costs down to a minimum, I had taken copious notes when IBA recommissioned the engine and equipped myself with a manual. The manual purported to tell you all that you need to know about marine diesel engines and the TLC that they require so, no excuses, I was to do it myself.

I should have known the book was misleading when it fell open at a page showing how you can position a small bucket under the fuel filter so that the diesel drops straight into it when you open the drain at the bottom of the filter housing. There was a picture of someone with clean hands tidily removing the filter and seals having just drained the diesel in the filter housing neatly into a receptacle stood underneath the filter housing on the clean floor of the engine bay. No oil or diesel on the gleaming clean uncluttered floor of this engine bay. Beautiful hands too — like those that grace TV commercials for skincare products. None of the normal signs of battle with the engine, no oil smears or skinned knuckles and half torn off fingernails. Unbelievable.

On Sundowner, the oil filter is too close to the bottom of the engine bay to get much more than a small yoghurt carton under it… and that has to be precariously balanced on the hoses that are part of the raw water-cooling system. The same applies to fuel filters. The first of the two fuel filters is inside the engine bay and 'around a corner' so you have to kneel on the floor of the starboard cabin with your head poked through into the engine bay to locate the filter. The drain cock is out of sight and awkward to reach so getting a spanner on it is quite an art.

The alternative to draining a filter into a can is to envelop the whole shebang in a plastic bag so that the filter, its content, the filter housing and anything else you have liberated ends up in the bag and not on the engine bay floor. However, even this is not as easy as it sounds.

When removing the number one fuel filter, I am ·kneeling uncomfortably and usually leaning well into the bay and I find it necessary to use one hand to brace me so that I do not overbalance. The other hand is busy using a spanner to unscrew the drain plug or the screws that hold the filter housing together. However, at some point in the procedure, it usually becomes necessary to clutch at the bag with the other hand as all is not going to plan. The bag and its messy content are about to spill onto the floor of the engine bay. As I do not have three hands this is the point at which I fall forward into the engine bay and head-butt some sharp protuberance of my unyielding diesel engine. So the whole pantomime is accompanied by odd oaths and profanities and there is a reasonable chance of plenty of blood and oil about the place — at least there is when I do it. On this occasion, Helen detected a higher than usual profanity count and enquired what I was grumbling about this time.

"Well, look at this," I said holding out a filter element thick with black treacly slime.

"Oh my God, don't hold it out like that. You're dripping the horrid stuff on the floor."

"Oh, don't worry about that, I'll clear it up later," I said swishing an old T-shirt vaguely around the floor. "It's this gunk around the filter. Do you know what it is?"

"Yes, it's nasty oily stuff. Put it in a black bag and bin it, why don't you?"

"No, I'm going to take it to show Kelvin."

"Well, he'll be pleased, won't he? I expect he gets to look at dirty oily bits of engine most days. He's going to think it's his birthday when you turn up with that."

"No, it's the stuff in the filter that's the problem. If you look the filter element is full of black stuff."

"That's what the filter is supposed to do isn't it filter out gunk?"

"Yes, but it's not usually anything like as bad as this. Normally, it's as clean as a whistle. In fact, I sometimes wonder why I bother changing it…"

"Yes… Well… I often wonder why you do half the things you do on the boat."

"Yes, well, this is different. I think this is the diesel bug!"

"The diesel bug? What's that?"

"It's a bug that lives in your diesel tank."

"A bug that lives in diesel? You're kidding me."

"Well, it's more than one bug. It's a whole lot of organisms — something like 150 different types of things, fungal growths, bacteria, stuff like that." (In fact, with the advent of biodiesel, there is something like ten times that number of species that will happily live in your diesel tank.)

I must admit I had wondered whether it was a ruse — a story put about by the chandlers that line the quaysides so that they can sell yotties yet more expensive gunk with magic properties that will fend off the diesel bug or this or that threat to their boat and their halcyon sailing days.

"What's the problem, anyway?" Helen continued. "The filter is filtering it out. Job done."

Kelvin confirmed later that what I had was the bug. "But why?" I wailed. "I do everything I'm supposed to. I keep the tank topped up so there is little air and condensation is minimal. I always add in the anti-diesel bug treatment that has been recommended. And plenty of it."

"Hmm, what is it that you use?"

"That blue stuff in the clear bottle that seems to be recommended by most chandlers round here."

"Ah, that disperses the water so the bug cannot live there anymore, but it doesn't actually kill the bug."

"Well, I was told that it's the best and anyway if the water is dispersed the bug can't live there so it will die."

"It was considered to be one of the best, but there are always improvements being made and there is some stuff on the market that kills the bug right off. You shouldn't normally need that. But you never know..." Kelvin paused.

"You never know what."

"Well, you never know whether the stuff you pick up from the mini tankers at the quayside or even in fuelling berths in the marina... you can never be sure that it isn't already infected — particularly at the start of the season when there has not been much throughput."

The course of action he recommended was to remove the tank completely (easier said than done of course) and scrub it out. Purging it and flushing it out with a number of different solvents including petrol among other things and cleaning out everything from the tank to the injectors.

"Why doesn't it happen in cars with diesel engines?" I asked him.

"I suppose in theory it can, but the boat is sat on the water getting cold at night and hot during the day — How big is your tank?"

"150 litres."

"What does the tank on your car hold?"

"50 or so."

"How much fuel do you use in a week on the boat? Ten litres? A tank full is a few months' worth of fuel — most of the time just sat around. In the car you're probably filling up twice a month. Maybe the stuff doesn't hang around long enough."

"So it's not that the stuff from the pumps in a garage is cleaner?"

"It might be. Faster turnover of fuel and all that."

"Well what are you going to do about it?" Helen wanted to know as we left IBA.

"Ahh... think about it..."

"Put it off you mean. What's there to think about? It needs doing — so you say. So do it."

"Well, can I do it? Do I need the professionals in to do it? Is it necessary to clean the tank out? I need to look into it a bit."

The advice I got was varied. It was the usual case of three yotties — six opinions. On the one hand, I was told 'change the filters and put in a killer dose - job done'. At the other extreme, the advice was 'dismantle it all, clean and purge everything in the fuel system and fill it with fresh clean fuel — omitting to say that getting fresh clean fuel in itself may be a bit of a lottery'.

I had to get back to the UK so I winterised the engine, closed off the tank stopcock, dosed the diesel in the tank with plenty of anti-bug medicine and left the removal of the bug as a start-of-season treat for myself when I returned.

Collecting a Car

What do you do in the winter when your boat is in Greece and you are in the UK? You can't sneak down to the boatyard and work on your boat and there is a limit to what you can bring back to the UK to work on. Though there is always something.

"There is catching up to do," Helen told me.

"Catching up?"

"Yes. Catching up with friends and family'. Come to that there is catching up with maintenance to house and garden," she said as she looked out at our overgrown garden.

I had hoped for a bit of paid work to compensate for depleted funds, but there was also an unexpected diversion.

I found myself in Stuttgart on a cold Monday evening on the last day of January. A German taxi driver was taking Johnnie Dangerous and I on a guided tour around Stuttgart when John remarked that he would like to see a 'traditional' part of town. "Where is the old quarter?" he asked. "We would like to see the traditional architecture and local life. You do have an old quarter, don't you?"

I was trying to kick him, but couldn't as he was in the front and I in the back. The driver took some time and effort to construct an answer which was delivered in good English and was diplomatic in tone but, stripped down to bare bones, it amounted to 'Well, we did have until you lot flattened them in the early 1940s'.

Germany 1 England 0

Some years ago, when John had bought a brand-new Mercedes, the company had offered to fly him out there to have a tour of the factory then drive his brand new car home to the UK. At the time, life was too busy for him to take time out so he had taken a rain cheque and was now cashing it in and had asked me along.

The trip around Mercedes Stuttgart manufacturing centre on the Tuesday was interesting, but the reception area rapidly got to me. There was the tasteful décor, there were the artfully placed exotic plants, lilies, rare orchids. There were the discrete Mercedes designer clothes — the uniform in which the staff were turned out. All expected. All very well. But the hushed tones used, the atmosphere of reverence — as if in some major cathedral or mosque. It all made me feel that, had I blurted out 'It's only a f*cking motor car factory', there would be screams and crashing as the elegant, designer-clad skivvies raised their hands to cover their mouths and dropped trays glasses, cups, coffee, and water on to the thick pile. I would be pinned to the ground by elegantly uniformed bouncers who murmured deferentially into my ear, "Sorry for the inconvenience, sir," in perfect English while they hastily scrubbed my mouth out with soap and water.

I mean, what is all this fuss about motor cars? We've all got one. Some of us have more than one. John at the precise moment of writing has four. I am not rubbishing them. They are pretty much essential today and I will even admit that there have been and are some that are works of art — all too few really. But when it comes down to it, they are just for getting about in. They make demands on the planet because they need feeding from increasingly limited resources and the exhaust that they leave behind pollutes the place. But I suppose even big G did not manage to sort that out. Many of his creations, particularly us, could be seen to have those same defects. Ah well.

I suppose I have to admit that I did not treat Mercedes with the reverence they deserve because I am not a proper male. I do not do golf or car magazines. I think it is some element missing from my DNA. A bit of genetic engineering would probably put things to rights, but there you go. Some years back, I was trying to check out which would be the best satellite navigation thingy to get for my wife's birthday. Although I checked to see if anyone that I knew was around, a neighbour caught me furtively riffling through the car magazines in W H Smiths to see if any had published a survey of these new gadgets. I was so embarrassed. As I remarked at the time, I would rather have been caught looking through the soft porn on the top shelves by my grandchildren than looking through the car magazines by a neighbour.

An attractive lady, in her late forties, rescued John and I from the Mercedes reception area at ten o'clock. She described herself as a technician and said that she was going to introduce John to his new car. A little bit of social foreplay took place and when she learned that John also had a Jaguar, she all but swooned. Surprising for a dedicated Mercedes technifrau. "What model?" she asked.

"Oh, it's the *xyz 1234 series B*," he answered.

"Ah, one of the best, but my personal favourite is the *kmz 309 series 2 version 9 with brass knobs on*," she said.

My eyes began glazing over. I mean you expect women to describe their favourite car as 'the powder blue one with the long bonnet', but no. That's more me. The technifrau has it specified chapter and verse.

"Sit in the driving seat," she commanded John. "And I will sit in the passenger seat and explain everything."

"What about me?"

"You can sit in the back," I was told. Then she added as some sort of a sop, "It is where the important people sit."

"Yeah, yeah."

"It is! You never ever saw your Queen Mum sat in the front seat."

"She did when she was out on her motorbike."

She looked puzzled then a small smirk stole across her face, "Ah the British sense of humour."

"No, honestly, we were near neighbours. We live near Windsor," I told her. "And she was often out and about on her Harley in her royal leathers."

However, I couldn't steer the technifrau from her course. She returned to her task of taking John through the controls, displays and gadgets — a task that she did very well but which was to take over one and a half hours to complete.

The car will stop you going to sleep. It will not allow you to pull out if there is a vehicle in your blind spot. It will prevent you from inadvertently wandering out of your lane. It will massage your back as you drive. It will switch your headlights on when it gets dark and dip them when there is an oncoming car. It will hold you firmly in place if you corner fast. You talk at it to make a telephone call, use the wireless, or set up a route on the satellite navigation system. It simply will not

171

permit a collision or so she told us. Mind you, John might see this as a challenge, a battle of wills.

"There are nineteen sensors in the cab," the technifrau told us. This figure will not be entirely accurate — we were absolutely deluged with statistics that day and I remember none of them. "The system uses the data they generate to detect whether your concentration is dropping, whether you may be getting a bit drowsy. If the car thinks you are going to doze off it will sound an alarm and show you a big cup of coffee in the display."

"It makes you a cup of coffee?" I asked dumfounded.

"No no," she was easily irritated by the dumb questions from the man in the back who had confessed to owning an old Toyota. "It is just a picture of a cup of coffee. It is telling you to stop and have a cup of coffee."

"What if I don't like coffee?"

"Haah," She exclaimed and turned her attention back to coaxing John through all the bell and whistles.

Eventually, we started off on our tour of Mercedesland. We saw the original car built by Carl Benz. A sort of trap, as in pony and trap, on three spindly wheels with solid rubber tyres and spokes — just like big bicycle wheels.

Our guide told us that it was the first motor car in the world. I cannot vouch for the truth of this. He went on to tell us, "When Carl Benz had completed and tested it, Mrs Benz," he said indicating a photograph of a handsome-looking woman, "She took it the following day, without his knowledge and used it to go and visit her mother." So, the first motor car journey in the world was made by that most maligned of the species — a woman driver. And it seemed she was a spunky sort who was quite happy to nick Carl's invention and use it for her own ends.

We went around the factory with a bunch of German Californians. One of them chattered to me enthusiastically about Mercedes, their cars, their technology. Eventually, he asked me the leading question: "Are you buying a car?"

"No. He is," I indicated John who was deep in conversation with our guide.

"And then you are driving it back to England?"

"No. He is," I muttered pointing at John again.

"Is he not going to let you drive?"

"Nah."

"What model is it he is buying? Is it the *xyz*-series?"

"Oooh, I dunno it's a big brown one."

At this point, he lost interest and rejoined his group.

Germany 1 England 1

The assembly line was fascinating. Robots did delicate tasks with unerring accuracy picking up large subassemblies from pallets — floor panels, dashboards, or sliding roof assemblies etc. They would twirl them round in the air to orientate them correctly and then move them in a path toward their final fixing place. The path often had to be quite complicated to avoid clouting the irregularly shaped subassembly on one of the many obstructions. The dashboard went in through the front left door of the car and, to get it through the doorway, it had to be twisted around as it was moved through. Then on the end of the long robot arm, it had to be located accurately in its destined position and fixed in place.

There were all sorts of variants of the model on the same production line; right-hand drive, left-hand drive, different colours, and different options, such as a sun roof. Each time a new car appeared in a manufacturing cell, the bar-coded identity of the car called the correct programs up to set the robots to the appropriate task for the car in front of them. They picked the correct parts from the correct pallet and put them in the correct place and the right way round. Then, when the robots had completed their tasks, the car was moved on and the next car moved in and identified.

The assembly line snaked back and forth and even up and down in the huge building. Yes, there were even cars moving above us and cars disappearing into another floor below us. The assembly line was miles and miles long. We were told how long, but I can't remember; it was all part of the hail of statistics we endured.

A Hip Job

The month after my trip to Stuttgart the main event was a hip replacement. What an exciting winter I was having. My hip had been giving me some problems for some time. I went and talked to my doctor and, a year later, I arrived at the appointed hospital at seven o'clock in the morning. Luckily, I was listed first for the op. I was settled into the hospital bed pretty soon and the surgeon/consultant/whatever you call them these days and the anaesthetist were in to see me. He, the surgeon, was a likeable young Glaswegian — a friendly smiling face and a gentle (for Glasgow) sense of humour. She, the anaesthetist, was equally charming and of a similar age, at least viewed from my seventy years perspective she was — a tall slim willowy blonde with a smile that easily dissolved into a grin.

The surgeon asked me to confirm that it was my right hip that was to be replaced. Having had a lifelong difficulty with right and left I pointed, "It is thissun". He wrote a short memo to himself on my right thigh in black felt-tip pen.

"I don't want to labour this too much," he said at one point in our conversation. "But modern procedures require that I inform you of the risks." He continued to list all the things that might happen to me if he cocked up the operation then told me that there was a negligible chance of any of those things happening. I was unsure of the value of that little discussion but apparently modern-day procedures deem it necessary.

I was not attempting to track time, but I think that by 8.00 or 8.30 a.m. I was on a trolley in the room that precedes the operating theatre. Three or four people including the anaesthetist were bustling around me while I received the pre-op injection and was positioned for the operation. I remember not much more for a while, but was told that I used my mobile to phone home about midday. Helen phoned the ward

174

somewhere round that time and told them she was enquiring about me and how my operation went.

"Ah, that must be the chap they wheeled past me a short while ago shouting out 'Have you got Wi-Fi in here?' Yes, I'm sure it went OK," the lady manning the ward desk reported.

I don't remember shouting that out at all. Maybe it was fabricated at my expense. In fact, the rest of the day was a bit of a blur as the anaesthetic gradually receded. When Helen arrived laden with grapes and other goodies, I was moderately coherent at some stages, incoherent at others and lapsing into sleep the rest of the time. She sat patiently with me for what must have been the longest couple of hours of her life.

The next day began my preparation for release back into the wilds of Berkshire. I was got out of bed and was taken for a short walk by the physiotherapist, just out of the double room I was in and across to the far side of the corridor to demonstrate how to use the crutches. I would not have thought it would need demonstrating. I saw Robert Newton hamming it up as Long John Silver in my youth and using crutches all seemed straightforward enough. All I needed was a green parrot that swore, well by cinematic standards of the fifties it swore, and I was away. However, there are techniques and, when thought about, they are common sense techniques but I find I still need instruction in common sense things. For the rest of the two hours of my maiden voyage, I alternated between a little bit of practice in the newly-instructed technique and a little bit of sitting in a chair doing a sort of can-can movement with my legs while attempting to do a crossword that blurred in front of my eyes.

I was more coherent for visitors the next day which was as well. I had four of them representing four generations.

Nicola arrived first. She swept in bubbling with laughter and laden with gifts from her family — cards, goodies to eat and a book describing how to teach your dog quantum physics. I don't have a dog. She has three. So I suppose that's a clear hint that she wants them educated — *By me?* She entertained me with the latest trials and tribulations of bringing up a family of three boys, two girls, three dogs, three horses, two sheep and a cat with asthma. We compared notes. She had previously undergone a far more intricate operation than I. It involved a sort of tiny scaffolding structure in stainless steel being installed around a small section of spine. "What I enjoyed was the morphine," she said. "But it didn't half make me talk nonsense. Dad, the nurses *pleaded* with me to shut up when I was coming to."

"Are you still on it?" I enquired gently. Helen arrived at that point with, I was delighted to see, Hollie our granddaughter and her daughter, Crazy Maisie. Maisie was quite obviously phased to see her great-grandfather in what appeared to be a floral nightie, but she attracted a great deal of attention from the hospital staff whose voices went up and up in pitch (as they do when talking to babies) until they could only be heard by dogs and bats. I slid into a defensive coma for a while.

The following day, the tutorial was 'Stairs and how to Negotiate them Using Crutches'. I had the advantage of a god-daughter who is a physiotherapist and thus I already knew the "Bad leg to hell and good leg to heaven" mantra, but found it surprisingly difficult to get up and down stairs with all legs and crutches operating in a smooth coordinated rendering of the BLHGLH technique. However, this does not mean it is actually difficult — it is more that, well, how can I put it… Let's just say that the words smooth and coordinated are not words that naturally come to observer's lips when I am the subject of their observations. The dos and don'ts were explained by the ever patient and informative staff. I remember being told the importance of not rotating the upper leg away from its normal plane of operation.

"Don't pivot your new joint."

"Why not?"

"Well it might come out."

"Oooh err."

"Dislocate," he explained.

"Yes, yes, I know what you mean. But why? You don't hear of it happening in a natural hip. At least I haven't."

"Ah well, firstly, the muscle and tissue that normally surround the joint have been ahh…"

"Savaged?" I offered unkindly.

"No," he frowned. "Stressed a little during the operation and they have to grow back and strengthen — that's why your exercises are so important."

"And secondly?"

I can't remember his answer exactly, but perhaps it was along the lines of "Well, it's a ball and socket joint and the good Lord has the advantage of growing the one inside the other. We manufacture the two separately and have to be able to insert the one into the other at some stage so the engineering tolerance is not as close in our case."

If the day of the operation was day zero, I think that my maiden voyage was day one (the Thursday) and the ascent of the north face of the stairwell was day two.

I was quite keen to get home on day three — I was unashamedly using emotional blackmail by day two. "It is my birthday — see — and, if I don't get home for it, the family will have it without me, drink all the beer and eat all the cake," I moaned. The staff were unimpressed. They explained that there were obstacles in my way:

- Medical staff have to be happy that the mend is progressing in the expected way and at the expected rate.
- I have been shown to be adequately competent with crutches and techniques for manoeuvring myself generally — a close call this.
- Bodily functions have to have resumed normal service.

The last point was worrying me a bit. A tumbler full of pills was presented several times a day — four, I think. Their purpose was explained by the nurse with each presentation.

"That pretty pink one is for so and so. The nice bright yellow one is for xyz. Those cute, ever-so-tiny-little ones do such and such," she would purr as she handed the rattling plastic tumbler over. By day two senna was part of the consignment. "To ahhh... get things, ah going," she added to her explanations.

"I can't be doing with this," I told Sharon when she phoned on day two. "Nothing's happening and I don't want the attention in that err... umm... area."

"Ooooh I know, Dad," she said. "I'm the same. They can do what they like from the waist up but below... Well I don't want it." Our conversation had taken a scatological turn as it frequently did.

I recalled the only other operation I had undergone.

"After that particular operation, I came to in the ward," I told Sharon. "And, once I woke up, a nurse came over to me and explained the dos and don'ts. One of the things she told me was that I was not to get out of bed. If I needed a pee or err uhm... worse, I was to call a nurse and she would give me a bed pan. 'Bed pan' I thought when certain biological urges started to set in, 'I can't be doing with that. I'm OK. I feel fine."

I am not sure why I have this attitude. Dignity? Well maybe, but dignity and I are not the best of pals; however, I suppose the idea of perching on a po on a bed in the middle of a crowded ward did not appeal — in spite of the pretty flowery curtains that could be drawn around the bed.

I continued. "I felt the need and the bog was just opposite, nothing could be simpler. I hopped out of bed and walked over to the door marked TOILET, went in locked the door and set about the business in hand. All went OK until I came to leave. I couldn't find the door. The anaesthetic was still doing something to my brain. It was a peculiar sensation. My mind was on some sort of holiday. I turned around several times in the small confined space looking for the damn thing. Eventually, I located it and staggered back to the bed to get a major bollocking from the nurse".

"Never fear, Dad," Sharon brought me back to the present day. "I am in Birmingham at the mo, but I will be back in time to call in this evening."

"Oh, I'll have sorted it by then," I blurted out rather hastily.

"Well if you haven't, we'll sort something out. I'll get you home for your birthday."

"Oh shit," I thought rather aptly as I put the phone down. "That's her on the case." I was afraid — I was very afraid.

Part of the release procedure was an X-ray of the finished job. I was wheeled through corridors to the radiology department. Two young ladies stood me up against a white wall.

"Look straight ahead with your legs straight... That's right, just right... Now which hip is it?"

I pointed, "The one painted yellow with the good doctor's notes on it."

"Quite right — just need to be sure," she said pressing buttons so a machine moved in to peer myopically at my right thigh. "Now stand perfectly still for a few seconds — do you think you can manage that?"

She disappeared behind a screen, pressed another button then after a 'click' and a 'whirr' she was out again. "Just want you at a different angle," she said guiding me to assume a new pose.

"It's like being the groom at a wedding," I commented.

She looked thoughtfully at me stood there holding my nightie daintily above my waist. "Strange weddings some people have," she muttered as she disappeared into the shed for a second click and whirr. I could see a large screen with images on it. The fact that they were immediately available and the general high technology of the place was impressive intriguing and alluring.

"That's it?"

"Yep."

"That's the X-rays on that screen over there?"

"Yep. Wanna see them?"

"Oh, yes please."

The console containing the screen was hung from an overhead gantry and was easily moved into my field of view. I was caught between wishing I hadn't asked to see it and the awe of the technology that made the execution of the X-ray and the instant viewing of it so easy. The dagger of steel with the ball on top neatly housed into the new artificial socket stood in sharp relief against the shadowy outlines of the hip bone now joined by the new implants to the thigh bone in my leg.

Sharon breezed in that evening with about an hour to go before the end of visiting time. "Job done?" she enquired.

"I don't like your choice of words," I growled back.

"Well? Have you?"

"Yes of course," I dithered.

"Bloody liar."

"No no… Well… That is... I am on the cusp so to speak."

"Hmm. I don't remember asking for that much detail. Never mind, I've the solution here," she put a huge bag of goodies and cards beside the chair in which I was sat. "Look just what you need," she said lifting a bottle of Guinness from the bag. "Purely for medicinal purposes."

"Am I allowed that?" I wondered aloud suddenly feeling a whole lot cheerier.

"Definitely. It will build you up buttercup."

At the second Guinness ("Now don't go overboard" Sharon had admonished) the nurse came in and I confessed "Just for medicinal purposes," I told her. She shrugged.

"Just make sure you tell the nurse bringing round the drugs," she advised.

And that was pretty much that. The Guinness having done its stuff, the passing out parade was on Saturday morning. There was a run through of my performance on the lower slopes of the stairwell by the physio. There was a signing of papers and handing over of packages and I was home for lunch. The running in of the new hip was well on schedule and really no trouble at all. Amazing when I thought about what had been done. A fact confirmed by my children...

David came around once I was home and said, "Do you realise the size of what they put inside you? We used to irradiate (to sterilise) them at Isotron. I was surprised how big and how heavy they are."

Debbie — his ex-wife — also came to visit and described the operation. She was a nurse at the local hospital and had witnessed a few. "There's a lot of very energetic heave ho involved," she told me. "And a lot of sawing and drilling to see out the old and bring in the new."

"Blimey, what do they do with the sawdust."

"Oh, don't worry, they wash it out of you."

"And do they hammer that spike into a hole that they have drilled in my bone."

"Well sort of. It's a bit DIY I suppose."

It's true what they say... Your children are an immense comfort to you in your old age.

Interestingly, one of my fellow swimmers from the early morning session at the local pool had his hip done at the same time as me. We met a few weeks later for a post operation progress check… Were we doing the exercises? Could we walk along that corridor? Up those stairs? etc. etc.' We met up after we had both been put through our paces and the sun being above the yardarm, adjourned to a nearby hostelry for a little light refreshment.

It turned out, that Tony had had his hip done under local anaesthetic.

"You're a braver man than me, Gunga Din."

"I didn't have much option. They discovered that I had a problem with the anaesthetic in a previous operation. They came to see me before the op and said it was either a local anaesthetic or pack my bags and head home."

"It must have been horrific."

"Well, they did put up a screen to hide the action at the other end so I couldn't see anything, but the noise was overwhelming. There was a hell of a racket going on, but I couldn't see or feel a thing so I didn't immediately associate it with me. I thought it was road works outside or something. But the noise was echoing around the room, I mean the theatre. There was nothing else going on in the room — I was the main event. It dawned on me that the noise was them hammering, sawing and dynamiting parts of my body!"

"Bloody hell. Sounds awful."

"Yeah, well, I found myself thinking back to my schooldays. How the brainboxes who were going to be going on to be lawyers, surgeons and so forth were never that good at practical things like metal work and woodwork and I'd got two of the bastards trying to nail my body back together!"

"Bloody hell, do you want another pint?"

"Is the Pope a Catholic?"

Hip replacement is seen these days as pretty standard stuff, but it certainly struck me as quite a task. The operation took about ninety minutes. My team did three hips and a knee that day.

I was an NHS patient in a private hospital so I experienced a bit of both prior to and during. It was interesting and thought provoking to see the two alongside each other. It must be immensely difficult to get a huge operation like the NHS to work efficiently. But it is easy to see private practice as cherry picking — it can make choices that the NHS cannot. And to me the private route is in essence a very expensive form of queue jumping. For certain operations, you may wait a week or two in a private scheme and months or even years in the NHS. Do the two sit alongside each other, or does the private scheme leech unacceptably off the NHS?

Return to la Belle France

We travelled to Greece by car, on several occasions, in spite of the fact that travelling by air was quicker and cheaper. Often, we justified it on the grounds of the luggage we had to transport such as a second hand tender that we had bought for a song in Blighty. We told each other that we would treat it as a sort of mini holiday, a relaxed car journey which could take in the countries and towns on the way to our destination. In practice, we didn't really do that at all. We were anxious to reach our destination and set about getting the boat in the water as quickly as possible and ended up scorching along autostrada rather than meandering through rustic villages.

The second season I miscalculated our departure time and that set the pattern for the journey. An overnight in a sleazy hotel in France, difficulty finding our hotel in Italy, a run in with jobsworths on the ferry from Italy to Greece and mishaps that continued when we, with some relief, arrived at the boatyard in Greece.

Helen asked me the day before we were to leave what time we needed to leave our house to catch the 8.15 ferry from Dover. I was struggling with a flu-like cold, didn't think about it much and replied "It's a good hour." On the basis of this, we left at six o'clock giving us one and three-quarter hours before check in. The journey was good at first. We had the one-hour thing fixed in our minds so no rush. We cruised below the seventy-mph limit. As it was Saturday the roads were quite empty. As we went past the Gatwick turn off the M25, Helen remarked drily, "Well, we've been going an hour now."

"Ah yes. We normally allow an hour for Gatwick."

"So, Dover is just around the corner then?"

"Err no it's a way yet. I did say a good hour."

"How much over an hour is a good hour then?"

"Ahh... It's about another hour yet."

"So a good hour is like… two hours."

"Hmm."

"Wouldn't it have been better to say two hours?"

"Probably…"

"Well, we're supposed to check in at a quarter to eight so we had better get a move on."

So the accelerator was floored. We drove the rest of the journey as fast as we dare. We arrived at Dover with only ten minutes to spare and were waved on as we approached the ferry. The wheels didn't stop turning all the way from home till we were parked on the ferry.

We disembarked in Calais around half past nine and soon shook ourselves free of the port and into the somewhat boring flat, largely tree-less countryside of that part of France. After about five hours, the countryside started to improve and get really quite pretty.

We had booked into a cheap hotel in Bourge-en-Bresse and, wonder of wonders, had managed to put the address into the car satnav first time. Bourg-en-Bresse, we had read, is located at the western base of the Jura mountains, on the left bank of the Reyssouze, a tributary of the Saône. It sounded nice enough. The cultured tones of the satnav lady took us off the motorway and into a run-down shopping-cum-industrial area. It was a tip. We drove around the block twice because when she said, "You have arrived at your destination." We didn't believe her the first time. We picked the hotel out the second time around. It was sleazy. No… Sleazy would have been good in comparison. But we were tired so it did. It had Wi-Fi and cold and cold running water — especially down the walls. But it was very cheap.

"It's a bit of a run-down area. Do you think our car is safe? Everything is on display," Helen asked. It was true. I had had to put the back down to accommodate an inflatable dinghy.

"Ah, it'll be all right," I said. "Anyway, that's the only option we have."

"Well go and make sure that nothing that looks tempting is on display," Helen urged.

The first thing I did was to lose my car key in a bush near our hotel room (don't ask) but fortunately I found it again — but the bush was bloody spiky so besides the flu-like cold I was now nursing serious wounds.

We wanted to make a reasonably early start the next morning so we went to bed quite early. As I was drifting off, I became aware of noise from the room next door through the thin walls.

"Christ, these walls are thin and some lucky bugger is having rumpy pumpy!" I said.

"What… what are you talking about? I was just dropping off?" Helen grumbled sleepily.

"Can't you hear it?"

"Hear what?"

"The bed squeaking next door. Our neighbours are at it."

Helen listened and the noise stopped. "It's stopped now. But it wasn't rumpy bumpy. That's just your dirty mind and your fevered imagination."

"What was it then?"

"Sounded more like someone sawing wood to me," Helen replied.

"In a hotel room? At night?"

"Why not?"

"So that's this year's euphemism for sex is it? Sawing wood?"

"It wasn't sex. It didn't last long enough."

"You obviously cannot remember the last time we had sex."

"No really… if it was sex, the woman can't have got much out of it."

"Who said there was more than one person involved?"

We tried to get back to sleep and I at least was on the cusp so to speak when a car alarm started up. Helen sat bolt upright, "Someone is breaking into our car," she shouted.

"Oh Hell. How do you know it's ours?"

"It sounds like ours. Exactly like ours."

"They all sound the bloody same. Anyway, it'll stop in a minute."

"No, go and have a look. I'm sure someone is stealing something from the car. It's that sort of area."

"What would anyone want to steal from the junk that we're transporting to Greece. No, you go and look."

"Why me? You're the man."

"Yes, but you're much braver than me," I grumbled rubbing sleep from my eyes and reaching for clothes.

I hobbled out pulling on my trousers. My shirt was sort of inside out and upside down — fuddled by sleep I hadn't been able to sort it out. The alarm had stopped as I had predicted. I walked around the car with my hands in my pockets — I had forgotten to put on my belt. If I had to run for it my trousers would probably drop to my ankles which wouldn't have helped. Nothing appeared to be amiss. The car had just decided to trigger off the alarm, it happens.

The next day, we woke early and were on the road by seven o'clock. We were pretty glad to leave the hotel behind and Helen was pretty miffed to drive past some quite nice-looking hotels just a little further on in the outskirts of the town.

"They look much nicer than the one we were in."

"Probably much more expensive."

"Tightwad."

Through Italia

The next stage of our journey was very beautiful; the green hills started to turn into mountains. Fast flowing rivers ran alongside the road. Snow-capped mountains towered over it — we were approaching Mont Blanc.

We stopped at a chalet-styled cafe for a coffee. It was warm. We sat outside and took in the scenery. The bug that we had both caught was being persistent and made us go into paroxysms of coughing from time to time. Mine was apparently man-flu so wasn't really much more than terminal hypochondria but, in spite of this, I decided a Lemsip would do me no end of good and so asked the girl behind the coffee counter for a cup of hot water. What I got was another coffee. So much for my French. I took my coffee back to the little table in front of the café. The café was in an elevated position above the motorway and a garage where we had just filled the car with diesel. It was a nice view if you ignored the garage and the motorway. I settled myself at the table and Helen peered into my cup of coffee.

"Your hot water looks a bit murky," she remarked brightly.

"It's coffee."

"I can see that. I thought you were getting a cup of hot water for your Lemsip."

"I thought I'd try it in coffee," I said twisting the top of the little sachet, pouring the powder into the coffee and stirring it.

"Ugh, what's it like?" she asked after I had taken a tentative sip at it.

"Just the job."

"I'm not convinced."

"It's not you that I am trying to convince."

We drove on through the Mont Blanc tunnel which took us through into Italy and then through more tunnels. The Italian side of the mountains was also beautiful with towns set in the valleys, and waterfalls cascading down rock fronts. Five hours later, we were at a hotel in the Italian town of Brescia.

Brescia, we read, is situated at the foot of the Alps and is the second largest city in Lombardy. It is the administrative capital of the province of Brescia and has been an important regional centre since pre-Roman times. An uprising against Austrian rule took place in the spring of 1849 earned the town the title of *Leonessa d'Italia* (Lioness of Italy).

Today, the engineering industry provides employment and the tourist trade benefits from the proximity of Lake Garda, Lake Iseo and the Alps. The city has sites which date back to Roman times but is mainly a mix of traditional and modern Italian architecture, along tree-lined avenues.

Finding the hotel was interesting. The satnav took us a most complex route. At one point, we went through the same streets twice — a satnav with a sense of humour perhaps. Then I found myself driving on the wrong side of a dual carriageway. This was more my fault than the machines'. I got the real left mixed up with the continental or surreal left. I have difficulties with left and right anyway and when your continental decides that left is right and right is left — well, the whole thing is mightily perplexing. An Italian in a car coming the other way explained the error of my ways by using his hooter, his lights, shaking his fists at me and, quite unnecessarily, nearly ramming me. I rapidly rectified the situation by bumping the long-suffering Toyota over the central reservation, shades of The French Connection — The Brescia Connection, if you like.

The satnav eventually told us that we had arrived and our destination was on the right; I couldn't see the hotel and carried on around the block until I found a place to park. We looked for the hotel on foot — it seemed safer. To Helen's relief, the hotel was luxurious compared to the previous one. The lady on the reception desk showed us our room and indicated where to park the car. It was two o'clock in the afternoon, it had started to pour with rain outside so we spent the afternoon in the room relaxing, reading, playing cards, and waiting for the rain to subside so we could have a comfortable walk around the locale.

The next morning, we decided to try and make our way to Venice using the secondary roads to avoid paying any more tolls. The road took us around the south end of Lake Garda. Rain drizzled from a grey sky but temperatures were in the low twenties. It was a slow journey with the normal stopping and starting that you get when driving through small towns with numerous junctions and roundabouts. We were sat in traffic much of the time. We passed miles of vineyards and some beautifully rustic clusters of farm buildings. Eventually, twenty miles from Venice, we decided to go on the motorway thinking it would take us straight to the commercial port in Venice, but we somehow missed the correct exit and found ourselves hurtling along the motorway to Trieste. No problem, we will get off at the next junction and sort ourselves out. The motorway system seemed to be newer than the in-car satnav so she didn't have a clue where we were. She showed us driving across wide-open spaces that were probably fields when she had her brain manufactured and prompted us repeatedly to do a U turn at the next opportunity.

"I am not doing a U turn on a bleeding motorway," I shouted at her. "You got me into enough trouble in Brescia you tart."

We had unknowingly entered a stretch of motorway without turn offs or intersections for miles. The longest such stretch in the world I shouldn't wonder. After what seemed like a couple of light-years, we came to a motorway exit. The roads were still a mystery to our trusty satnav — as they were to us. We had resorted to our road atlas of Europe but that was about the same vintage as Sonya the satnav and thus about as much help. However, we found road signs — an excellent invention — and after going the wrong way, at least once, were back on the correct road to Venice.

The Minoan Lines ferry boat on which we were booked was berthed at the ferry port and queues of cars, campervans, lorries etc., were waiting in disorderly lines for the command to surge forward into the bowels of the boat. Dominant were German number plates closely followed by Austrians. Our column was waved forward. *Oh goodie, action,* but then we were held in a line just before the open maw of the boat while campervans took priority. We waited twenty minutes in the hot sun while leering drivers swept past us in enormous houses on wheels.

We drove on to the boat and were then told to stop. Helen was told to get out and go up to reception on a deck a couple of decks above the one on which we were currently parked. Helen wanted to organise what we would take from the car for our 24-hour ferry journey. She did not much care for the peremptory attitude of the staff and said, "I want to go with my husband and park the car."

"You go to reception. He will follow."

She grabbed our overnight bags and made off with a creditable parody of goose stepping and waited at the door for me, but the very bossy young girl — Greek, but with more than a trace of the jackboot — came over to Helen and told her that she was to go upstairs.

"I am waiting for my husband," Helen told her.

"You must go," the girl re-iterated firmly.

"I am not going anywhere without my husband."

"YOU WILL GO. Your husband will go up by another way. You meet upstairs".

Helen reluctantly did as she was told and went up an escalator on the boat to the reception area where she checked in. A porter guided her through the labyrinths of the ship to our cabin. She dumped the bags, returned to reception and sent me a text to tell me to join her there — and then started to panic as she did not get a response.

I did not hear the text arriving at my phone. My mobile was somewhere in the car, but I suppose the ambient noise on the car decks precluded my hearing it go off. I struggled out of the car and collected the bits and pieces that I supposed I was to take to the cabin and made my way to reception.

When we met Helen checked me out for essentials — namely, whether I had bought my mobile. No, I hadn't. It was still in the car.

"You had better go and fetch it."

"It's not essential."

"What if we are in different parts of the ship? You're always wandering off."

"Doesn't matter. We've both got a key to the cabin."

"Supposing I want to communicate with you and I don't know where you are?"

"Leave a note in the cabin. I'll pick it up when I'm next in there. I'll probably spend most of my time reading anyway…"

Helen noted the pause and looked me up and down, "So where's your book?"

"Ah…. well… I think…. err I do believe that I've left it in the car."

This seemed to be not far short of a disaster as we were captive on the ferry for 24 hours now, so admitting defeat, I set off back to the car decks.

"Don't forget to bring your mobile too. Here. Wait. I'm coming with you," as I disappeared back down the companionway.

The lift was blocked by a surly steward.

"We want to get to the car deck. Which floor is it?"

"You cannot. The decks are shut."

"We have to… medication for my husband."

"Shut and locked. Sorry."

"He will die and it will be your fault," said Helen improvising wildly and walked into the lift.

The lift offered a few decks. We tried the lowest on offer and walked into the engine room much to the surprise of two of the grease stained below-decks crew. The next deck up looked familiar. We walked towards the bow of the ship surrounded by huge lorries and clattered down a couple of flights of stairs and there we were. The car park was not shut and locked so we had been fibbed at and were able to retrieve books and mobiles before returning to civilisation.

We settled down by a huge window in one of the lounges and watched as the boat moved off past the familiar sights of Venice, the water busses, St Mark's square, the gondolas, the beautiful city.

Unwrapping Sundowner

We docked in Igoumenitsa at about nine o'clock next evening and arrived at the boat yard around ten thirty. I fetched a ladder and we clambered on board and set to opening hatches to let air into a very hot and stuffy Sundowner. We unloaded bedding and very little else from the car before we turned in as midnight approached.

A cloudy sky greeted us the following morning. Good. Good for working in. Not too hot. The cold light of morning revealed mildew over the plastic work around the ports and elsewhere. It was much worse than previous years. Should I bring the dehumidifier from home next year? I had bought it for use on Tethera and it did a good job. I had it on a timer so it took the moisture out of the air in the middle of the day when the temperature and water content was likely to be highest. But I was able to get down to Gosport regularly through the winter to do odd jobs and check on things like the dehumidifier. Not so easy when the boat is in a different country where there are regular power outages.

The outside of the boat was covered in a thin layer of red dust, sand from distant deserts. A hose down of the exterior was a top priority otherwise the stuff would be trod everywhere.

We were expecting someone to arrive at nine o'clock that day to deal with the diesel bug and commission the engine. I had decided not to risk my new hip early in the season so left to the professionals the tasks that might impose stressful contortions to my hip. I phoned at nine thirty to be told that we had not confirmed the booking so they were not coming. I had received an email in response to my emailed request which clearly stated that we had been booked in for nine o'clock that day. It was definite in tone and made no mention of requiring confirmation.

"Well, when can it be done then?" I asked.

"Not until next Monday I'm afraid."

"Oh brilliant — that's when we have arranged to have the boat launched." I took the date, but was determined to do it sooner if I could - meantime I went to the office and cancelled the launch.

By late afternoon, we had completed a lot of work on the boat and started cleaning mildew off the plastic surfaces. The early morning cloud passed and the day heated up until a thunderstorm at the end of the day provided a welcome respite from the sticky heat leaving the air cool and fresh in the early evening.

I was anxious not to lose all my precious (about 200 euros' worth of) diesel so I spent some of the day asking around about other means of solving the problem. I spoke to Yianni the yard owner and Barbara, the proprietor of *The Ionian* magazine, both of whom had many contacts.

The next day Spiros appeared. Yianni had said he would have someone who had expertise in this matter come and talk with me in the morning so I assumed (wrongly it turned out) that this was he.

I asked Spiros what he could do for me.

"I can do everything," he told me expansively. "Anything to do with boats I can do."

'Oh dear' I thought, 'the sort of claim that sets alarm bells ringing'. He spotted that we were in the middle of rubbing down the hull to prepare for a coat of antifouling. The fact that we were both blue with the dust of the existing antifouling and perspiring heavily was a bit of a clue — and it was obvious that neither of us was enjoying it much. "I can do antifouling, epoxy coating, antifouling, engine service, antifouling, anything," he told us.

"How much would it cost for you to antifoul this boat?" Helen leapt in.

"Yes, but the problem is…" I interjected.

"120 euro for the labour…"

"Ah, but what I am most concerned about…" I spluttered.

"When can you do it?" Helen was brooking no interruption.

"Let me just make a phone call. I think I can probably do it tomorrow."

"Yes, but the problem we really want solving is our diesel bug," I blurted out at last. He was already on the phone to somebody or other.

"If he's prepared to do the antifouling for 120 euros, he can have the job. I'll find the money," Helen said forestalling my next objection.

"Yes, tomorrow," Spiros said finishing his call and stuffing his mobile back in his pocket.

"Done — we've got the materials. So just 120 euros," Helen sealed the deal.

"Ok. Tomorrow at 08.30 then," Spiros turned to me. "And I can deal with your diesel problem."

"How do you do it? Do I lose the diesel?"

"No, we process it; filter it through special carbon filters. You will lose perhaps a litre but when I have finished you have clean tank and clean fuel."

"Is this what they call diesel polishing?" I asked. The author of an article in Practical Boat Owner had told me of this in an exchange of correspondence that I had had with him.

"No. Different process. Better process… in my opinion. More… more… eco-friendly."

We talked and Spiros described the process a bit more. He did seem convincing so I thought, 'What the hell. We'll give it a try'. I'll change the filters after a month or so to see if there is any evidence of the dreaded bug remaining after the treatment.

It turned out that Spiros was not Gianni's man. Gianni's man and Gianni had turned up at Sundowner, but spotted me engaged with Spiros — a rival concern — and departed. Oh dear. I had sparked too many people up to search for a solution to my problem and now possibly had to pour some oil on troubled waters. In fact, Spiros was one of Barbara's contacts.

In due course, the hull was abraded and antifouled by a couple of Polish gents that Spiros farmed the work out to. The diesel bug was dealt with by Spiros himself who also turned up with a tap to replace a leaky one in the galley. I decided to re-commission the engine myself in spite of the new hip and ran it up. Everything looked good for the launch, but there was one other task that was to be carried out before launch — a thorough check out of the holding tank.

The Holding Tank and the Austrians

The previous season's problems with the holding tank led me to do two things:

(1) Give the boat a good clean down, removing floorboards and whatever else was necessary to get to the deepest darkest recesses. My, that was fun.

(2) Take the holding tank and associated plumbing and valves to pieces to see if there was anything that could be the cause of intermittent blockages. That too was a thrill a minute.

The plumbing for the heads and holding tank took the form of the usual plastic hoses secured by jubilee clips and they required heating to expand them in order to disconnect or reconnect them. I did not have a suitable heating tool. I also had to remove both the door and the frame of the locker that housed the holding tank in order to remove the tank itself — necessary if I wanted to inspect it thoroughly. Some of the screws that held the holding tank in place were almost inaccessible so your grip on them was extremely fragile and so it was going to be pretty easy to drop one of them into the virtually inaccessible void under the floor of the heads while attempting to remove or replace it.

However, I did eventually get the tank out and it was pretty clean. I decided, having hosed it through, that I would leave it in the sea overnight for a good soaking prior to a final clean through. It was fairly heavy and an awkward shape, so I found it easiest to carry any distance by making a kind of cradle out of rope and hauling it on to my back. Walking out of the yard with a large black plastic container on my back I must have looked like some seriously mutant tortoise that had gained the ability to walk on two legs. I certainly got the attention of the dogs who followed me as if I was the pied piper. They were barking as loud as they could and drawing unwelcome attention to my progress through the yard.

"Oi mate, what's that on your back?"

"It's my holding tank."

"Ugh."

"What are you doing with it?"

"I am taking it to the sea to wash it."

"Ugh."

"Not near the slipway I hope."

"It's clean. It's quite clean."

"Well, what are you washing it for?"

"Well there are some calcified solids..."

"Ugh."

"Please don't do it near the slipway."

I put the tank in the sea and tied it to a broken down disused jetty next to the slipway. I washed it out using what implements I could, then I left it in the water.

The following morning, I felt that a dawn raid might be necessary to avoid the attentions of fellow yardees who seemed to be less than enchanted by my carrying my holding tank about. It was perfectly clean, but not a pleasant thing to be contemplated — especially by the ladies of the yard.

I went down to the sea at daybreak and stood for a while watching fishing boats come and go and contemplated the view across the water to Preveza. It was a lovely daybreak as usual. The sky was clear but for a few wisps of cloud and it was pearly pink in the east. Pink to slate grey mountains ranged around the limits of my vision to the north east and south. Early fishermen went about their business. Boat noises came clear across the undisturbed early morning water.

They ranged from the barking of an inadequately silenced motor to the comforting tump-tump-tump of slow revving diesels. Some of them purloined from some land-based vehicle and creatively conjoined to the boat. After standing a while in a sort of reverie, I got down to business. I gave the tank a final clean through, untied it and lifted it out the water. I hauled it onto my back and set off back to the yard where I was soon getting the undivided attention of the dogs again. Above the general shindig that they were kicking up, I could hear someone shouting at me — oh dear.

Just inside the yard gates was a large traditionally styled wooden ketch with a respectable sized bowsprit and a wheelhouse aft. Perched on it were the couple that owned it — two Austrians.

"Excuse me, sir."

I walked up to the boat until I was below them, "Ya?"

Thinking this indicated a fluency in German they immediately launched into German. In fact, this is one of the very few words I do know. The rest are equally useless from the point of view of having a conversation. 'Please', 'thank you', 'railway station', 'television' and 'zoo' — what sort of conversation does that give you? I disabused them of their misconception and the conversation continued in English.

"We arrive late last night and we found a ladder. We climbed into the boat to sleep. Now we wake up. Is gone. Someone, take it."

I began unstrapping the holding tank. I had thought that my carefully contrived harness was perfectly acceptable to health and safety, but I had difficulties unloading and had a passing image of two Austrians up on their boat watching helplessly as an Englishman equipped simply with a large black plastic tank and a length of dirty rope garrotted himself below them...

"What is that on your back?"

"It's my holding tank."

"Ugh."

"Yes, I've already had this conversation — several times."

"You are putting it down there? Please not."

"Look. Do you want this ladder or not?"

They debated this. Obviously not a straightforward choice. Then,

"Please. I need the toilet so can you hurry."

I crossed the yard to where the spare ladders were usually stored, stood against a wall. There were none there. Hell, there was always some there. I would have to go around the yard looking. The general convention is that if there is a ladder laid up against a boat there might be someone up in the boat so don't take it (obviously this didn't apply to my hapless Austrians). So I was looking for one laid flat on the ground somewhere. Not so easy to spot in the long grass and general detritus of the yard but, eventually, I fell over one and was able to rescue the marooned Austrian couple.

With the Austrians rescued from their predicament I was able to resume my journey back to Sundowner with my tank back on my back and the baying hounds of Aktio snapping at my heels. Dishevelled freshly woken folks emerged from cabins to find out what the general disturbance was all about.

"What's that on your back?"

"It's an octopus trap."

"What have you been doing with it?"

"Catching octopus."

"Really?"

Although it was a sort of a lie, I had wondered whether I might find an octopus in the tank in the morning. It was the sort of place they might crawl into. If I did, I could have rescued some of my now wrecked kudos by barbecuing it at the yard barbecue tonight — freshly caught and cooked local octopus — ah well, it was not to be.

On Speaking Italian - and a Frog

I had befriended an Italian couple, Georgio and Daniella, on *Vagabond*, a ketch alongside Sundowner. They invited me aboard for a drink one evening. We had scant grasp of each other's language but, as is usually the case, a bit of drink — and they had a particularly revolting schnapps-like concoction that they seemed anxious to get rid of — and communication was improved by a sudden and inexplicable grasp of the language. Needless to say, talking loudly, flamboyant gesturing and crude drawings were brought into play to augment the spoken word.

My son-in-law (well, strictly speaking, my grandson-in-law), Stu, came across during my time in the yard to complete a glassfibre job. When he had completed his allotted task, I decided that, as a reward for his efforts, Stu should meet the Italians and so returned their invitation. We had a very communicative evening on board Sundowner in which Welsh was thrown into the mix of English, French and Italian with obvious improvement all round. Why French? Well I have this theory that French and Italian are much the same. Compare 'Parlez Francais' with 'Parliamo Italiano'. See what I mean? It's just got to be a bit more elaborate and have a few more 'i's and 'o's about the place. So 'voiture' (car) quite obviously becomes 'voiturio'. Easy peasy. It didn't seem to work awfully well. But that was probably due to my pronunciation. But we struggled through in spite of all that and learned a little on the way.

Names were quite easy and they knew mine and I knew theirs so I pointed to them and told Stu, "Daniella, Georgio." Then at Stu and told them, "Stuart."

"Stu," Stu corrected me.

"Ah, Stu," Dani repeated then she enquired. "*Vostro figlio?*"

That took some fumbling in the 'Dunces guide to Italian' till I concluded that they were asking whether he was my son.

"No, uhm granddaughter's fiancée. How do I tell them that Stu?"

"Don't ask me, mate."

"What's grandaughter?"

"Haven't a clue."

I looked for, but didn't find, the word for granddaughter in the very limited compilation of useful words and phrases at the back of the guide. It told me how to ask for the next dance or a cure for diarrhoea but not what the word for granddaughter was. However, I found that the word for daughter was *figlia* so tried to get across the concept of granddaughter by pointing at myself "*figlia*" then indicated dropping down a level with my hands and "*figlia*". They looked puzzled. Hmm, they must think I'm telling them that Stu was my grandaughter which clearly didn't fit. He didn't look feminine enough — the half day's growth of beard said no. I resorted to drawing the family tree — or enough of it to show Hollie who I linked to Stu with a dotted line and said, "Fiancée."

"Fiancée? Ah fidanzata," asked Dani.

"*Sì fidanzata*," I confirmed thinking that sounded about right.

She pointed at the depiction of Hollie on the drawing and said "*Nipoti*" or something similar.

"*Nipoti,*" I mused then pointed at her and George. "*Vous nipoti?*" in a heady mix of French and Italian.

"*Si. Uno nipote. Voi?*" she said pointing at me, "*Voi quanto?*"

"What's she saying," asked Stu.

"I think she has told me that she has one grandchild and has asked me how many I have." We had not got down to the level of grandchildren in previous conversations — too taxing by half.

"Go on, tell her," chuckled Stu. "What's the Italian for twenty-seven?"

"Can't remember. Twenty is something like *venti* I think."

"*Venti? Venti nipote?*" Dani picked up.

"No," I said. "*Vingt-sept*" resorting to my theory about French and Italian being the same language with minor mods and then after a pause, thinking they must have learned to count in Greek, "*Eikosi epta.*"

"*Ventisette!*" she exclaimed and turned to George losing me in a torrent of Italian. Drinks were poured and toasts were proposed. God knows what they were saying, but the word *Congratulazioni* needed little translation; although, at this stage in the game, I was no longer anything much to do with child producing so why congratulations were due to me I could not fathom.

Stu went home and the Italians launched the following day so I had nothing but a frog for company. No, not a French person, but a small amphibian.

Climbing onto Sundowner one morning, the frog greeted me at the top of the ladder. I wondered how it had got there. It couldn't have clambered up the ladder. The frog was small, but beautifully marked. It was not much bigger than my thumb. Had it got onto the boat when we were stern to on a jetty sometime last season?

The frog was not too keen on being caught. It went to ground in my gas locker but I eventually caught it and carefully took it down to the long lush grass beneath the boat where I felt sure it would rather be happier. I then went over to Ian on Cariad to discuss the matter over a little light refreshment as we are inclined to do when faced with an imponderable question — the mysteries of the universe, whether to go to Panos Taverna tonight, that sort of thing.

"What I reckon happened," Ian said after determinedly sucking the last from his tin of Mythos. "Is that your frog got picked up by a bird for breakfast and wriggled free just as the bird flew across Sundowner." We agreed that that was probably the explanation and settled for supper at Panos Taverna.

The next day, the same thing happened. The frog was there glaring at me as I got to the top of the ladder. He was, not to put too fine a point on it, hopping mad.

"It takes me half a day to get up that blasted ladder of yours… and I've just got up there… and what do you do, but take me straight back down. Don't even think about it today. You don't know what it's like being a small frog in a boatyard."

It was true. I didn't know what it was like being a small frog in a boatyard. However, the secret of how he got aboard was revealed. Sticky feet, suckers or something very gecko-like. He demonstrated sprinting up and down the ladder for my benefit. I offered him a beer.

"Don't drink," he told me gruffly. "You're getting us frogs confused with them newts. Drunken layabouts. Don't deserve to be called amphibians."

I thought of correcting his English, but let it pass.

In the early hours of the following morning, the gas alarm went off waking me and probably most of the boatyard. I shot out of bed and switched it off. Then it hit me. It was the frog. That's why he favoured the gas locker. He was addicted to the stuff and he had been tampering. He only favoured my boat because they were French next door and they would catch him and eat his legs and he would have to spend the rest of his life bumming around.

I posted a notice in the recreation room with a picture of him and inscribed underneath.

WANTED DEAD OR ALIVE 'MAD FRED' THE CLIMBING FROG

The public are warned not to approach him directly as he is a known gas addict and could be violent. Contact the authorities and they will arrange for special police units to apprehend him and frog march him off.

It is a pity I put that last bit in. Nobody took me seriously.

Outboards and Raw Water Pumps

Helen arrived back from Blighty in time for the launch. Besides all the usual preparations, we had to deal with an outboard motor that would not start, a broken seacock valve, and a malfunctioning gear change mechanism for the Volvo engine. We had shortened the season because of the need to be signed off from the hip operation before we set off for the Ionic so we were anxious not to delay the launch too much and only fixed what was absolutely necessary. We managed to launch just over a week later but with a leaky raw water pump and an anchor chain that was starting to look as though it needed renewing. When we had installed a new windlass the previous season, we had been told to renew the anchor chain as well. We were told that the old worn chain would cause more wear on the new gypsy than a new chain would. We had not done it as we were already seriously over budget as usual. Perhaps now was the time.

Helen was not happy.

"We are launching with a water pump that fills up the engine bay when we run the engine, an outboard motor that won't start and an anchor that we may lose if we anchor!" she told the family in a long email detailing the trials and tribulations of the season thus far.

The launch was early afternoon on a Friday. The forecast was for north-westerlies at force three or four. Gianni and his machine turned up to put the boat in the water at about two o'clock. We moved away from his jetty mid-afternoon and were able to enjoy our first sail of the season through clear blue waters of the warm Mediterranean. We made the Lekas bridge late in the afternoon and puttered down the canal that runs from Lefkas down to the Inland Sea. We enjoyed a relaxed sail in the expanse of water between the mainland and Lefkas and dropped anchor in the Vlicho lagoon at about half past seven. We stayed there swinging at anchor for several days while we started to resolve some of the problems that we had launched with.

One of the problems was, of course, the outboard motor. Eventually, I gave up trying to start it and phoned Second-hand Geoff who seemed to love tinkering with outboards and asked him whether he would resolve the problem for me.

"I've retired," he told me.

"Jesus Christ. You? Retire? Has the world stopped spinning on its axis? What's happened to all that junk... ah... merchandise that you used to preside over?"

"Sold it all to Andreas in Nidri."

"Bloody hell, I thought that he ran a half decent shop."

We moved the boat to Nidri to sort out the outboard and the raw water pump and do a bit of shopping. We arrived late in the afternoon and I took my outboard to Andreas who specialises in outboard motors ranging from small ones like mine to big things that you need a crane to lift.

An engineer was going to turn up early the next day to look at the raw water pump which had resisted my efforts to find and remedy the cause of the leak. Shortly after we had tied up, a large Sunsail catamaran crewed by eight or so South African youths moored up alongside us. They went out on the town for a little light refreshment late in the evening and arrived back in the early hours well refreshed and noisy. Their conversation was not that loud but one of them in particular had a high pitched almost girlish laugh that penetrated. Another fell in the water at one point and the girlish laugh went on and on. They quietened down a bit when remonstrated with, but the damage was done and it was difficult to get back to sleep. The conversation though muted went on so when I got up at about six o'clock, I didn't feel any obligation to be quiet.

The engineer turned up at half seven to look at the raw water pump.

"The seal has gone," he told me.

"Yes, well, that is what it looks like to me but I only renewed it last year," I protested.

"Did you renew the drive shaft?"

"No. Should I have done?"

"Well, there may well have been wear there too," he muttered about bearings, seals, a worn drive shaft. My brain started hurting so I told him to take it away and mend it.

Immediately, he had departed Helen and I ran our various errands I had to get some dosh from an ATM, call in on Danny at IGR to sort out the matter of a new anchor chain (bloody expensive), a new boathook (I had broken the old one), fuel filter and various other sundries including the potion for killing the diesel bug. I collected the boathook and the diesel treatment, but chain was out of stock and new stock would not be arriving until mid-July. I finally went back to Andreas to see if he had mended the outboard. He had promised to have it ready by midday and had pointed out to me that the problem with the outboard was oil in the fuel tank. I got a telling off for that. Apparently, I really shouldn't have turned the motor upside down to empty the petrol from the tank.

It was getting on for one o'clock when I got aboard the dinghy to go and fetch our outboard motor. I had walked the motor over to Andreas' workshop the previous day but had to rest it several times — not because of the weight, it's pretty light — but because the thin ridge that one hand was gripping was uncomfortable. It was a two-hand carry if I was to avoid gripping the grease besmeared drive shaft and keep the thing upright. So, today I thought, I would take the dinghy to the outboard rather than the other way around. I could row the dinghy to a pontoon just by the workshop, tie it up, collect the mended outboard and simply drop it on to the dinghy then motor the dinghy back to Sundowner. Simples.

One thing that I realised as I was rowing the dinghy was that I had forgotten the safety cord that you attach between yourself and a cut off button so the engine cuts out if you fall overboard. The engine won't start without it — or something like it.

'Never mind', I thought. 'I can fashion something that will jam the button in the 'drive' position. I have done it before with a bit of string'.

A second problem occurred to me as I was dismissing the first. It would be tricky lowering the outboard on to the transom of the dinghy from a position above it — stood on the jetty. This type of outboard has to be kept vertical. It could, said the manual, be rested on a particular side, but I had been warned not to rely on that. Keeping it vertical and lowering it onto the transom from the jetty then securing it was not going to be as straightforward as all that — mostly because I still felt a bit cautious about the new hip and didn't want to stress it too much if it could be avoided. The danger of dislocation that absolutely forbade a right-angle bend for the first twelve weeks was now a thing of the past, but I still felt that I should be a bit careful. I persuaded myself that a better option might be to beach the boat on the shingle shore beside the jetty with the bow on the beach and the stern in the water so that I could drop the outboard into position and still keep a firm hand on it until I had clamped it in place.

I changed course and rowed the dinghy towards the beach. What had looked like normal water was in fact a layer of an inch or two of water over mud. It was a struggle. I was virtually rowing the boat through mud. It would be easier to get out of the boat and tow it ashore. So I did. I launched myself straight out of the boat into thick sticky mud. I struggled ashore just avoiding going flat on my face in the mud on several occasions while trying to move forward while the mud had a firm grip on my feet. In fact, the mud had such a firm hold on my crocs that I lost one of them fairly early in the proceedings.

'It doesn't matter. They are cut and worn and close to getting thrown out', I told myself as I reluctantly let the mud keep it. I struggled on and found that the muddy shallows extended along the shoreline all of the way to the jetty. I struggled back onto the boat and sat on the side of it using feet and oars to work it out of the muddy shallows into deepish water once again. Eventually, with mud spatters all over the dinghy and myself, I got it alongside the jetty. I 'handed' it past other dinghies moored alongside until I found a slot on the jetty in deepish water and clear of the mud. I tried to clean the mud off but only managed to spread it more thinly around a larger area. I was just re-arranging it really.

After I had finished my rather pathetic attempt to clean both myself and the dinghy, I tied the stern to the jetty so that I could hopefully lower the outboard on to the transom. I scrambled out and sat on the jetty dangling my legs in the water for a minute while I swished around with my hands to wash the tenacious mud from my feet and shins.

Having done that to my satisfaction, I picked the two bundles of rubbish out of the dinghy and walked back to the bins which were actually nearer to the jetty from which I had started out. I should have told Helen to take them herself when she said, "Would you pop these in the bins while you are there?" she was, after all, much nearer to them than I now was. However, the plan was to do as much walking as possible to keep the new hip exercised. You can only really do that ashore so that I was OK with the suggestion. However, now shoeless, I had to hobble along pathways of sharp granite chips and, after collecting the outboard, would have to do so carrying that.

I collected the outboard — along with a few bollockings about the lack of appropriate care and attention that I had exercised on it — from Andreas who had, as good as his word, mended it.

"Always keep the machine upright. There was oil in the carburettor and the combustion chamber. Only do up the filler cap and the air vent finger tight. Use the choke at starting if necessary, but put it in straight away when the engine starts... etc."

He had a grizzled English assistant. A gold earring shone through an unkempt mass of black and grey greasy hair. His face, brown as a conker and creased as a walnut, bore a couple of day's stubble. He looked like one of Long John Silver's band of brigands but, seeing my shoeless state, he offered to help me out to the jetty with the motor — mainly to get away from and to have a grumble about his boss.

"He gets more fucking miserable as each fucking day goes by," he told me referring, of course, to Andreas who indeed had objected to his assistant leaving the premises to help me out.

"Why do you put up with it?" I asked after enduring his tirade for a while. I had always found Andreas more than helpful.

"It's a job init? But if he pushes me much further, I'll find another fucker though."

"Been out here long?"

"'Bout ten years... nah probably twelve... lost fucking count."

"Not going back to the UK then?"

"Nah. Fucking place pisses me off."

"Why's that then?"

"Long fucking story, mate."

Beside his rather limited range of adjectives he sounded like one of those expats whose main reason for living abroad was to escape money problems or woman problems, or most likely both... or the law? A murder rap perhaps? He looked the part. Fortunately, by then, we had the engine mounted on the transom and secure.

"Better not fucking start it till you get clear of all these fucking mooring lines," he advised me. I thanked him, thinking 'my thoughts precisely' and rowed carefully into the side of a smart new blue hulled Beneteau.

"Yes and you too," I replied to the Beneteau owners who were sat rather grandly in the stern enjoying a lunchtime snifter. Or they had been until I assaulted their bloody Beneteau whereupon they seemed to get exceeding vexed and call me all sorts of rude names that would have made Long John Silver's mate blush. I pushed off and rowed into clear water. The motor started first time.

"You've been a long time," Helen greeted me as I pulled the dinghy to the stern of Sundowner garrotting myself on the mooring lines of the neighbouring boat. "And you are in a bit of a state. Sit on the stern and clean yourself off before you come aboard. What have you been doing?"

"Just been out enjoying myself my little treasure."

Party Time in Port Atheni

Daniella and Georgio had told me that, once launched, they made for the Gulf of Patras, Corinth or the Peloponnese where there were numerous nice places away from the popular and, at times, overpopulated bays and harbours in and around Kefalonia, Lefkada, Ithaca, etc. I did not expect to see them during the summer. Because we planned to stay around the area and head no further south than Zakynthos. However, a couple of months or so after I had launched Sundowner, we came across them again. We had Nicola, our daughter, and her family on board and Helen wanted to show them the charming village of Katomeri so I had anchored up in one of the popular bays on Meganissi. I went ashore to put our rubbish in a bin and was about to launch the tender to return to Sundowner when I was hailed by a familiar voice. It came from a small white ketch that had been anchored in the bay when we had arrived. I had not taken much notice of it but now saw that it was Vagabond.

"Hey George," I plunged into the water forgetting that I had my specs on and so spent a few minutes scrabbling about for them blindly on the sea bottom before I could proceed further.

"I sleep in Vagabond and I hear you — your voice as you come in," he said as he took the dinghies painter and secured it to a cleat on Vagabond.

"Oh crikey, was I that loud?" I thought and was rewarded with an image of us coming in crashing splashing and shouting as we dropped anchor and took a line ashore. We must have seriously disturbed the tranquillity of the small bay. I scrambled on board Vagabond and sat awhile chattering to them as best we could manage, which had not improved any since our last social occasion.

And so it was, in an expansive mood, with a couple of glasses of wine inside me that I invited them onboard, "Hey, look, you must come aboard Sundowner meet the family — or some of them." Of course, it was an amalgamation of drawing, waving my arms about and frugal bits of English, French and Italian that conveyed this simple invitation.

Swimming back to shore to collect the tender, this time keeping my spectacles safe, it struck me that we had no nibbly things and I was not sure about wine. I fumbled in my waterproof pouch and found I had twenty odd euros so sprinted to the little shop at the head of bay and came back with a couple of bottles and some crisps. I rowed hastily out to Sundowner.

"Where's your ma?" I asked Nicky.

"She's just gone below for a zizz."

"Oh hell. Do you think she's asleep yet?"

"I should think so, she's been gone for five," Nicola said eyeing the clinking carrier bag and raising an eyebrow. "When's the party?"

"Uh, I've invited the people on that boat over there aboard for a drink. They're old friends. Well, I was next to them in the boatyard and... Well they've met Stu," I ended lamely.

"But not Mum?"

"Er no."

"Well, you go and wake her up and I'll organise things up here. When are they coming?"

I looked at my watch. Time had flown, what with my shopping trip and all. "Oh hell. Five minutes. Are you sure you don't want to wake her up? I can set things up..."

"No, Dad," Nicola grinned. "It's your party. Enjoy."

I went below and woke the sleeping Helen, "Ah, I've invited some people on board for drinks," I told her.

"Oh, that's nice," she said sleepily and shuffled herself more comfortably into her bunk showing every sign of returning to sleep.

"No, you can't go back to sleep they're coming soon."

"Oh hell," she unshuffled a bit and rubbed her eyes. "What do you mean soon?"

"Fairly... well, actually... very."

"Define very." She went from sleepy to frosty in a nanosecond or less.

"Five..." I looked at my watch, "Well four minutes."

210

"FOUR MINUTES!" Helen sat up suddenly cracking her head on the low part of the ceiling and fixed me with a glance that could have frozen hell over. Charlie and George were descending into the saloon, sent by Nicky to pack some of their detritus into their cabin.

"Who are they? Do I know them?"

"Oh, yes. Well, sort of. I've told you about them. The Italians next door to me in the boatyard."

"The ones that don't speak a word of English?"

"Yes. Well they do have some... and they are very good at mime... and... Well, yes, those Italians

"Great. Fucking great!"

I heard Charlie clatter up the companionway, "Pops has invited some eyties aboard and they don't speak English and g'ma used the "F word." I could hear Nicola and Alan trying to suppress laughter without total success.

It turned out fine, although I still got my dressing down after the event. Dani's gesticulation was as creative and animated as ever, her big round eyes nearly popping out of her head. With a generous rum and coke inside her, Nicky discovered a hitherto unsuspected talent for Italian and matched Dani pop-eyed gesticulation for pop-eyed gesticulation. Georgio and Alan discussed fishing in great depth and with a great deal of mime. George and Charlie rapidly bored with the whole thing and returned to their interrupted bombing of each other from the bow of the boat.

On the Putty in Amvrakikos

August is quite the busiest month of the year around the islands of the Ionian Sea. The number of boats is up — small boats, large boats, very large and seriously over-the-top boats. Speedboats and motorboats buzz around the popular bays. Floating gin palaces anchor in what, a month before had been a quiet backwater, and get out their toys — jet skis and the like. In the popular resorts like Nidri, water sport is being advertised and loud music is blasting out from the water sports centre. Water sports customers are being towed around on water skis, inflatable rubber rings, big yellow six-seater bananas and anything else that can be inflated and towed. Up above, a pair of spindly legs dangles from a harness attached to a parachute that is being towed by a launch with the word PARASCENDING emblazoned on its side.

We decided to spend some time around the Gulf of Amvrakikos. The gulf is largely off the holiday maker's radar mainly, I suppose, because it is the mainland and does not have the romance of the islands. But it is quieter and populated with turtles, pelicans, dolphins and even flamingos. Second-hand Geoff had advised us, "Try it. Amfilokhia at the far end of the Gulf is like Greece was in the sixties." So we anticipated a quiet relaxing period of exploration — quite wrongly as it turned out.

There was next to no wind as we left Preveza and motored slowly into the gulf. The water was disturbed from time to time by a turtle surfacing momentarily to gulp air then returning to its underwater world. At one point, we stopped the engine and just drifted for fifteen to twenty minutes to see if the turtles would stay at the surface a little longer if the engine was silenced. No deal. By Aghia Laskara, we had picked up a bit of breeze and hauled the sails up. We sailed on to anchor in the lee of the small island of Vouvalo for lunch and a swim. We chose to overnight in a bay just east of Koukoumitsa — a small wooded island off the town of Vonitsa — an island that is prettily linked to the mainland by a white stone footbridge that is lit at night.

The next day, we moved the boat to the quayside at Vonitsa in order to stock up with bits and pieces. We walked up and around the castle that overlooks Vonitsa and admired the views across the gulf that it offered.

We ambled back to the quay. The boat moored next to us was an attractive French-flagged wooden ketch. It did not look old, but the style suggested that it was built along the lines of some traditional French craft. The couple on board had been making quite a fuss of the local dogs feeding them with scraps but they seemed to be a bit standoffish as far human beings went. As many do, the French couple would leave their shore shoes on the quayside at the end of the passerail so that minimal abrasive grit from the harbourside would be walked on to their glossy varnished deck. However, one of the dogs they had been cultivating took an interest in the shoes and was chewing one as we approached. Worried that he might run off with it, I shouted to the couple, who were inside the cabin, "Monsieur. Le chien mangez votre ahh... oh fuck what's the French for shoes?"

"Ah, chaussures," he explained grinning at me as he emerged from the cabin.

As I talked to Henri, one of the dogs that he had cultivated came up. I made a fuss of him so he parked himself on my feet, licked my hands and reached up to lick my face.

"Don't let him do that," Helen hissed.

"Do what?"

"Lick your face."

"Why not?"

"Well, he has just been licking his backside for starters. Why they do that?"

"Ah lick their backsides," said Henri. "Is after they have been licking us. Is to take the nasty taste away!"

The next day we set off for Amfilokhia at the southeast corner of the gulf. It was a pleasant day. We anchored for lunch in a nice spot off what appeared to be a small private beach. We saw a number of turtles and a pelican — no dolphins though. The Emu describes Amfilokhia as a village with a small harbour where a yacht can go alongside at the north end of the quay. Village? Busy noisy little town more like. Fetch up on the harbour wall? Not likely. The wind blows a hoollie into the harbour most afternoons and I would prefer not to be moored up against the harbour wall during that, even with an anchor out as the Emu advises. After inspecting some pontoons that seemed to be for smallish local craft rather than visiting yotties, we backtracked out of the harbour and found a nearby bay which was quiet and provided shelter from the northwesterly that was building.

For the next three days, we pootled around the gulf and spent the nights anchored in bays. Finally, we headed for Menidhion at the north east corner of the squarish gulf. According to the Emu, Menidhion is "A small village and harbour that attracts a few local tourists." When was he there last? It seemed to me to be a fully blown tourist resort with crowded beaches, tavernas along the shoreline, hotels and apartment blocks.

The harbour, as he remarks, is really only suitable for small yachts. We decided to anchor overnight outside the harbor at the head of Ormos Kopraina where there was good holding in about five metres of water. We were near the mouth of a small harbour and sat watching the sun go down over distant mountains behind the low-lying marshland that surrounded us. The wind dropped to give us a peaceful night with strong winds forecast for the following day.

I woke at dawn, made coffee then fiddled around with the laptop in the cockpit as the sky got lighter. The dongle that I had was essentially a mobile phone circuit that plugged into the laptop. Reception in some areas was too poor for it to be of use. However, it was OK where I was anchored and I was able to access the Poseidon website which showed a quiet start to the day, but building to gale force eight during the afternoon and sustaining that until mid to late evening. We pulled anchor at seven o'clock and, due to the fact that there was only a light breeze, gently motorsailed south more or less parallel to the coastline to our first waypoint that I had set off the outlet of the river Arakhthos. There were herons fishing on the shoreline. It was a peaceful morning with only the occasional fisherman puttering by in the distance. We maintained a lookout for turtles, pelicans and of course the elusive dolphins that we had, unusually, spotted only once so far this season. Pretty soon the depth was less than ten metres. 'Hmm funny', I thought having set a course that should keep us in more than ten metres of water all the way. 'Never mind. Perhaps the charts are out of date, banks of silt at river mouths are changing all the time. Or perhaps my plot was wrong. Slow down and make sure the depth doesn't reduce to less than five metres. That will give us ten foot to spare'.

I saw something ahead that might be a turtle and I shouted to Helen who was below, "There is something in the water over there, looks like a turtle... but it's not moving."

Helen came up equipped with the binoculars, "Turtle my foot, its mud." I looked down at the depth sounder display.

"1.7 metres! Fuck!" I put the boat into reverse as we gently slowed and stopped with the echo sounder showing somewhat less than the boat's draft of 1.7 metres. We were parked in our own slot in the mud like a bicycle in a rack.

I tried to reverse the boat. This can work. You can reverse out of the slot you've carved if you react fairly quickly, but she was not having any of it. The mainsail was up. The breeze was just forward of the beam pressing the boat gently onward into the mud but not strong enough to cant the boat over so I shouted Helen to pay the sail out and drop it. Helen released the rope clutch without tightening up the topping lift so the heavy old aluminium boom came crashing down. There was a bit of commotion with both of us saying, 'Oh deary deary me' a few times. Helen hung on to the main halyard and I hauled the boom back up with the topping lift. Then she let go of the halyard and the sail came down. There was a lot of flapping about on the part of both us and the sailcloth. Battens got caught up with the lazy jack stays and it was all a bit of a mess, but we managed to stuff it fairly rapidly — albeit a bit untidily — into the stackpack bag on the boom.

That done, the next thing was to try and kedge ourselves out — taking the kedge out in the dinghy with one end of the warp secured to Sundowner and dropping it behind the boat at the maximum length of the kedge warp. Unfortunately, the dinghy was a bit deflated with quite a bit of water in it, but I got the kedge planted and raced back to

Sundowner in the sad shrivelled tender. I started Sundowner's engine again and put it into reverse at pretty high revs while Helen tried to winch in the kedge.

"Nothing's happening," she shouted. "I cannot pull any harder. Let's swap jobs. You come and work this winch and I'll sit and play with the throttle control."

So we changed places to little avail. The kedge warp was bar tight and the boat was going nowhere. We were well and truly stuck. The water was shallow enough that we could see the track through the mud that the keel had made.

Not being able to shift the boat we were in a bit of a dilemma. The weather was due to increase rapidly during the afternoon. The forecast showed it as westish which might enable us to put some sail up and heel the boat enough for the keel to lift clear of the mud and we might get blown clear, but then again, we might get driven further on if there were further mud banks to leeward. Best call for help.

The first call was to Spiros who was fairly local, but all I got was an answerphone. I left a message and phoned IBA to see if they had any bright ideas. I got through to Kelvin and told him that we were aground. I gave him the latitude and longitude of our position reading it off the GPS and told him what we had done so far in attempting to extricate ourselves. He said he could get someone out to us and the line went dead. I rang back and got John who passed me to Mike. I gave him the information that I had given Kelvin and told him that it looked a little as though we needed assistance, but that I had told all this to Kelvin and was cut off so was not quite sure what if anything was happening. He said he had better tie up with Kelvin and he would then ring me back pronto.

I now decided that I had better take a look at things. The long paddle of a rudder on Sundowner is not as deep as the keel, but still pretty deep. If that was in the mud and we forced it back through the mud, we could damage it. Though what we could practically do about that was unclear, apart from keeping the rudder straight and praying. I was dressed in a respectable pair of shorts so I clambered out of them, Helen passed me my mask and in I went. It was not very clear with all the muck that we had stirred up, but clear enough to see shoaling to left and right and in front of us. The rudder was well clear of the bottom. The track we had carved in the mud was about two metres long. If we could get back along it, we would be all right, but it looked like there might be further problems to leeward. It was difficult to tell in the murky water.

I came back onto the boat as the phone rang, it was Tom from IBA.

"Hi Rob, how are you?"

"Yeah OK... Well not OK.... In a bit of a pickle actually."

"Look, I am getting ready to leave..."

A small boat was heading towards us. I was caught quite literally with my trousers down, and not to mention covered in mud. The boat containing an old Greek was almost with us. Some of these traditional old Greeks are not that cool about wanton nudity. Helen was shouting and waving a pair of shorts at me while I was trying to talk to Tom.

"Put these bloody shorts on. There's an old boy just about to come aboard," Helen shouted. I tried to put the shorts on with one hand while carrying on a phone conversation with Tom with the other. These are swim shorts with the built-in netting knickers. So I managed to get both feet in one trouser leg. I pulled them off and started again and got my feet tangled up in the netting.

Eventually, I gave the phone to Helen telling Tom to hold off for the moment. I extricated myself from my trousers, put them on properly and piped the old man aboard.

Helen, in the meantime, was being warned by Tom that the old boy could ask for salvage money from us if he assisted us. He said he would call us back in five minutes to check what sort of state we were in.

The Greek told us that he was a retired merchant seaman and he knew what he was talking about, or that is what we thought he was shouting. He then told me to let down the main anchor and he would take it out in his boat while I let more chain down allowing him to plant it behind us like the kedge. We would then operate the windlass, the ships motor, in reverse, winch in the kedge and he would pull us with his launch all at the same time. Helen wanted to change jobs again as I had her back on the windlass while I played with the throttle and pressed the winch up button — ever the gallant gentleman!

But it worked. Our hearts were in our mouths, but Sundowner slowly began to move. Between us, we gradually edged the boat astern.

Helen attempted to phone Tom to say he was no longer needed, but the phone was out of charge! She plugged it in to charge it up then could not find Tom's number. The phone rang and it was Tom. Helen told him we were now afloat; he said great, but that we should check the keel and the keel bolts for seepage. 'Jesus Christ' she thought, 'could the bolts really be loose?' She thanked him for his help and he repeated his warning that some Greeks had a reputation for charging a lot of money for helping boats out of trouble.

"Right," she said. "What would he suggest as a reasonable amount?" Tom thought about it and suggested 100 euros.

The Greek and I were now struggling to get the kedge up. It would not come as hard as we tried. We were getting in each other's way and had different ideas. I was shouting orders to the poor man who was trying to help us. Helen was saying, "*Ef haristo poli,*" with great emphasis and frequency so I would get the message that I was being a bit short with the Greek and could do with being a bit more polite. Although we were afloat, we were still in very shallow water so there was not much room to play with. Our main anchor was still down to hold us secure, but neither the main nor the kedge were shiftable. I had the idea that we were sat on them so I jumped in the water to see if I could see what the problem was, but it was as murky as hell with all the stirring up that we had been doing. I got back on board and tried to communicate with the Greek to let the kedge go — he still had it on the Genoa winch and it was bar tight. He got the idea when he saw me tying a fender on the kedge warp as a float and we dropped it free. The kedge and the main anchor must have been braced against each other and possibly twisted around the keel as we were now able to manoeuvre the boat with some freedom and get it anchored in four metres of water. The Greek then got into his boat and went off to rescue our kedge anchor. He brought it over to us. The exercise was over. Now for the settlement!

I asked the old gent what we owed him. He shook his head and said what sounded like *tipota* (nothing). I got Helen to get 50 euros and offered it to him. "*Ochi, ochi*" (No no). He started fishing around in the bottom of his boat. We tried him with some tins of beer. He shook his head and presented us with a plastic bag of fish that he had been sorting out in the bottom of his boat. He grinned and waved us a cheery good bye as he took his boat off towards Amfilokhia. So… far from paying serious salvage money, we got a free fish supper in addition to his help. One of the old school, without a doubt.

We anchored that afternoon back in the bay beside the island of Koukoumitsa off Vonitsa and purged the mud from ourselves and Sundowner. I watched a straggly line of large birds making their way across the gulf in the distance. Something about the straggly line, their broad wings and the shape of the bird made me think flamingo; although, surely, they were a long way from their natural habitat. Surely you saw them in Africa? They were too far away to make out salient details such as the shape of the beak but I later found that there was indeed a type of flamingo seen in Greece. So flamingos they were then.

Later, we barbecued the fish and sat in the cockpit eating it. We watched a turtle busying about the bay surfacing from time to time among the yachts that were laying at anchor in the bay. We bet each other that we knew where he was going to surface next. In the dusk, the lights on the arched stone footbridge to the island were lit. Beyond it, the Venetian castle above Vonitsa was floodlit. A perfect end to a day that had started rather less than perfectly.

As we left the Gulf of Amvrakikos the next day, we were treated to the sight of dolphins out on a spree — or that's how it appeared to me. Leaving Vonitsa bay, we rounded Ak. Panayia keeping well clear of the shallows and an uncharted reef and we headed west towards Preveza. About half a dozen dolphins crossed our paths. Two large dolphins that seemed to be in the lead most of the time were launching themselves out of the water and high into the air in what seemed to be an exuberant show of high spirits. There was a heavy snorting sigh of exhaled air as one surfaced near us then slipped back underwater leaving rings of heaving water behind it. Sometimes, in this sort of mood, they will come and investigate a boat that happens to be in their vicinity but they didn't pay much attention to us on this occasion. They were headed for the fish farm that lay on the west side of the promontory of Ak. Panayyia. One of the men who staff these places was feeding his captive fish. The water inside the cage of netting was a maelstrom as shovelful after shovelful of food pellets was thrown into the circular enclosure. Nets above the cylindrical enclosure protected the captive fish from predators from the sky. Tough netting around the vertical walls of the cylinder and across the bottom kept out aquatic predators — bigger fish and dolphins.

The dolphins were not going to penetrate the defences. Maybe sometimes they got lucky, but they must have known that they were not going to get at the fish — they are intelligent creatures that regularly demonstrate creativity and the ability to learn. Their boisterousness suggested something else was afoot.

"Can you hear that chaps?"

"Yeah what is it?"

"Come on chaps… It's feeding time at the fish farm."

"Yeah, but that's no good to us. I bashed myself silly trying to get through their netting last week."

"Never mind, let's go and annoy them anyway."

There was one man on an odd-looking boat that the fish farms use — little more than a small raft with sacks of food pellets on it, a crane and a motor. As we passed, and left the fish farm behind, the lone fish farmer was surrounded by half a dozen dolphins busying themselves about so they looked like a dozen. The ringleaders were still leaping out and crashing into the sea splashing copious amounts of water in his direction. The others were circling and diving, dorsal fins like sharks on the prowl, before diving below, presumably to pull faces at the panicking captive fish.

Frikes

We have a number of friends in Frikes on the island of Ithaca. Our relationship with the village dates back to our back-packing days. That and the fact that it has a more 'villagey' feel than the pretty harbour of Kioni next door made it one of our favourite harbours in this neck of the woods. Like Kioni it is a favoured overnight stop for the flotillas, so we don't stop there much once the season really gets underway.

Once we had the boat, the whole family (or those that made it to Sundowner — our summer residence) were introduced to the village, the villagers, and the walks into the hills and along the coast. George, who with his mum and dad (Nicola and Alan) and his brother, Charlie, were one of our first visitors, and even rescued another visitor who had come in on a day hire motor boat. The man, who I think was a Greek, breezed in on his hired boat, tied it up to the jetty for small craft and repaired immediately to the nearest taverna (the Rementzo).

The tying up was less than expert and the late afternoon/early evening gusting that is a characteristic of the harbour took control of the boat, undid its rather flimsy mooring and moved it off in the direction of the harbour entry. Zorba the Greek, to his credit, was on the case straight away. He pulled off his shirt revealing what was more of a family pack than a six pack but, splashing into the water, made a pretty creditable 50-yard dash to the boat. However, once he got there, he discovered that he was out of puff from his Olympian freestyle splash and further, the high freeboard of the day hire launch meant that he was unable to haul himself out of the water and into the boat. He found himself holding onto his day hire launch and with no vestige of control, being propelled out of the harbour by the increasing wind while the spectators, transfixed by the drama, did nowt. George untied our tender, fired up the outboard, and pursued the knot of struggling man and boat out of the harbour and eventually brought them both back to safety.

As long as I have known Frikes, the place to moor up for the night has been alongside the harbour wall on the inside of the mole. A mole in this case being a weather break made out of rocks rather than a small subterranean animal. You can also lie alongside the road on the south side of the harbour, but it is noisy; some of the space is shallow and a lot of it is taken by local boats and their mooring lines. My prime position behind the mole is right next to the harbour entrance so I can slip out easily even when the harbour is full of flotillas that — like as not — will not be leaving till mid-morning. However, for some years this position boasted a notice that asked you to leave the location clear during the afternoon for the day trip boats that arrive from other islands and spill out tourists for a couple or so hours.

The day trippers swarm into the local shops, tavernas, and bars and you can hear the happy 'ching kerching' of cash tills. So, generally, the locals will understandably clear you off if you are in the way of such day trip boats. Sometimes it all happens a bit late. We had tied up there on one occasion; we had seen the daytrip boat using various other spots in the harbour on previous occasions and so regarded the notice as one of those that no longer applied, but was still there because no-one had yet got around to taking it down. We went ashore for lunch and some light refreshment and indeed we were told the Nidri Star, which was the only day trip boat calling in at the time, was no longer in the habit of using that particular spot on the quayside. Everybody, except me, decided to shake down their lunch by walking to Kioni — the next port to the south, about an hour's very pretty walk. I opted to shake down my lunch by snoozing in the afternoon warmth. I had no sooner dropped off, it seemed, than there was a knocking on the cabin roof. It was a taverna owner.

"You have to move," he informed me.

"Why?"

"Nidri Star comes… coming"

"When?"

"Now," he said pointing over my shoulder. In my semi-soporific state, I had not registered the thumping of a large boat engine and the shouting and yelling of the crew which was mainly in Greek but, I suppose translated to 'fuck off, yottie'. There was the large dark bulk of the Nidri Star reversing relentlessly towards me.

"If it hits me, he's in the wrong," I thought, but then discretion took the better part. I threw off the springs, rapidly slipped the forward mooring line then dived back into the cockpit. I started the engine and slipped the aft line then pulled out from the narrowing gap between the Nidri Star and the harbour side like a melon pip being squeezed between finger and thumb. Fortunately, there was a couple on a Countess 37 that was the appropriate size and build to take me laying alongside. They happily took my lines. I giggled to myself as I secured myself alongside — the crew would think I left Frikes without them when they got back.

I walked back out along the mole to collect my abandoned lines which someone had thoughtfully coiled up for me. The captain of the Nidri Star sat beside them on a bench seat.

"Did you not read the notice?" he asked pointing.

"Yes, but you don't usually come in here," I countered. "I have seen you moor off the ferry ramp and off the north harbour side before."

"This is reserved for me," he said. "Sometimes, I go elsewhere if there is room and the weather favours another place."

"But that's confusing," I said. "I think you just saw a yottie in your spot and wanted to be awkward."

"Parakalo?"

"Oh, forget it. No harm done I suppose."

"No, you not forget," he said. "I try to help these people." He waved imperiously at the tavernas and shops of the harbour. "They need the business. You try help me help them."

'Pompous git', I thought as I threw my springs over my shoulder and flounced off to the giggles of his crew.

The Mediterranean tradition of mooring stern or bows to the harbour is not advised along the mole in Frikes due to the poor holding for the anchor that holds the bow or the stern off the harbour wall and the possibility of strong winds in the late afternoon or evening. The convention of mooring alongside is preferred. The boats are tied fore and aft to strong mooring rings or concrete bollards that are securely anchored in the concrete of the quayside. I feel comfortable with the arrangement. It feels a safe and secure — a British way of mooring. However, it is also understood (though not by everybody) that you permit other boats to moor alongside. A number of boats may be rafted out from you with the drawbacks that that will entail.

There is a new stretch of harbour wall along the north-east side of the harbour that looks inviting. However, this stretch of harbour wall is exposed to the wash from the ferries that frequently exceed speed limits as they hurry north to Igoumenitsa and then Italy or south to Patras. This can throw boats about a bit leading to mast clashes and even hull damage against the new ferry wall. At the time of writing, the ferries seem to have slowed due either to the successful fining of those who exceed speed limits or the escalating price of fuel. Notwithstanding this, the inside of the mole is much sought after.

There are boats that you bump into from time to time and gradually friendships are formed. It was in Frikes that we first met Goldeneye and her owners Bill and AnneMarie. We had successfully found a place inside the mole right next to Goldeneye. A 40 ft Bavaria rocked up and wanted to moor outside Goldeneye, a 36 ft Westerly that already had another 36 ft boat alongside. Some disagreement ensued. The convention is not to moor larger boats outside smaller boats. The larger boat may place excess stress on the smaller one particularly in high winds and Frikes often gets a strong late afternoon wind howling down the valley that opens up into the harbour from higher ground. Of course, if the larger boat is a lighter build and the smaller a well found boat the issue becomes a bit blurred. The contretemps on this occasion involved a certain amount of shouting but was eventually resolved with extra fendering donated by the outer boat adding extra protection between the smaller inside boat and the quayside. Most of the folks gathered around helped to push Goldeneye away from the harbour wall against the weather that was pressing it on to the quayside so that the fendering could be inserted.

Once the ruckus was over, Bill and AnneMarie invited adversaries and helpers on board for a little light refreshment. I later returned to Sundowner after gratefully accepting their hospitality and was told,

"It's astounding how men can be shouting at each other one minute and then, when someone offers them a beer, they are all friends again."

"It seems an eminently sensible way of repairing relationships that have been rather stressed," I replied. The disagreement notwithstanding, we both made friends with Bill and AnneMarie over the following seasons, bumping into them here and there.

Episcopi

The searing heat of August had given way to more gentle warmth as we moored up alongside Goldeneye in Episcopi on the island of Kalamos in early September. The afternoon sea was bright with glinting silver highlights on the blue sea that changed to turquoise in the relatively shallow waters along the coast. The trees on the slopes leading down to the bay partly concealed the houses built up the rocky slopes that overlook the harbour. The vista was a myriad of greens — dark greens, light greens, the shimmering silvery green of olive trees. Houses and gardens had cascading bougainvillea and other vines, fans of palm leaves and, randomly scattered among it all, erect Cyprus trees pointing firmly at the unbroken blue of the sky. Oleander, bougainvillea, hibiscus, and roses add splashes of colour everywhere.

Epscopi is a quiet hamlet. There are no shops. If you want shops, you have to make your way around the island to Port Kalamos. Busses? No busses. You better have arrived with your live-aboard cycles and puff and wheeze your way along the road — rough at times but with lovely views through lush green conifers. The other option is to catch one of the few caiques (water taxis or busses) that ply between the islands of Kalamos, Kastos, and the town of Mitikas on the mainland. From Episcopi you can see the white buildings of Mitikas edging the coastline across the blue shimmering sea.

The only source of refreshment or nourishment in Episkopi is a small bar that is open during the peak months of the summer. The choice is limited (burgers, sausages or chicken kebabs the last time we were there), but inexpensive and it is a nice place to be. You can sit there and admire the view across to Mitikas or look down on the harbour. The harbour is small, and you use pretty much the full width of it to lay anchor chain if you come in stern or bows to. This means that the prevailing wind can place you in danger of running onto the far shore when picking up the anchor. There is not a lot of room. Four or five modern yachts is usually the maximum you will see in port at any one time. One can also drop anchor in the bay that leads into the harbour. The holding is good but you have to be prepared for a bit of rock 'n roll in the night when a swell is quite likely to roll in.

Eucalyptus spread shade at the waterfront. Decorative palms, the fat trunks of which look like giant pineapples, add to the exotic look of some of the gardens and, of course, grape vines decorate the frontage of houses and sprawl over trellis work everywhere. The summer sees the houses occupied but mostly they are holiday homes and only a handful of people (half a dozen I am told) stay through the year serviced by caiques from Mitikas. Up behind the port, a walk overlooking the sea takes you through shady conifers to the ruins of an old monastery. The road also leads to Kalamos Town on the other side of the island. It is about a seven-mile walk.

Having moored Sundowner stern to, run out the passerail and made everything shipshape so to speak we decided on a walk that took us up the only road out of the village towards the monastery. It rose steeply between the houses of Episcopi. Their gardens were coloured with bright bougainvillea, red hibiscus, roses and other less easily identifiable blossom. They also sported crops of glossy dark purple aubergines, large beefy tomatoes, oranges, lemons, figs and pomegranates that were bursting apart to show their multifaceted honeycomb of flesh and seeds. Above Episcopi, the road levelled out and ran east some distance above the shoreline. We walked through shady pines of a type that are supposedly unique to Kalamos — with wild mint, oregano and thyme in the hedgerows. We admired the view over the sea to Mitikas and the mainland and eventually reached and stood admiring 'Castromonastiro' and the view beyond it. It was an impressive building with largely intact external stone walls with high internal arches that supported wall-top battlements.

On our way back from the monastery, we decided to try to find the spring in the hills above the village. We had been given directions by a German lady from a large motor launch that seemed to spend a month and a half in Episcopi each year. I had spoken to her while she filled some bottles with water from the tap above the harbour.

"The water is good?" I asked.

"Oh ja. It is spring water," she told me and added. "You can walk up to the source of this water."

"Oh, that might be interesting. Where is it? I might go up there later"

"No, not this afternoon," she told me.

"Not this afternoon? What's wrong with this afternoon?" I said bridling a little at the rather peremptory manner that seems to come naturally to some Germans.

"Too hot."

"Oh, we'll take floppy hats and there are plenty of trees for shade."

She shrugged, "If you must... but you need to take water." She looked me over like a school ma'm regarding an errant pupil and seemed about to say something about mad dogs and Englishman when her gaze alighted on my feet.

"Ahh... but not in those."

"What's wrong with my feet? They are a matching pair and, actually, the only pair I have," I said truculently.

"Not your feet, your shoes. Flop flips, they are not good. You need good walking boots."

"Haven't got any. We'll be all right. These are special mountaineering flip flops — Japanese walking boots."

"You need better. There are snakes!" She warned us darkly and gave me directions to the spring and the snakes.

We found the stone path that she had referred to quite easily and walked up it taking care where we placed our flip-flop-clad feet. It was certainly hot in the sun, but conifers offered occasional shade. The clatter of cicadas mingled with the harsh caw of large black crows and the chittering of smaller sparrow-like birds — probably sparrows.

It was about forty-five minutes before we heard the gurgle of water. A rocky promontory and some bushes blocked the source from view until I pushed through some foliage and there was somewhat disappointingly a brass tap and a length of plastic pipe sticking out of a rock face. No spring gurgling from the stony ground into a pool and off in a clattering chattering spring down the hill. The black plastic pipe disappeared down the sloping countryside doubtless to the two or three freshwater taps in the harbour. The tap dripped into a large stone sink that had been placed under it. But what really got my attention was a large long black snake draped along the black pipe over the sink. It was a big snake. It looked at me and I looked at he and I briefly wondered what was going to happen next.

"Stay where you are," I shouted at Helen who was a little way behind me and likely to come crashing through the bushes at any moment. "There's a bloody big snake here."

At my shouting, Helen appeared through the bushes and the snake moved like greased lightning toward me. I leapt about six foot into the air and hung there as long as possible. However, the snake was just heading for shelter and disappeared under a nearby bush while I returned from free fall with all the dignity of a near seventy-year-old landing on his arse.

"Your new hip doesn't seem to have impaired your athletic prowess. I think you have just broken the world record for high jump from a standing start," Helen gasped between paroxysms of laughter as she helped me to my feet.

"Uh, I thought it was coming for me."

"Coming for you? I think the poor thing was petrified of you landing on him."

Walking back down into the village, I was aware of a terrible thirst as we approached the small bar.

"A drink? I think we've earned it," I ventured.

"You've a bottle of water there in your hand." We had taken water on the walk, in spite of being tempted to ignore the admonitions of the German lady. We tend to do that anyway but we had remained firm on the question of flip-flops.

"Water? It's been warmed by the sun. A cold beer is what I'm thinking about."

"As ever!" Helen snorted.

"Hey Amstel. Over here," AnneMarie called from where she and Bill sat in the open-air bar.

"See, AnneMarie has nicknamed you Amstel — and we've not known them long."

"That's probably because she knows we used to live in Holland."

"It's because whenever she sees you, you've a tin of Amstel in your hand."

The afternoon was turning into evening as we sat in the bar with Bill and Annemarie, putting the day to rest.

The Rat

The following morning, I noticed something had taken a bit of a chunk out of a peach in a fruit bowl on the saloon table. Helen noticed it too. "You haven't been indulging in your penchant for sneaky midnight snacking," she remarked looking pointedly at the peach in question.

"Nope."

"Well, what has taken a chunk out of that."

"Probably wasps."

"Wasps my eye. Bloody big wasps."

"If there is something like that in the offing it attracts a lot of them."

"So they work in gangs."

"Well…"

"And at night? And we didn't notice this big gang of wasps that somehow found their way through the mosquito netting and attacked our fruit bowl."

"They probably did it yesterday and we didn't notice, while we were out for a walk."

"It wasn't done when we went to bed last night."

"I didn't notice."

"I did…" She retorted and continued. "So your money's on a huge gang of nocturnal wasps — probably peculiar to Kalamos… just like the pines."

"Well, if it's not wasps it's probably a mouse or a rat."

"Arrrghh," Helen shrieked. "Don't tell me we've got a rat on board!"

"All right I won't... But we probably have."

It was worrying. There is the question of hygiene. They tend to eat anything remotely edible that they can find leaving what they have not managed to eat in a very dubious state because they defecate absolutely everywhere they go. Even worse, in many ways is their habit of chewing through insulation on electrical wiring — just to keep their teeth in good order if you please. This can lead to electrical short circuits that can lead to fire which you really don't want on a voyage.

Later that day, we heard some rattling and scuffling. The rat — or whatever it was — was up and about and doing damage somewhere. At first it seemed to be coming from the battery locker. Imagining the rodent gnawing away furiously at electrical insulation I removed the seating cushion and the wooden cover exposing the three large batteries but no rat.

"It's coming from that locker," Helen pointed at a locker above the battery locker. It held cooking dishes — possibly some with a residue of fat or cooking oil that it might find attractive. I opened it cautiously and saw a flash of something furry. I started removing the contents of the cupboard bit by bit imagining the heavy breathing of a fierce cornered rodent. Eventually, one circular metal dish was left stood on its edge at the back of the locker. The intruder was surely behind that. He had been quiet for a bit. He had become a *he* in my mind. I was beginning to know him as "Ratty" ('Don't get too familiar with the enemy', I told myself).

Had Ratty sneaked out somehow without my noticing? I made to withdraw the dish gently. Mistake. I should have smacked it hard against the wall with my fist. That might have stunned the rat so that I could get at him and swaddle him in the old towel I had in my hand for such a purpose then dispose of him somehow, somewhere. However, I opted for the soft approach of snatching the dish away and clobbering the rodents and confusing him by wrapping him in the towel. As soon as I disturbed the dish, the rat came streaking out like a man-eating rodent on a mission. He flew through the air with his front legs akimbo, claws stretched towards me, eyes focussed on my throat and venom dripping from his fangs. I stepped back from my precarious balance atop the edge of the battery compartment yelping profanities and fell on my back on the floor cracking my head on the heads (shower room) door. Ratty fell in among the batteries. "Aw fuck it. I nearly had him there," I groaned.

"Nearly had him my eye," shrieked Helen. "He nearly had you."

"Where did he go?"

"In the battery compartment."

We looked, but the bugger had gone to earth in one of the many nooks and crannies designed in by boatbuilders as a safe haven for rodents so the boat owner can't possibly get at them.

"He was quite light coloured for a rat," I observed. "Looked like somebody's pet rather than vermin."

"You can keep him for a pet if you like. I'm off back to Blighty in a couple of days."

"No no... Still needs getting rid of... Before it chews through an electrical cable."

We were diverted by a crash and a splash and some shouting outside. We hurried out into the sun and peered over the edge of the cockpit. The foaming water indicated that something large had fallen in. Bill's panama hat was floating on the surface indicating that it might have been Bill. He came up coughing and spitting beneath the hat so that the act of surfacing re-instated it at its usual jaunty angle on his head. Bill is a dapper dresser. He manages what I never can — to look tidily turned out on a boat — hell, I cannot even manage that on land in the most benign of situations. And there he was, having fallen in the water, coming to the surface still turned out in his immaculate dress code.

"Are you OK, Bill," shouted a worried AnneMarie.

"I'm fine. Just thought I'd escape from the heat for a bit," said Bill reaching for a handhold on the stern of Goldeneye.

"Shaken but not stirred — very James Bond," said Helen laughing unkindly at his discomfort; Bill has a passing resemblance to Sean Connery. Bill attempted to casually haul himself back onto the boat, but rather marred the coolness of his recovery from the undignified ducking by cracking his head on the passerail as he pulled himself up.

A stiff drink was taken, for medicinal purposes only. On Bill's part, it was to subjugate the pain of a cracked rib — he had hit the passerail on the way down. On my part; well, you can't let folks drink alone, can you? Besides, it helped to stop me laughing unsympathetically at his distressing experience. We discussed his cracked rib then, when we tired of that subject, my rat.

"We had one last year," said Annemarie.

"How did you deal with it?"

"I couldn't stand the idea of a trap so we just made sure that there was nothing to eat and left the boat open until it buggered off."

"How did you know it was gone?"

"It said goodbye. It said it wasn't coming here again. The service was awful and it would make sure all its friends were aware of its opinion of the place. No food, rough company, poor customer service, all the usual," Bill explained.

"Yes, he had all his worldly goods and chattels bundled up in a big red handkerchief with white spots. We saw him set off along the passerail back to terra firma with his bundle tied on the end of a stick that he put over his shoulder," continued AnneMarie. "It was very sad."

We gave up in the idea of getting any sense or helpful suggestions from either of them and left for Vlicho that day. The village had a shop or two and, in one of them, we found a very medieval looking rat trap.

When you get a rat on board, you have to decide how to get rid of it. If you poison it, it will probably go off and die in some inaccessible place and will lie there festering. It has got to be a trap of some sort, or else the alternative that AnneMarie and Bill successfully tried. Ensure that there is no food on board then open everything up when you are in port and it should eventually, hopefully, desert ship. We opted for the trap. We set it and went up into the cockpit. Within an hour, I heard it snap shut and sure enough the awful contraption had the rat in its uncompromising jaws. I drowned the rat and the clean-up began.

I prepared Dettol, bleach and God knows what else. I got down on my hands and knees and scrubbed lockers, flooring and every surface. At last the boat smelled clean… it was… must be… clean.

Poisonous Spitting Toads

By September, Helen was back on the boat to help me put it away at the end of the month, or the beginning of the next if we felt so inclined. The weather is frequently lovely in September though there is the occasional storm. The shortening days are usually filled with a balmy warmth rather more restful than the intensity of July and August.

At anchor in one of the less busy bays, I swam in the sea in the early morning as the sun began to break the horizon. The water seemed chilly, but that may have been me getting spooked. When I dived under the water it was dim, silent, and all I could see were little more than shadows. As the sun rose higher warming the air, a moderately large fishing boat puttered in from somewhere out to sea in the half light and dropped anchor outside the harbour. A large rowing boat stacked high with wooden boxes set out from the fishing boat. It creaked and splashed its way to shore to where a pickup was waiting for a catch of about 18 boxes of fish, and squid.

The day's activities were planned over a breakfast of omelettes and coffee — we had decided to treat ourselves and had breakfast at a taverna near the shore. At one point, I went back to the boat to get a chart in order to check distances. On the way back, I heard a deep chirruping coming from a low clump of plants bearing yellow flowers. The plant was low — a bit like primrose or coltsfoot I thought, but growing along the salty shoreline rather than in a hedgerow. The noise sounded as if a toad or a frog was hiding in the foliage and calling for a mate or simply protesting at passers-by.

I had heard the noise when passing the same spot earlier and decided on this occasion to unearth the chirruper. I pushed the plants aside roughly where the noise seemed to be coming from. The chirruping stopped momentarily... then something spat viciously leaving a great green lumpy gob of slime on my arm. There was some force behind the spit. I vaguely recalled that there were such things as poisonous toads who are apt to defend themselves by spitting venom at prey or perhaps anything that they perceived as a threat.

I thought that the toads were native to South America rather than Greece, but being of a cautious (not to mention cowardly) disposition, I hurried down to the water's edge and washed the venom from my arm in the sea. It was probably harmless enough, but there was no point in risking an irritating rash or worse.

Unfortunately, my activities had been observed from the taverna.

"What were you doing in the sea?" asked Helen.

"Washing some stuff off my arm."

"What stuff?"

"Green-yellow, slimy snotty stuff."

"Ugh, I don't want to know any more," Helen said, but Johnny Dangerous did. So I had to explain my close encounter with the venomous toad which excited some interest.

"Venomous toads?" he asked. "Surely, they are from Africa or somewhere."

"Yes, well… perhaps South America."

"What are they doing here then?"

"Well, I'm not saying it was a toad. But I heard what might have been a toad or a frog and it spat at me."

"Hmm, pity you didn't catch it," concluded Johnnie D.

"Him… catch it. I had to defend him against cockroaches in Crete," Helen scoffed.

"Catch it — I didn't even see it!" I said — offended.

"So it's just a product of your imagination? Why were you washing this gob off your arm then?"

I explained that I thought that I had better wash the spit off in case it was a nasty irritant. I was accused of rank cowardice in the face of small imaginary amphibians and John challenged me to point the nasty little creature out to him.

On the way back from the taverna, I armed myself with a stick and lead the others to the clump of yellow flowers. The chirruping was still emanating from round about the middle of the clump. I foraged around the area from which the noise was coming with my long stick and sure enough there was a splat and a great gob of spit soared past my right ear, and I was standing as far from the clump as my stick allowed. The gob hurtled so far and so fast that Helen thought that it was the animal escaping.

"No, no. I will make it do it again," I said gingerly poking around with the stick and producing another splat. This time, it hit the small wall behind the clump of plants particularly viciously.

Now I had the nasty little toad fairly accurately located and could perhaps move it out into the open. The first ejaculation had indicated that the toad, if indeed it was a toad, had thought that it was being attacked from the right. I had then prodded an area further back and to the left. The poisonous toad had responded by gobbing at the wall behind it, obviously under the impression that enemy forces were now moving in from behind it.

I explained that I had the venomous brat cornered and we should be able to see it soon. I got Johnny D to stand to my left and cautiously rustled the plants to the right of the creature explaining that I had worked out exactly where the toad was located and that, if he stood where I suggested, the venom would whistle harmlessly off to my right. I explained that the creature was getting pretty miffed by now and that it might well be venomous.

The toad spat directly at Johnnie. It must have been his gaudy Bermuda shorts which had upset the toad. Johnnie asked whether I could get it to do it again, but this time at myself rather than him. I waved my stick around in a rather diffident manner — my assessment of the location of the beast was now suspect. Nothing happened. Then a waft of breeze disturbed the plants and gob of venom came flying out again, but this time I saw what was happening. My venomous spitting toad was a seed pod. As the flower starts to die, the pod grows — we could see them in various stages of development in the same clump of plants. The pod ends up looking like a gooseberry — round, green with small hairs and the wilted flower just a brown tag at the end of the green globe. The ripe pod is pressurised and, when jostled, sufficiently it ruptures at the weakest point (where the pod joins the stem), the pod flying in one direction and a gob of glutinous jelly containing seed flies off in the other. The spit is the plant propagating its seed. I tried to look it up later. I used the internet which made the results a bit suspect, but the closest I could get — not being a botanist — was some form of lesquerella or bladder pod.

The end of another season had arrived and at the time we were still making the journey by car. We caught the overnight ferry from Igoumenitsa to Venice so that we arrived in Venice early in the morning. Although it was early, the water was usually already busy with water busses, water taxis, delivery barges and all manner of commercial craft. This season we noticed a number of rowing boats practising a technique, peculiar to Venice as far as I know, where the rowers stand in the boat facing forwards and push the oars rather than pull them. "It looks rather odd to me," I said.

"Seems perfectly logical to me," remarked Helen who likes to sit facing forwards to row. "Can't understand why you always sit back to front. You can't see where you're going."

We looked down from the ferry at the familiar sights — St Mark's Square and the ranks of gondolas at the waterside moving gently in the confused wake of the water traffic. We slowly moved past the entry to the Grand Canal and on to the rather less glamorous ferry terminal.

Once off the ferry, clear signposting soon got us on to the autostrada across northern Italy. By late afternoon, we were at the Mont Blanc tunnel. "You should be keeping your speed down to 80," I told Helen.

"I'm only doing 70."

"Kilometers."

"Well, I don't know. It's 70 on this dial."

"You're reading the wrong dial — it's the inner one that gives the speed in kilometres per hour."

"I can't read that — it's too faint. We are well behind the one in front. Cost us 35 euros to use the tunnel — we should be able to do the speed we like."

I managed to cajole her to drop her speed to 50 mph — well my nagging and the fact that we were rapidly closing on the car in front did the trick. "Those little blue lights indicate how far you have to be behind the car in front," I told her but, nonetheless, at the end of the tunnel we were flagged down by a spotty young gendarme in uniform brandishing a print-out of a picture taken by their speed cameras with Helen hunched aggressively over the wheel and the legend '120 kph. Fine 55 Euro' quite clearly printed below it.

"There you are," I grumbled, "35 euros to get in and another 55 euros to get out."

Helen seemed to be toying with the idea of just running the very young officer over. I managed to persuade her that this would probably result in an even higher fine if not a garrotting.

The rest of the journey was relatively trouble-free. An overnight stop in Dijon then back to the drizzle of Blighty in October the following day.

The Silent Suitcase

There was always discussion on whether we should travel to Greece by road or by air. A flight was cheaper by far once you had factored in overnight stops, road tolls, diesel, ferry fares, etc. You could, however, take it as a break and linger a while in places like Lake Garda, or Venice. Against that was the relentless and sometimes furious drive along busy motorways. A positive was the fact that we could throw lots of odds and ends and fairly bulky items into the back of our Toyota hatchback. One year it was a gas cooker, another it was an Avon inflatable dinghy. This year it was a petrol-driven generator that provided 240 V a.c. and a 12 V feed. This latter proved controversial. I thought it would be useful for when our sagging batteries were giving us problems and the laptop needed a boost.

I floated the idea with management first.

"But those things are so noisy and big," argued Helen. "Where are we going to store it on the boat?"

"Andy's got one and says it is very quiet, and no bigger than his briefcase. The type he's got is currently on offer at a place in Portsmouth."

"Oh well that's it this year then. We will be mooring up in nice peaceful bays and disturbing the peace."

"Ah. Mostly if we are in a bay there will be as much noise coming from building projects going on around the place."

"Vlicho, yes but not places like Little House bay... or Seahorse Bay."

So I went to Portsmouth and brought a generator back with me. Helen watched bemused as I struggled in with the brute.

"I must check out Andy's briefcase," she said wryly. "If it's as 'small' as this it's a bloody big'un."

I unwrapped it and took it outside the kitchen door and put oil and petrol inside it to check it out. We didn't want to find out that it didn't work when we were out in Greece. That had happened with the cooker. We installed the cooker only to find one of the gas rings didn't work which led to lots of phone calls to the dealer back in Blighty to enable me to repair the fault.

Checking the generator over, I primed it and pulled the start cord. Nothing much happened and I could sense Helen grinning behind me. I pulled it a number of times. Still nothing. I could sense the grin widening. I fiddled with the choke. Nothing. Then just as Helen was about to intervene it started.

"Jesus, that took a lot of starting... And what a racket..."

"Ah it'll be all right once I get the knack of it. But, yes, it's not what I would call quiet."

"Well, shut it down then you're deafening the neighbours — not to mention me."

It got taken out to the boat and used and referred to sardonically by Helen as 'Andy's quiet briefcase' which degenerated to the more alliterative, 'silent suitcase'.

On our way out to Greece, we frequently stopped in Annemasse and I came to dislike the place. It was a nice enough place I suppose, and it seemed a good place to stop on our chosen route for a number of reasons. However, in the first year, we had not been able to find somewhere to stop due to the launch of a European football tournament. The next time we chose to overnight in the place, we pre-booked a hotel to avoid the same thing happening again. However, the satellite navigation thingy that we were using put us in a place where we could not turn around, due to the one-way system; there was no on-street parking and, although the hotel was nearby, it was the wrong way down the end of a one-way street. The satnav, thinking that it had parked us, shut up shop. So we had to try to loop around the block to the hotel. Narrow streets and the one-way system conspired against us. We eventually got to the hotel totally strung out and mentally frail.

The following year, we booked a different hotel that, according to the description on the web, was near the outskirts of the town and very easy to find. It was no easier than the previous one — in fact, it was almost next door to it. The satnav once again landed us somewhere else in a maze of unfriendly streets and shut up shop.

"Bloody GPS," Helen said when we eventually pulled into the hotel car park. "I don't know why we didn't use mine this year."

"I don't think yours does Europe — not without a special chip."

"We should have bought a chip. It's a much better GPS than yours."

"Well, we're here now."

"Not without an awful lot of stress."

"Ah well," I told her. "Worse things happen at sea."

"That is not a great deal of comfort," she retorted. "Seeing as that is exactly where we will be in a week or two!"

The next day, we anticipated a fairly long but straightforward drive through the Mont Blanc tunnel and across northern Italy to Venice. We got up early and hit the road for the tunnel where we paid the fees and were issued with the bits of paper advising us of upper and lower speed limits and what to do in a crisis. We drove into the tunnel and, in a flash, the windscreen steamed up.

"For Christ's sake, the air conditioning is wrong — do something about it," I shouted at Helen. The misting up was so bad that we really could see little more than glimmers of light through it and, to keep from a head-on collision, I was running the car tyre sides along the kerbside and winding the window down to try and get some idea of what was in front. I was conscious that we were going nowhere near as fast as the lower limit, but unless we could get around the problem with the windscreen, we would have to stop. Helen hit every button on the air conditioning/climate control/air flow dash in turn.

"Can't you get the thing working properly?" I yelled.

"I've tried everything… I don't know what to do, why don't you try the windscreen wipers?"

"Don't be daft, what will that do?"

Helen wiped the inside of the screen experimentally to clear it. Nothing happened. The condensation was on the outside. I fired up the wipers and we had a clear view immediately. I suppose that it was relatively warm and humid in the tunnel compared with the snowy slopes outside so immediately the windscreen, super-cooled by the outside air temperature, hit the atmosphere inside the tunnel, water vapour condensed on it.

Although Helen, as usual, drove down to Greece with me to "unwrap" the boat, I spent the early part of the season on my own. A birth was due in the family at the end of April so there was no way Helen would be out for the launch that year. In Italy, we stopped a few days on Lake Garda — a brilliant idea on Helen's part, but which I took to with ill grace wanting to be on Sundowner rather than peering at the lake through the March drizzle. Eventually, we drove on to Venice and caught the Patras ferry that took us down the Adriatic and dropped us off at Igoumenitsa at the north end of the Ionian Sea before continuing on to Patras. So we spent twenty-four hours on the ferry before an hour of motoring south along the coast road took us to Aktio. The coast road took us past nesting storks, lakes and wetlands that were dark and mysterious in the early morning mist, and at one stage a tortoise hurrying across the road to the safety of the verge — a naturalist's paradise I should think.

Helen spent the few days before her flight back organising cabins, lockers and galley. She checked the sheets pillowcases and clothing that we had sealed up and left on board in black plastic sacks. Most of them seemed to have survived the winter without mildew or similar problems. I ran Helen up to Igoumenitsa in early April for the first ferry of the day to Corfu and the first Easy Jet flight of the season from Corfu to Gatwick.

Spring was breaking around me as I set to the list of tasks that I wished to complete on Sundowner. The snow caps on the mountains in the distance diminished in size as the days went past. Hedgerows were ablaze with myriad colours of wild flowers. From time to time, a herd of cows would wander into the yard to graze and then be seen off by the half dozen yard dogs who seemed to be there to do just that. Apparently, there was contention between the farmer who didn't see why the cows shouldn't graze wherever they liked and the yard who did. There were stories of cows doing damage with their horns but the only transgression that I witnessed was a round brown cow pat — a welcome mat that one of the cows had left at the foot of our ladder. A donkey, who also had a place in the yard, would wake me up in the morning with that harsh distressed sounding braying that donkeys make. At night, the toads in the nearby marshes would chatter in rasping belching croaks right up till last light. Behind us was the Gulf of Amvrakikos surrounded by mountains and blessed with pearly pink sunrises.

I was in daily contact with Helen to check the progress towards the imminent arrival of our third great-grandchild and other domestic news. During a call, in mid-April, she told me that there had been a volcanic eruption in Iceland on Wednesday night that had sent plumes of ash thousands of feet into the air which was now hanging in a cloud over the UK and mainland Europe. Air flights were suspended by order of the government.

"Ahh, it'll disperse in time for Johnnie Dangerous to make his flight over," we told each other. Johnnie Dangerous was coming out to help me with the launch and to spend a week or so on the water. That was the plan anyway but, surprise surprise, it didn't happen that way.

Two days later, the weather had not pushed the volcanic ash away but the weathermen were hopeful. Another couple of days and it was still there. It was touch and go[2] whether John would make it and there was dissension in the ranks. Could it be that HM Government were being over cautious? A plane had flown up and taken a look. "It's OK up here! What are they on about?" but the ban was not lifted and eventually it became clear that even if flying were resumed there would be enough confusion and backlog that John would not make it and, if he did, might not make it back on time. He cancelled.

---

[2] The phrase "Touch and Go" owes its origins to the east coast bargemen who sailed the rust-red sailed spritsail barges otherwise known as Thames barges. These barges, 100 ft or so in length, were often sailed by just a man and a boy. They plied their trade in the tidal waters of the Thames Estuary and the south east of England generally. Beating up some of the narrow Essex and Suffolk rivers, they would have to take advantage of as much of the width of the river as possible and so would leave going about until they just touched the mud in the shallows. On a falling tide, this put them in some danger of not quite being able to go about onto the new tack and getting stuck on the putty until the next rising tide floated them off. On reaching their destination, they would describe the sail up as touch (the mud) and go (about).

Fitting Out Again

On the boat, I continued preparing for the new season — oh frabjous joy. On the first night aboard, the gas alarm had gone off. It makes a dickens of a racket — a bit like a burglar alarm. It probably woke the whole boatyard at about three o'clock in the morning. It seems to happen from time to time. It is supposed to detect gas, but I think it is also triggered by a lot of other things, freshly applied paint or resins for example. The result is that it eventually gets switched off… so it's an incredibly useful device… another shrewd investment.

The next night, it was the fridge that kept me awake. It started to make a harsh knackered-bearing sort of a noise in the wee small hours. What was the noise? I thought I understood all about fridges when I left school with physics "O" and "A" levels among my all too few achievements. I could draw a diagram of a refrigeration system and explain how it worked. But that was 2,000 years ago. Did the noise indicate that damage was being done? I didn't know so I eventually turned the fridge off anyway and restarted it once or twice during the following day. There was no change. An engineer was coming out to see me in a few days he could give me his expert opinion. On the morning of his arrival, I switched the fridge on. It worked perfectly and continued to do so until the launch date.

A couple of days later the engine was recommissioned and was OK except that the audible alarm was not working. This was a bit of a pest as the visual alarm lamps are not exactly in the field of view being at the foot of the wheel console and too dim to make out on a normal sunlit day in the Mediterranean.

I replaced the audible alarm with a buzzer that was delightfully loud. 'That should grab my attention if the engine starts to overheat, stops charging the batteries or whatever' I thought to myself, but concluded the exercise by checking out the alarming system. It was bad news again. Not all the visual alarms worked so, although the audible alarm would tell me if something was going wrong, I would not necessarily be able to tell at a glance what was going wrong.

The alarms are integrated into an ECU (Engine Control Unit I think). This incorporates some intelligence (it's a Volvo so not a lot) and is not easily bypassed to build my own alarms. A new one will cost (it's a Volvo so a lot) so there was a little situation to sort out.

Thus, as the proposed launch date got closer my chances of being ready for it seemed to get further away and things were not going according to plan. A hatch that required mending wouldn't dismantle — the usual yacht builder's masterstroke of dissimilar and inappropriate metals in a saline environment.

Even the laptop ganged up on me. Twice it gave me a message on boot up that amounted to.

"I am distinctly unwell. I may even be dead. Shall I diagnose what's wrong with me and try to repair myself?"

I told it yes. It told me that it was going to take some time and it may reboot several times. I went for a walk in the sun to prevent myself from hitting it with my big adjustable spanner which for some reason I had picked up and was gripping rather tightly.

When the laptop returned to normal working, my iPod wouldn't charge from the USB ports. It was flat. It told me so in no uncertain terms. This was the instrument that was going to get me proficient in Greek and Italian. I had a course of each on it. I tried it in another USB port in case it was the port that was the problem, but it just lay there gasping 'I want electricity'. I plugged it into the mains adaptor that came with the damn thing. It just lay there, 'Please connect me to some electricity. I must have electricity'.

"What about my Italian and Greek lessons," I remonstrated, but it lay there with its eyelids fluttering. 'Electricity' it rasped hoarsely.

I looked at a nearby pylon and considered shinning up it and connecting the bloody thing across 30,000 volts and saying, "Is that enough for you, sir," but no. It was time to put down the adjustable and go for another walk in the sun.

The forward navigation lights had given up on me at the end of the last season. The cause of the problem was a rather makeshift join in the electrical cable. However, on close inspection, the light assembly was also pretty near the end of its useful life. It would have been handy to have got a direct replacement, but they seemed to be a discontinued line so I bought another assembly that should do the task but, of course, the bracket was almost exactly the wrong size and shape so I made a little wooden bracket and we had navigation lights again. Super, but now I discovered that the outboard motor wouldn't start, but what the hell: I had oars and, anyway, at present, no dinghy... or rather, I had a dinghy but it needed repair.

I phoned Nikos — the local expert in the high-tech rubber that the dinghy was made from — who said he would collect my dinghy on the same day but didn't. So when he didn't turn up at midday the following day which he had said he would when I phoned him about not turning up on the previous day, I thought: 'I'll get the boat ready for launch and I will sail down to Lefkas with the fucking dinghy and get it into his workshop there'.

I did all the prelaunch things then went into the office and asked if they could launch me tomorrow morning. Themida said yes, but she could not tell me when because Gianni was busy with his new big hoist. "New toy syndrome?" I asked.

She firmly put me right on that then brightly remarked, "You will have to pay us first — no cash, no splash".

"Fine, a credit card is OK isn't it?"

"Yes, but we have to make a surcharge of 2.7%."

"Really? When you first launched me I paid in cash but then, a couple of years ago when I didn't have the readies and asked whether I could pay by credit card, you said that you preferred it to cash and there was no talk of a surcharge then."

"Ah, well, these things change."

So I told her that I would be ready for launch tomorrow whenever it suited them and she said they would work out the bill and present it to me before today was out, which didn't of course happen.

I got back to the boat and lashed up an elaborate hoist to get the dinghy up on the deck of Sundowner. After two repaired hernias, there was no way I was trying to get it on board without a pulley system to reduce the strain. The hoist was made up from lightweight blocks from my dinghy sailing days and miles of string so hoisting the thing up from the ground was a bit of a performance.

Then I tried to phone Nikos to tell him that I would be bringing the dinghy to Lefkas on the morrow. However, when I attempted that, the Greek phone told me that I hadn't got enough credit to make the call. So I checked the credit on my UK mobiles and neither (why the hell do I have two?) seemed too healthy so I set about topping up, but then my Greek mobile rang. It was Nikos to say that he would be round in a half hour to pick the dinghy up; could I be at the boat yard gate to guide his man to the dinghy? I re-lashed up my hoist and tortuously craned the dinghy back down to ground level. I then went to the gate to wait. An hour passed and no Nikos. I was beginning to think, 'I am going to have to hoist the fucker on to the boat again and find someone else to glue it together'. But he turned up... Ninety minutes late.

A New Season

On launch day, Sundowner was first in Gianni's list. I heard the launch machine being fired up about eight thirty. Gulp. Have I done everything? A few minutes later the tractor appeared with the trailer/launcher in tow and came to a halt just past Sundowner. Gianni then reversed pushing the trailer and angling it in the confined space between the rows of boats. He worked it under the boat as yard hands released the props around the bow and moved them out of the way. The centre of the weight of the boat is aft somewhere between the engine and the keel so the front props are not taking much weight; they are just there to keep the Tupperware monster upright.

Pretty soon the carriage was worked under the boat and the trailer pads raised each side of the keel so the trailer was taking the weight of the boat. The boat was raised slightly and the whole shebang was then manoeuvred slowly and carefully out of the berth. Once out of the berth, the tractor and trailer stopped and Gianni's assistant 'Lanky Gianni' took the remainder of the antifouling and a brush to paint the areas concealed by the props when it was in its berth. Then with a roar of engine, the tractor unit pushed Sundowner along the yard between the rows of boats and down to the slipway.

Lanky Gianni motioned me to board when the boat was in the water and he and his colleagues were holding the lines. I hopped aboard and went below to check everything was tickety boo — no water coming in — before they finally withdrew the trailer from under the boat. I was away ten minutes later and reached the outer marks of the Preveza channel on the hour so 'Good', I thought. 'I should make the 11 o'clock opening of the Lefkas Bridge'. It was not to be.

I nearly got run down by a boat as I turned to the south at the lateral marks at the exit from the Preveza channel on my way to Lefkas. Two boats were coming toward me as I was coming from where they were

248

aiming for. As we got closer, the first of the two who was going like a bat out of hell seemed to be making a beeline for me.

I thought at first, 'There's someone at the helm, I can see his head, so he will take steps to avoid me. It's my right of way. He is on my port side he can see my red port light — or he could if it were lit — and red meant stop when we are both under motor.'

As we closed, he did not seem to be interested in altering course. 'Perhaps he doesn't know the rules under motor', I thought to myself. Everyone knows the rules under sail, but sometimes one suspects that under motor some are a little rusty. This might be the case. If I had my klaxon by my side, I could have given him a blast. Five short ones, "Your intentions are unclear," would have been correct I suppose but just one long one would have got his attention. But the damn thing was below and we were too close for comfort. I took avoiding action and as he steamed past. I shouted but to no avail. There was no-one in the cockpit. What I had thought was a head was a small outboard on the stern rail — well some peoples' heads can be funny shapes. He had wandered downstairs to make a cup of tea or something I assume. Lesson 1: If you're going to go for a P or a T check out what's likely to happen in the next ten or so minutes. Lesson 2: Always keep your trusty klaxon by your side.

I tootled on in the direction of the Lefkas swingbridge, but halfway there, I became aware of a coastguard launch heading for me. What did they want? Ships papers? Oh hell, I hope I can find them; things had got a bit disorganised just before the launch. They stopped and bothered a boat that was about half a mile in front of me who immediately changed course. Then they came for me.

"Head that way. West," they shouted.

"But I want to go to south to Lefkas," I shouted in response.

"No, you must go that way... That way," they shouted pointing emphatically west. Perhaps I was heading for shallows, I shouldn't be. I looked at the echo sounder. The shallows extend quite a way out from the shoreline, but I was in deep enough water I was well clear of any danger of that nature.

"Why?"

"Shooting... shooting," they shouted.

I rapidly took their advice and set a new course almost due west. Gunnery practice rather than local hostilities I assumed. When I seemed well clear of the area that they appeared to be patrolling, I resumed a course toward the bridge across a slightly rolling sea. I gunned the engine a bit but the diversion delayed my arrival at the swingbridge that connects Lefkas to the mainland too late for the eleven o'clock opening. I dropped anchor to wait for the midday opening and I was moored on Lefkas quayside by twelve thirty.

I was moored up in Lefkas town to stock up on provisions, but the next day moved down to Lygia — a quieter place overnight — and waited for a phone call from Nikos to tell me that the dinghy was repaired. It was a nice place to stay a few days and gave me the opportunity to catch up with an old friend Makis at his taverna. Nikos phoned a couple of days later and brought the dinghy down to the harbour. It was ready except that the floor board had to be inserted.

Last year, when the inflatable floor gave up the ghost, we had a carpenter in Ithaca make up a solid one from marine ply. He used the leaky inflatable one as a pattern so it was a nice tight fit. It worked wonderfully and the tender was firmer; it felt more like a rib than an inflatable. But inserting the floorboard now required a bit more heaving and grunting.

I decided not to risk the new repair by putting the floorboard in on the rather rugged Lygia quayside so I towed it behind the boat and made my way down to Nidri next day. The quayside at Nidri is nice smooth concrete. However, there seemed to be no room on the Nidri quay so I anchored opposite in Tranquil bay to see if anyone pulled away to give me a spare slot to moor in. I soon got bored with waiting and thought, 'I'll put the floor in while afloat — it must be possible n'est-ce pas'. Helen, still in England, disagreed when I spoke to her on the phone. "You'll fall in the water you fool," she told me. I took that as a challenge.

I got the solid floor out from the forepeak which was a struggle and then I had to drill holes and fit fittings to match up with the inflatable version — we had not done that last year and managed perfectly well without so why the hell? Oh well, there were various reasons that I will not bore you with now. So I drilled these holes and fitted the fittings on the saloon table praying silently, nay loudly, that I would not accidentally drill right through the bloody thing into the saloon table. Having done that to my satisfaction, I then struggled to get the floorboard up the companionway (a close fit) through the cockpit and into the tender.

The new floor was a tight fit in the tender so with the tender on the water and me in the boat this was an exercise which had me nearly in the water on several occasions. I dropped the swimming ladder into place so I could brace myself off the top rung of that. After struggling for some time, I decided that the only way to deal with it was to let the tender down a bit so it was more flexible. What seemed like an hour later, I still couldn't manage it in spite of the fact that I had bled air out of the tender several times and it now looked quite a sad little boat. Finally, I decided that the floor had to come out and I would row ashore as best I could in the half-inflated tender towing the floorboard behind and get the thing on dry land where I surely stood a much better chance of getting it in.

I had put the tender on a long painter so I could spin it around and get to all the parts I needed to from my perch on the stern of Sundowner. The long line seemed to have wound itself around the bathing ladder. I hauled the ladder up. No, it was not the ladder, it was the rudder. I put a heavy shackle on the line so it would drop down along the line and drag it down and off the rudder but it didn't. It dawned on me that the line must be hooked above the leading edge of the blade in front of the stock. Nothing for it, but an early season swim so goggles on and in I went. After that debacle, which seemed to offer much amusement to a young couple in a posh looking Beneteau anchored nearby, I thought: 'Stuff Tranquil Bay. Tranquil my armpits. There doesn't look to be a decent place to go ashore; anyway, I'm off to Vlicho where I can anchor near a reasonable place to get the tender ashore.' So off I jolly well went and anchored near the Hippocampus — a favourite taverna.

I heaved the floorboard out of the tender and put it on a short line behind the tender — no more long lines for me. I deliberated whether to inflate the tender, but decided not to; I would only have to deflate it again once ashore to get the floor in.

251

I bundled pump, seat, oars and other necessities into the tender then got in myself. It didn't half sag in the middle in its half-inflated state and it rowed spectacularly badly. It was like trying to row a half dead jelly fish. The Hippocampus was bouyed off. Not yet open for the season. I could not see Gianni to ask permission to use his jetty, but there was a concrete slipway nearby. It looked smooth enough, so I made for that. There were jagged rocks at the foot of it. I managed to avoid impaling the tender on them. The jetty was slippery, but I managed to scramble out of the tender on all fours with the dirty painter between my teeth. It was a bit of a battle and blood was drawn, but I won in the end. I inflated the tender and rowed gently back thinking: 'My, doesn't this row nicely now'.

The car was of course still in the boatyard in Aktio, but we wanted to base ourselves at Vlicho this year so the next task was to collect the car from the boatyard and get it to Vlicho. The most inexpensive way was to use the local bus service. I caught the afternoon bus from Vlicho to Lefkas then another one from Lefkas to Preveza. There was a marked contrast with the busses that we had experienced when we first started visiting Greece in the early eighties. Nowadays, they are air conditioned. Then they had not been and, in the heat of the day, we were often sharing a down-at-heels coach seat with a person and maybe livestock such as a chicken or a baby goat. I left Vlicho in the air-conditioned comfort of a very modern coach. At Lefkas bus station, I caught the Preveza bus that took me across the swingbridge that I had come through in the boat and the bus headed along the road below the ramparts of the Venetian fort that looks down imperiously on the cars and lorries scurrying along the road to Lefkas.

The hedgerows of the Spring countryside were resplendent in yellow, pink, scarlet and cornflower-blue flowers. We entered Aghia Nichalaos across Cleopatra's bridge and turned left at the far end along the country road to the airport. I got off the bus just past the airport and before the toll tunnel. There was a ten-minute walk to the boatyard.

I collected the car and backtracked from the boatyard past the airport, through Aghia Nichalaos over the swingbridge on to Lefkada island, through Lefkas town and on along the coast to Nidri finally arriving at Vlicho where I parked it at the waterside in the shade of a eucalyptus tree.

Crossed Lines in Lefkas

About a week after the launch, I made my way back to Lefkas in Sundowner. My insurers had insisted that I got a rig check carried out some time this season — some insist on a rig renewal every ten years, but my current insures seemed happy with a check carried out by the local professionals.

By the time the check had been carried out, and I had collected my certificate from their office, it was surprisingly late in the day. I had intended to head for the south of the island but I thought: 'the hell with it, I will stay tonight and treat myself to supper at one of the rather good tavernas in the back streets. I will set off for more tranquil waters tomorrow'.

I woke just after six the following morning and thought: 'I might as well go now'. I quietly took the passerail (gangplank) in because my Danish neighbours were still asleep — I could hear one of them snoring. On the other side of me was an old man with a delectable young girl from the far east (Thai child bride?). I didn't like them, but not because I was jealous of him. It was more because, late in the evening while I was sat in the cockpit savouring the evening prior to going below, there was a sudden gushing sound and a revolting unmistakable smell. He had dumped his holding tank in the harbour. "You dirty bastard," I yelled and whacked his boat with a boat hook, but he had remained below all shut up with his child bride.

Now, in the quiet of the morning, I slipped one of the stern lines and stowed it. It was on the leeward side, was slack and thus doing nothing to hold the boat. As I slipped the second stern line, the weight of the chain dropping moved the boat forward out into the harbour, but the light wind was also influencing things. It was taking the boat rather near a big floating gin palace that was parked near me, but I had allowed for that. Pulling the anchor in would clear me — no problem, everything was under control. I walked up to the bow nice and steady. It's important to be calm and measured when working single handed. If you run about you are likely to trip over things and there is nobody there to pick you up, dust you off and wipe the tears from your eyes. Of course, the first thing that happened was that the anchor chain jammed on the windlass. I returned rather more briskly to the cockpit and put Sundowner in a position where she should stay clear of the gin palace for long enough for me to sort things out.

I walked faster but calmly to the bow and freed the jam. Up came the anchor with half the mud in Lefkas harbour in a dollop on top of it and, low and behold, someone's bloody anchor chain. I reached over to see if I could manually clear the chain but it was a long reach down to the offending chain and the chain was too taut to lift off my anchor. I only succeeded in caking my hands in mud. I trotted back to the stern and took a spare line from the stern locker trying not to smear mud all over the place.

The wind had changed direction and I was closing with the gin palace again. The owner had emerged and was watching me closely. It was difficult to tell whether he was a helper or a shouter. If I got close to his boat, he would either help by fending off if required or he would just shout at me to go away. I would probably find out soon enough.

I took the line back to the bow with a bit more urgency and secured one end of the line to the pulpit. It became clear that the chain belonged to the Danish boat. They had been woken by the noise of my anchor picking up their chain, which probably resonated through the hull of their boat. Two of them appeared on deck rubbing their eyes blearily. One of them shouted helpfully, "Excuse me, I think you have picked up our anchor chain."

"Yes... I know... I have... It would help if you let a bit of anchor chain out for a mo," I shouted back.

"Our bow will go round."

"Well... Start the motor and hold your boat off the quay against your stern lines."

"Pardon?"

"Oh, forget it."

I managed to haul their chain up far enough that by hanging off the bow like some sort of bedraggled trapeze artist I could pass my line under the chain. I tied the free end of the line to the pulpit. With both ends tied off and the line looped under the offending chain, I dropped my anchor below the held anchor chain and then was able to manually pull my anchor in clear of the other boats chain. I stowed the anchor on the bow roller and undid the retaining line to drop their anchor chain back into the water. By this time, half the mud in Lefkas was all over me. I looked like a native of Nigeria as I ran back to the stern to take Sundowner away from the gin palace. Then I let Sundowner drift a bit in mid harbour while I leaped down the companionway and washed off the worst of the mud.

Crossed anchor lines are not an uncommon occurrence with the Mediterranean penchant for mooring the boat at right angles to the quay ("stern to" or "bows to") rather than alongside — as is usually the preference in the UK. The argument is that it is easier for individual boats to come and go. If boats are moored alongside each other, and rafted out side-by-side from the quayside, then the inside boat normally has to wait for the others in the raft to clear before she can release her mooring lines and move off.

One can, if space around the rafts permits, run lines from the outer part of the raft around an inside boat that wants to be away earlier than the others and slip it out. However, "slipping it out", although it sounds simple, involves much grunting and puffing, fending off, pushing and pulling, easing and tightening of lines and, unless due care is taken, the occasional damaged stanchion or even damaged hand. With a "stern-to" moored boat all you do is slip the two lines holding the stern onto the quayside and move off pulling in your anchor line as you go. If it is moored bows-to then the same approach, slip the bow lines and take in the kedge anchor as you move out. At least that's the theory.

In fact, not everybody manages to lay their anchor in a nice line so that it ends up straight out from the bow of the boat, perpendicular to the quayside; especially, as is often the case, there are bends and angles in the run of the quayside. A lot of lines end up a bit crooked and, especially in harbours like Gaios, the charming main port on the island of Paxos, where there are a few changes in the run of the quayside, crossed lines are likely. They are normally not difficult to deal with and it is more constructive to agree with the offending boat what's to be done about it rather than just hollering: 'You have dropped your fucking anchor over my fucking chain' as sometimes seems to be the preferred approach. It is important, when leaving, to pick up your anchor cleanly and vertically — work the boat towards the anchor so that when it breaks clear of the bottom you are directly above it and you can lift it clear vertically and with reasonable speed. If an anchor is not picked up cleanly and is dragged across the sea bottom, it can hook under the chain of another boat — or, come to that, anything else that is lying on the sea bed.

From time to time, you will pull up your anchor on leaving to discover that a neighbouring boat arriving after you the previous night, has dropped his anchor chain across yours. If he is aboard, he will be aware of this as the noise of the two chains working against each other will transmit along his anchor chain and he will hear it. If he then fires up his motor and uses a gentle thrust so the two lines attaching the boat to the shore are stressed. In reasonable conditions, this is normally enough to hold his boat off the quayside while he lets out anchor chain so that you can bring it to the surface without ripping his anchor out of the sea bed. You can then usually hold his chain by passing a length of line — or a hook with a release — under it, untangle and drop your anchor clear, then recover it and release his line and, with a cheery wave and a thank you, signal that you are clear and he can re tighten his anchor chain. Of course, the cheery wave and the thank you are sometimes replaced by belligerent shouting: 'Next time you come in, make sure your fucking anchor line is straight', or similar; however, that's all a bit unnecessary really. Other matters may complicate the situation. If there is no-one on the offending boat, or there are strong cross winds, the procedure can be more difficult. General ignorance can add to the confusion. Lack of meaningful communication can also complicate matters if, say, one boat is from the Czech Republic and doesn't speak English and you are from England and speak no language apart from English.

The word, gently, is important in the above. Charging about on full throttle while trying to remedy this sort of problem is likely to make it worse. I have seen the over enthusiastic use of bow thrusters — the electrically driven propellers that exert a sideways thrust at the bow — get a boat into deeper doo doo than he was in before the thruster was brought to bear on the problem. I have seen, and been party to, over use of the engine to get one out of a fix.

Just a Thong at Twilight

After my anchor problem in Lefkas, I made my way down to Nidri. I needed laundry doing and managed to find a place on one of the charter company's pontoons at the end of town near a laundry lady. When I arrived on the pontoon an old friend, Gerry, took my lines and asked the usual questions.

"Where have you come from then?"

"Lefkas."

"Don't much like Lefkas."

"Oh, I quite like the town. Quite interesting and quaint in places. Nice little tavernas in the back streets."

"Yeah, agreed. But ain't it noisy at night?"

"Ah not my favourite place to overnight," I admitted.

"But you did?"

"Yeah. Had to have a rig check done, insurance company and all that…"

"Change your insurers mate," chuckled Gerry as he clambered back on his boat.

"Well, it's as well to have it done every so often, so I had Waypoint do it but it all got a bit late. In the end I couldn't be arsed to pull away so stayed the night."

"Oh, oh and what did we get up to in Lefkas then?" Gerry asked rather pointedly.

Puzzled, as much by the intonation as the remark itself, I looked up from coiling the ends of the mooring lines. Gerry was looking down at my tender that had come to rest between my boat and his. I followed the line of his gaze and there, caught onto the outboard bracket on the transom was what looked like a wisp of some sort of seaweed. On closer inspection, it was a small lacy thing — more a thong than a thing actually.

"How the hell did that get there?" I stuttered.

"You tell me bonnie lad," Gerry said raising his eyebrows.

The penny dropped "I was moored next to a boat with shorts and that sort of thing hung on the rail. They must have fallen off into the tender some time during the night."

"Them's canny short shorts! What class of person was on this boat you claim was dangling their smalls over your dinghy then?"

"Elderly gent with a young Thai wife."

"Were they his or hers do you think?"

"Definitely hers. He was not only about three times her age but three times her size as well."

"Hmm… I hope he or she didn't pay much for it."

"For what?"

"The thong thing of course. The builder didn't half skimp on materials. So what nationality was this dirty lucky bounder then."

"I don't know. They were talking a language I didn't understand or even recognise."

"Ah, that'll be English then. Did you not speak to them? That's unlike you."

"Well, they seemed rather standoffish and I had no reason to. At least not till the morning."

"What did they say in the morning then?"

"Nothing. They weren't up when I left. But I meant to have a go at them because just as I was drifting off to sleep there was a gush from his boat followed by an unmistakable stench. The sod had released his holding tank in the harbour."

"Are you going to give them back then?"

"What?"

"The knickers you nicked."

"Look I didn't nick them. Anyway, how can I? I'm not going back to Lefkas to do that, he will probably have left anyway. They're going in the bin. Dirty sod deserves to be fined at least a thong for releasing his holding tank."

"Should have reported him to the port police."

"Yes, I know, but it would have been my word against his in the morning."

"Should have got out of bed and frog marched him to the office."

"They wouldn't want to know at that time of night and I was trying to get some sleep in Lefkas for God's sake."

I didn't stay on the mooring long. I got fed up with Gerry wandering around singing the refrain, "Just a thong at twilight" over and over again.

Greek Easter Sunday

Stocking up with stores in Lefkas, I had bumped into the proprietor of a taverna that we occasionally ate at in Geni. We had exchanged pleasantries and chatted for a while and on parting he invited me to his Easter Sunday lamb roast.

"Why Gianni that's very nice of you," I gushed and promised that I would be there. As the day approached, I began to get a bit apprehensive.

I talked to Helen on the phone, "You must go if he's invited you." She insisted "It would be rude simply not to turn up."

"It sounds like a family do though. I don't know the protocol. I don't know the language."

"Come on. We've been going to Greece for years. You always seem to be able to make yourself understood."

"Oh yes. I can say. 'Hello… How are you?… It's hot (or, less likely, cold) today…' but then they launch into Greek and I have to slow them down and try to explain that I don't really speak Greek, but have a few stock phrases and that's them, all used up."

"Ah well, take it as opportunity to learn."

"Thanks a bunch. That's easy for you to say sat back in Blighty. But what about protocols? Do I take something? I asked Lucy and she suggested lilies."

"Ooh, that sounds a bit funereal."

"Yes, but then, she suggested a bottle of plonk and that's a bit 'coals to Newcastle' but I suppose…"

I spent several days trying to absorb enough Greek to converse and indeed practiced it at every opportunity, but these dummy runs were mostly met with blank stares and pleas for me to speak English. It was not wildly encouraging.

On Easter Sunday, I dropped anchor in the lagoon at Vlicho near to the Hippocampus and put on my reasonably presentable going ashore gear. I then took the outboard from its mounting on the stern of Sundowner and got dirty oil on my hands. I mounted it on the tender and went below to wash my hands thinking, 'I should have thought about that. If Helen was here, she would have told me to deal with the motor and then showered and then put my best bib and tucker on'. Fortunately, I didn't seem to have smeared the stuff anywhere else and I got into the tender getting the seat of my trousers wet with the salt water that the dinghy had accumulated since the last time I emptied it, 'I should have thought of that too'.

The outboard started after a few pulls and I motored the short distance to the Hippocampus jetty hit it rather hard, bounced off it and managed to grab hold of it on the second attempt. I scrambled up from the tender in a somewhat undignified manner. I was warmly greeted by Gianni who introduced me to his family rapidly dispelling my reservations about the event. Goodness knows why I was at all apprehensive. I have been coming to Greece for years and the friendliness and hospitality of the Greeks is legend.

I was introduced to various yotties who he had invited along. I met Geoff from Staffordshire, Colin from Shepperton, and Pauline, a blonde Essex girl from Southend via New Zealand. Geoff and Colin addressed her as Lady Lefkas — so she was one of the regular expats then. There were also a couple of Germans.

Gianni had roasted lamb on a spit, and the long table at which we all sat was laden with dishes of tzaziki, stuffed vine leaves, green salad, tomato salad, thin fried slices of courgette fried in a very light batter and sprinkled with oregano, and other traditional Greek mezzes.

It seemed a pity to pass up an opportunity to put all that sweated learning to use so I tried to converse with the family in halting Greek, and when I really could not muster appropriate Greek (which was a lot of the time), English. I knew from previous conversations that Gianni caught some of the fish and octopus that he served up himself so asked what he used; nets? line?

"No no. Harpoon." He described the technique that I had seen in practice in Vlicho and one or two other places. At one point, the

German joined the conversation. He had been around the world and fished for big fish, sailfish, marlin and so forth. By the sound of it, he probably had a cabinet full of stuffed killer whales on his yacht!

"Do you know how I get the really big ones on board? The ones that would be a hazard threshing around on deck? I kill them first when they are still in the water. I kill them without even touching them. Do you know how I do that?" And he waited for our astounded enquiries then, when they didn't come, told us anyway.

"I always take a bottle of the local cheap hooch with me," he told us. "Usually rum — but it would be ouzo if I was fishing here. It doesn't matter much as long as it is a spirit. I pull the beast up right behind the boat so it is flapping about mouth open and pour the hooch in. A glass full and it is dead within seconds."

"Hmm and marinated at the same time."

"I wonder if it dies happy?" Colin mused. "I mean do fish get pissed or is it just mammals?"

"Mammals? Get pissed?"

"Well, I know animals get affected by booze like us. I have seen a drunk giraffe."

"What here in Lefkas? Bloody strange parties you get to mate."

"No don't be silly."

"Who's being silly — where did you see a pissed giraffe — you must have been mistaken, they just look pissed when they are running about the place.

"No, I saw a clip, on U-tube, they had been eating fruit that had fallen to the ground and fermented."

"Oh, the internet — you don't want to believe everything you see on the internet."

Two of the dishes that Gianni had put on the table contained what I took to be ripe plums. They weren't. They were hard boiled eggs dyed deep red. At one point, the German picked one out of the dish and started to crack it on the table. Pauline, who seemed to be a regular friend of the German couple, made him stop.

"It's got to be done properly."

The proper way, it transpired, was for two of us to hold our eggs then bash them together. One of them cracked and the owner was out of the game so could eat his egg. The other with the unblemished egg had to take on the next challenger and so on until there was a winner — a bit like conkers without the string.

I left as the afternoon was giving way to the evening, and the bangs of Easter fireworks were becoming more dominant. I left educated as to the Greek version of conkers — 'Easter conkers' I suppose — the German way of killing big fish, and not a lot further forward in my mastery of the Greek language.

"Watch out for the giraffes, mate."

"Oh, do shut up."

"No, they hide out up in the trees round here. Regular hazard. They jump out at you when you are least expecting it."

Crewswap

We were at anchor in the lagoon at Vlicho on the last night of my son Barry's week in Greece. Getting him onto his plane home from Corfu meant a car drive up to Igoumenitsa to catch the early ferry. Having experienced ferry strikes that, in the past, had left me stranded on one island when the plane home was to leave from another island in a couple of days, I get a bit paranoid about travel. One such occasion, many years back, saw Helen and I having to hire ourselves a caique from Ikaria to Samos — good fun, rough seas, but expensive.

I telephoned the port police at Igoumenitsa to check that the ferries were running — "No strikes. Weather a bit strong but the Corfu ferries should run," they told me confidently.

We needed to allow time to get ashore in the dinghy in the dark and complete a two-hour drive and allow for other contingencies. I set the alarms on my watch and both the mobiles.

"Bit over the top, Dad?" enquired Barry.

"I don't trust myself not to snug down and drop off again after stopping one alarm so I set several and put them all over the place."

"It's all right. I won't go back to sleep."

"You? You've been known to sleep through alarms. I suppose we should have sailed up to Corfu then we wouldn't have to worry about ferries."

"Why didn't we?" asked Barry.

"Well, that would have taken a couple of days off your week and there were places to go down here."

"Ah, don't worry, it won't be a problem. If the worst comes to the worst, I'll stay here."

Just before five o'clock in the morning Barry and I loaded ourselves into the tender by torchlight. The first thing that happened was the outboard motor, or rather it didn't — it would not start.

I checked the fuel tap. It would not have been the first time I had forgotten to switch the fuel on. However, the fuel tap was on.

"It's only a short distance I will row. Shine the torch over here," I told a bemused Barry as I started to fiddle with the webbing that secures the oars in the bottom of the tender.

The wind was up a bit and the under-inflated tender was not so much bobbing up and down in the water as slurping from one wave to the next like a drunk surfer who had never quite got the knack of it. I cursed myself for not topping up the air in the tender the night before.

I undid the webbing and started undoing the line that, being a belt and braces man, I had also used to secure the oars.

"Hold the torch still. I am trying to undo a knot and I can't see the bloody thing."

"Everything is moving about. It's difficult." Barry complained and added, "Why don't you just use the webbing rather than tie them in as well?" He asked.

"It's called Mr Bean goes sailing," I told him.

"It's just like apple bobbing," he said as he watched me struggle with the bits of string in the bottom of a tender that was partially filled with water, partially deflated and lit with a dim flickering torch.

"What do you mean? It's like apple bobbing? Where did that come from?"

"Well, it's like that dreadful party game you made us play when we were kids. Do you remember? You tied our hands behind our back — there was no child help line in those days — then you made us fish apples out of a bucket of water with our teeth."

"Don't talk such nonsense."

"Well, it's a variant of bobbing apples — bobbing for string in a boat full of water, or something. Here let me tie your hands behind your back. It's fun, honest."

We struggled ashore, tied up the tender where, with a bit of luck, it would not be impaled on a sharp rock or on one of the nails that were stuck out from shuttering that was still in place a year after the new section of jetty had been completed. The weather was becoming quite blustery.

We arrived in Igoumenitsa with plenty of time to get a ticket and get Barry onto the seven thirty ferry. I then had a wait for my sister who, now that I had a yacht in the Mediterranean rather than the wild and windy shores of the UK, had booked herself and a couple of her friends in for a week or so of drifting about in the sun. 'She's in for a bit of a shock', I mused as I settled with a cup of coffee to await her arrival on the next ferry in.

The next ferry arrived. No Ruth. I went back to the harbourside café and got another coffee while I attempted to ring her on the mobile. I got through after what seemed an interminable time watching the wind build. It was blowing fine white spume across a very troubled sea.

"I thought you were on the first ferry out?"

"Missed it. We're on the next one."

"Well, thank the Lord for that."

"What's wrong? It doesn't matter. We're on holiday. No rush."

"Well, it's blowing up in case you hadn't noticed. I have left the boat at anchor and I am anxious to get back to it."

"Well, we are on the next one. It's all we can do, so stop worrying."

"Talking common sense when there's a good panic to be had. I can't be doing with it," I clicked the mobile off.

Ordinarily, the wait would not bother me. I was used to waiting around at Igoumenitsa. There were one or two bars where I was beginning to get known and I could have a chat and make a cup of coffee last for an hour or so. But the weather was getting nasty. Of course, that did not mean the same was happening down in Vlicho, but the forecast had warned of strong winds in Vlicho in the afternoon and now I would not be back until mid-afternoon. Would Sundowner's anchor hold? Vlicho was pretty good holding but boats had been known to pull their anchors in a stiff blow.

By mid-morning, the seas between Igoumenitsa were white with spray and spume. Periodically, a very strong gust would come through. Now, as I watched, a tree lost a large branch in the wind. It came crashing down on the pavement and covered a parked car. It was reminiscent of World War II films where a tank that had been crashing through the Ardennes had just emerged from the trees covered in the tree branches that it had collected en route. I was getting anxious. What was happening down in Vlicho? As soon as Ruth and her friends appeared, I bundled them unceremoniously into the car and we hit the road.

At Vlicho all was well. It was blowing a hoollie but Sundowner was held, albeit bucking and rearing at anchor like a startled stallion. The quickest way was to take one of the girls in the tender and bring Sundowner in stern-to at a space on the north end of the jetty. Ruth stayed on the jetty to take the lines as we came in and her friend Pauline came with me in the partially inflated tender. Once aboard, we secured the tender to the midships cleat and prepared the boat for a stern-to mooring and then upped anchor and set about it.

Back on the jetty, Ruth was wading about apprehensively on the jetty. The water was over the jetty so it was difficult to see exactly where the edge of the quay was. A tall youth from Sail Ionian was busy telling Ruth that we couldn't park there because he was going to bring one of their boats in there. Ruth told him not to get his fashionable pantaloons in a twist, we would only be there as long as it took. In increasingly wild conditions, we reversed Sundowner in to the quayside dropped anchor and threw the lines at Ruth who managed to find the quayside rings which were hidden under the water that was flooding the quay. Having secured Sundowner, I got the car and reversed it out along the jetty around the right-angle at the head desperately hoping that I knew where the edge of the jetty was — I could not see it. We transferred bags from car to boat.

"OK. That's us on board," Ruth shouted through the wind as she took the last of the bags.

"No, the cardboard boxes in the cabin need to go into the car boot," I yelled back.

"What…"

"Well, otherwise, we'll be tripping over them. You won't want them in your cabins and I certainly don't want them in mine."

"No, I mean what are they?"

"Tools and stuff that are only needed when the boat's in the yard."

"You need organising, you do."

"No, I don't. Helen's arriving in a couple of weeks. That'll be as much organising as I can poke up with."

I had planned to anchor near the Hippocampus which, like other nearby tavernas, has a jetty that you can moor the tender to. We could row or motor across, relax, have a drink. I planned to brief them on the things they needed to know over a nice meal and we could talk through plans for the week.

The briefing was done over a meal cooked aboard — best laid plans and all that. We anchored near the taverna as planned, but the wind was still rising. Our tender might not have made it against the wind to the taverna jetty, and I was fairly concerned about the anchor holding.

We had been having problems with the toilet — I suppose I should call it the heads. During the winter, I had made another hole in the hull and fitted extra plumbing and valves so that we could bypass the holding tank if it became blocked. However, the bypass valve leaked and while waiting for a replacement, I had set the bypass permanently to the 'emptying into the sea' position and sealed it up.

"Anyway, about the toilet," I told them. "It is busted so it's OK to use it at sea, but when we are in port we have to be, ah, um, discrete."

"What do you mean — discrete?"

"Well, some things don't matter but more serious things… ah… well they are to be avoided."

"What?"

"Ah… I mean… well…"

A moments silence then the penny dropped.

"He's talking about number twos. Don't do them in port — at least not on the boat."

They grinned at my discomfort and put up with the situation even though we were storm bound in Sami for three days. Heading up the channel between the islands of Ithaca and Keffalonia after we left Sami, the rain came down so heavily we lost sight of both islands and had to rely entirely on my hand-held GPS and my reckoning. We were aiming at sailing around the head of the Ithaca and heading for the islands of Kalamos and Kastos but it was so stormy and the visibility was so poor that we decided to pull into the relative shelter of Polis Bay on the north of Ithaca, drop anchor and have a rest. Once secure, I told them to get below and dry off. We sat in the cabin with rain lashing down on the deck and supping hot soup — just like your average summer day on the Solent.

Unfortunately, they did not get taken to the places like Meganissi and Kastos which was a shame, but they left a comment in the visitor's book about searching for toilets in the early morning mists so they obviously enjoyed themselves.

Spooked in Sofia Bay

Helen's son, David, with his partner, Debbie, and his son, Ben, enjoyed a fortnight idling around the Inland Sea in late July. One of our ports of call was the bay of Kalo Limani on Keffalonia. It was marked on the charts that we were using as Kalo Limani but, according to a road map of Keffalonia, it was Sofia bay. Commonly enough, the name of a bay depends upon whether you are in a car or a boat.

We had re-provisioned ourselves in Sami on the same island and topped up on water and diesel. We left after lunch anticipating the usual increase in wind and a reasonable sail in the afternoon, idled around the bay of Sami enjoying sailing opportunities that the freshening breeze gave us and then, as the afternoon progressed, we tacked up the Keffalonia-Ithaca channel and into a little bay between Aghia Efimia and Fiskardo.

The bay is a favoured place for lunch or an overnight stop. A road winds around the headland, past the bay and back up into the hills, but I've rarely seen traffic on it. However, there is a small taverna beside the road as it runs along the south side of the bay. In the holiday season, you will usually find three or four groups on the pebble beaches and three or four yachts at anchor in the small bay.

There are two beaches at the head of the bay and these are separated by a rocky promontory on which two buildings stand. There is usually no sign of life in either building, but one is freshly painted from time to time. The other is tired stone and may not have had occupants for years. The pebble beach at the north end is not used so much, but the other larger beach is often populated by a few families in the afternoon and into the evening.

Once we had anchored, we sorted the boat out for an overnight stop, stowed the mainsail, frapped down the halyards that would otherwise clatter against the mast overnight and put down the bathing ladder for a swim in the clear blue water of the bay. As I towelled myself down after a cooling dip, Ben was using the binoculars to look around the bay and muttering to himself.

"What's up Ben?"

"I don't like it."

"Don't like what?"

"That thing by the gates of the house up there. It looks like one of those things they put clothes on in shops."

I looked. The house had what looked like a white mannequin enshrouded in a blue gown standing at its front gate. David took the binoculars from Ben and had a look. It was indeed a mannequin.

"What's the problem Ben? It's just a mannequin."

"It's horrible — it looks spooky."

"Ah I see. It's those late-night films you watch with your mates on sleep overs isn't it. I've told you not to watch them and now they've come back to haunt you in a manner of speaking."

"Are we stopping here tonight?"

"Oh yes. It wouldn't matter if we didn't, it's probably following us. I think I saw it in Sami last night," David teased.

"Oh, shut up, Dad."

"Don't wind him up, David," Helen admonished.

"No, it's all right son. Grandmas got plenty of garlic you've just got to sleep with a necklace of it round your neck. And me and your Pops will take it in turns on sentry duty. We'll make sure no harm comes to you."

"I wish I hadn't mentioned it," grumbled Ben, but his eyes drifted over to the mannequin from time to time during the evening.

I woke just before sunrise without having to fend off mannequins overnight. The sky was getting light and the air beginning to warm. Goats that had been silent through the night were working their way down the rocky scrub-ridden slopes on the north of the bay and bleating from time to time. Two fishermen who had been conversing since they arrived at five thirty were at the water's edge fishing. Their muted conversation carried across the water. By seven o'clock, Helen was up with me and brought a cup of coffee up. There were two other boats in the bay. One, a white sloop with a deck wheelhouse, lay at anchor with a line ashore secured to trees at the head of the bay. The other boat was large, over 50 feet, dark blue, stylish and Italian flagged. Unlike the white sloop, there was evidence of life aboard. The engine started and, totally nude, the Italian walked to the windlass and started to take the anchor up.

"It's a good job Ben isn't up," I muttered to Helen. "That's an even scarier sight than the mannequin." The Italian appeared to be the only person on board. He had laid a lot of anchor chain and as he took it up the boat moved towards us. I watched ready to take evasive action, but the anchor broke out of the water a few metres from us and the bow, now released, was turned by the light wind as he walked back to the cockpit with the anchor dangling beneath the bow and just cresting the water. The engine revs increased slightly to give him steerage and boat swept past us on an arc that turned her through 180 degrees and took her gently out of the bay with the engine muttering softly in the early morning. He turned and waved as he passed — the crack of his bare arse visible as he sat at the helm.

"Just like Terry Jones at the organ in Monty Python," I said to Helen.

"Ugh," she responded.

As the noise of the engine faded from the bay, relative silence resumed. The only noise was the rattle of water over the pebbles of the beach, the occasional bleat of a goat and the quiet conversation of the two fishermen on the shore. They were discussing the austerity measures that the Greek government was taking. A harsh clanging of a tin being beaten with a stick broke the silence and the goats clattered and bleated their way across the shore towards the houses on the shoreline. The gruff bleats of older goats mixed with the shriller anxious bleating of the few youngsters in the herd. A big stately looking goat with a luxurious grey coat and a black satanic face looked like the main man in a herd that sported a mixture of browns, whites, tans, blacks and beiges in all sorts of shapes and sizes.

A Fish in the Works

It was a year for problems with the heads. On the penultimate day of David, Debbie and Ben's stay it gave up altogether. The pump would not pump water into the bowl. It appeared to be jammed solid as though something had jammed up the mechanism. As Debbie had discovered, the problem we blamed her. It seemed the right thing to do.

While Helen took them to the airport to catch the flight home the following day, I took the whole shebang to bits. I studied all the rubber flaps, metal discs, plastic passageways and chambers and tried to work out how the bloody smelly contrivance worked. I could see no reason why it shouldn't. I fiddled with it, cleaned it, put it carefully back together again. It still didn't work. You could force a bit of action on the flush cycle and, with the dribble of water, black flecks came into the bowl. Among the other disgusting odours was the distinct smell of dead fish.

I hadn't thought about the seawater inlet so far, so I supposed that I had better do something about it so I undid the flexible seawater inlet pipe that connects the seacock to the pump. It sounds simple but it wasn't. As with taking the pump to bits, screws that I needed to get at were very nearly inaccessible.

Eventually, however, I managed to release the pipe from the pump inlet. I peered down it and there staring bug-eyed up at me was a small and very dead fish just about exactly the diameter of the pipe. The poor thing had been pulled up the seawater inlet by the pump and jammed fast in the tube where it had been for approaching 24 hours. I gingerly put the pipe to my lips and blew until I heard air bubbles coming out into the sea at the far end. I peered down the pipe and could see the fish no longer. I had given it a burial at sea. I tried ineffectively to wipe the smell of dead fish from my mouth. It clung on.

'That's cleared it', I thought and reconnected the inlet pipe to the toilet. I pumped again. The pump was still jammed. I took the tube off once more. The fish was back again sucked up by the pump and staring at me with its bug eyes made larger, I presume, by the partial vacuum to which it had been subjected by my attempts at pumping the toilet. I had blown it down the tube out of sight, but not out of the tube. I blew down the tube again and this time I continued to blow for quite a while after I heard bubbles coming out of the outlet. 'I must have cleared it by now', I thought as I peered down the tube recoiling slightly from the overpowering whiff of decomposing fish. I optimistically reconnected pipe to pump. No joy. The pump still jammed up. It needed another cycle of decoupling the pipe blowing down it then reconnecting it and pumping it.

Eventually, the fish had started to fall to bits and the pump was able to draw it near enough to the end of the tube for me to extract it with a long thin screwdriver. Having given the kiss of life several times to a pipe that smelled strongly of decomposing fish, I showered and brushed my teeth. The smell seemed to be hanging on. I rewashed my face, rebrushed my teeth, gargled with TCP, took the last can of beer out of the fridge, drunk it in virtually one swallow, laid down in a darkened cabin, shut my eyes and tried to pretend I couldn't still taste and smell dead and rotting fish.

My rest was brought to a close as I heard Helen clamber on board five minutes later.

"What are you doing in there on a nice day like this?" she shouted from the galley.

"Well, I've just sorted the toilet problem and I'm recovering from the mental and physical stress of doing that."

"Don't be so wet. I've got something nice for dinner. Guess what?"

"Oh, I don't feel that hungry."

"Don't be silly. You will when you see it. There was a big fishing boat in at Lefkas…"

"Oh no…" I groaned.

"Yes, there was. He had some beautiful fish so that's what we've got for dinner."

275

Anchor Drag in Vlicho

A couple of our friends, Annie and John, were with us for a week. They had sailed with us on Tethera back in Blighty from time to time. At the end of the week, we made for Vlicho as the car was there and we were going to run them to Preveza to fly home the following day. In advance of arriving, we had checked with Vlicho Yacht Club to find out whether the England/Germany game in the World Cup would be showing. It was. We secured ourselves a place on the quayside so that we could get the gear off the boat with ease the following day. It was going to blow a bit and we were moored stern to presenting the side of the boat to the weather but we had our anchor planted firmly. All seemed good, but the trouble was that a large neighbouring boat had not got quite as good a hold on the sea bottom.

The boat was Italian flagged and was a traditional looking wooden ketch about 60 feet long, but heavily built and looking a bit in the style of a Turkish Gullet. It had high topsides — so a lot of windage. We were in its lee and with each gust the boat sagged downwind towards us. The two or three young men who seemed to be looking after the boat were retensioning the anchor chain, but it appeared that they probably had not got enough chain down. The anchor was not holding very well. I eased out our windward stern line to put a bit more space between us.

"I think that we are going to have to do something about this. It seems to be leaning further towards us on each gust," I said.

"There is room the other side of them. They would be leaning away from us if we re-anchored there," suggested Helen.

"With the antics they are getting up too I think I want to be well clear of them. We are 13 tons. They must be 70. They'll crush us if they lose it."

An even more vigorous prolonged gust came through closing the gap between the bow of the Italian monster and a Moody moored just downwind of us. The Moody, like us, was holding well so we were going to be the filling of an uncomfortable kind of a sandwich if things continued in this vein.

"Right, we had better do something about it now," I said.

I took off the leeward stern line then freed the windward one which was doubled to the shore ready to slip. John went forward to pull up the anchor. The windlass had given up the ghost and so it was a matter of taking up the anchor chain by hand — slower than just winding it in on the windlass. We waited for a lull and when it came, we slipped the remaining stern line while John pulled in anchor chain and I eased Sundowner forward keeping clear of the Moody and its anchor chain that the weather was pushing us on to.

Once the anchor was up, we found a spot where we thought there might be a little shelter. It was still windy, but the anchor seemed firm and survived some fairly intense blasts as well as the initial tug with the motor. I judged it safe to go and watch the game.

John scrambled into the tender and took the two girls ashore then came back for me. We made our way along Vlicho waterfront with me giving the boat a worried glance over my shoulder from time to time. It seemed stable and the weather seemed to be quietening down.

The Club was packed — mainly with Brits, but also a contingent of Germans. The game had already kicked off, but nothing much was happening as seemed to be the way with the England team at the time. Not wildly interested, I settled down with my beer and wondered about Sundowner in the wind that was raging out there. Perhaps I should go back to the boat — 'No don't be paranoid' I told myself, 'she seemed pretty secure when we left her. I'll just have a look from time to time'.

The Vlicho Yacht Club is run by Ruari and Vicky and it turned out that Ruari, a hero of the hour when hurricane winds hit Vlicho in the September of 2011, was keeping an eye on the boats on the lagoon. After ten minutes or so, someone shouted from the bar, "Is the owner of 'Coral' here?"

"Yes," a worried looking man got up from a nearby table.

"She's broken anchor and is adrift," he was told.

Helen turned to me, "Poor chap. We're OK, aren't we?"

"We are, but I'm not sure about the boat."

"I meant the boat."

"I know. It was a little joke."

"Very little. Microscopic. What are you going to do about it?"

"The joke? I think it died of natural causes."

"THE BOAT, for chrisake: is it OK?"

"Hope so. Seemed secure. I'll stick my nose out in a minute and have a look."

It was another five minutes before I heard the shout, "Owner of Sundowner."

"Oh, Hell's bells and buckets of blood."

Helen and I left the bar and ran for the tender scanning for Sundowner as we went. We spotted it as we scrambled aboard our tender. It was halfway across the lagoon. On board was Martin, an acquaintance whose native territory in the UK was the Menai Straits but who, like me, spent summers in the Med and fitted out his boat in the Spring in Aktio.

Martin hailed me as we got near, "Rob! Where's the switch for your windlass?"

"It doesn't work," I hollered back. "It's bust mate." We reached him, thanked him and asked him whether Sundowner had hit anything on her little solo jaunt.

"That cat over there," yelled Martin pointing at a white catamaran that looked like a live-aboard boat. "But no damage — it was all fairly gentle and the fenders did their job."

"Thank God for that," breathed Helen as we scrambled aboard.

"Yeah, but we had better still go over and talk to them once we've got Sundowner secured. It's lucky you saw it happen, Martin," I said as I fired up Sundowner's engine.

"Aye. You're about the third to have pulled, in a manner of speaking, and each time there has been a blasting of hooters from folks who have spotted it and I've gone up on deck in case I was in line. When I saw Sundowner trolling off on her own, well I got in my tender and caught her up."

"Well, ta Martin"

"Ah you'd do the same, I'm sure."

"We're lucky that you were around."

"You're lucky that my outboard started. It's not been too good at that of late."

"Another thing on your list then?"

"Oh. It's been there for ages."

Martin got back in his tender and I set about taking up the anchor he had laid.

"Don't you trust Martin's anchoring?" asked Helen.

"He's sound, but I'd rather do it for myself."

"Well, your last effort pulled out," she reminded me — quite unnecessarily I thought.

"I think I'm going to lay her alongside the quay. There's a fishing boat just pulling out."

"Oh dear, what about his lazy lines?"

"We... you will just have to look out for them."

Helen had a point. Local fishermen and occasional other boat owners with regular spots on the quay side put out mooring lines from an anchor or other mooring with the lines tailed off on the quay. Sometimes there could be a bit of a network of lines. If it was unclear how they were laid it was best to avoid them for fear of tangling a line around the prop.

We secured Sundowner alongside at the vacant spot left by the fishing boat as darkness fell. The weather had caused the jetty to flood. There is very little by the way of lunar tides in the Ionian, or the Aegean. There are still rises and falls in water levels, but the major influence is usually the weather — barometric pressure, onshore wind, that sort of thing. But I wondered as we splashed along the quayside whether the quay was sinking. It would not be the first time. There were quays where this had happened in other places in the Ionian.

We arrived back at the bar just in time to hear that Germany had ousted England from the World Cup 4 - 1.

Lefkas — My Bogey Port

What is it about me and Lefkas? Once again, shortly after the 4-1 defeat by Germany, I left looking like a native of Nigeria. Helen had temporarily deserted me on one of her trips back to Blighty and I had moored stern-to on the Lefkas quayside to pick up some supplies before heading off for Aktio. I was packing them in their appropriate lockers below when a German group in a Bavaria came in on my starboard side. Some bumping and thumping announced their arrival and when I came up into the cockpit they were tying up.

"I am OK here, ja?"

"As long as you haven't come to discuss football," I told him. He grunted and returned to tying up his bits of string. As we spoke, a bunch of Brits on a Jeanneau came in to moor stern-to on my port side. I got onto the harbour side and took their lines as they came in.

Sometime later, I was ready to go; the Germans had left their boat to go into Lefkas to go raping and pillaging or shopping in the town, but I warned the Brits next door that I was off. It was about a quarter of an hour before the Lefkas bridge opened, so plenty of time. Close all hatches and stow everything that is likely to fall over — after all I was taking to the open seas — all the way to Preveza! Take the passerail in and secure the main halyard that I have been using to hold up the passerail — as is my wont. Remove the snubber from the anchor chain. Start the motor and put in Olivier's fuse (project to investigate whether the voltage drop across the diode splitter is what is causing problems with the battery management system). Move the tender from the bow so that it trails aft and doesn't complicate matters when I am pulling the anchor chain in. Then I am in the cockpit taking in the leeward aft line as it is slack and is not really doing anything.

"Do you want any help?" called the skipper of the Jeanneau.

"No, I should be all right — though you might care to fend off, I am on my own so the departure may be a bit clumsy," I said casually coiling and putting away the leeward aft line. "The anchor chain will drop once I start releasing the other aft line and should take me out nicely. Once I am clear of you lot, I can start to make a nice clean pick up. There's no wind to speak of."

"You've obviously done this before."

"Oh yes," I said putting an air of casual nonchalance into my voice — difficult with a mouth dry with nerves.

Sundowner slipped out neat as you like between the two boats, but then it became obvious that there was a cross over. The anchor chain rattled as though running along another chain and the chain of the boat moored on my starboard side was shaking and rattling too. Normally, the co-operation of the boat whose anchor is across yours helps the situation but, of course, the German-flagged boat was deserted.

I was in the middle of trying to raise the offending chain to the surface when a heavily accented voice asked if I would mind moving up the harbour a bit so they could get out. It was a Danish-flagged boat the other side of my German friends.

"I am rather stuck on this bloody chain that your neighbour has kindly laid across mine."

"Pardon, but we want to catch the bridge."

"Me too."

I managed to move out of their path for long enough for them to get away but was closing on the boat whose anchor chain was giving me problems.

Once the Danes were clear, I was able to resume the attempted recovery of my anchor but the Brits were now getting agitated. Their chain was rattling too indicating to them that I was crossed with theirs as well. However, I could now see the chains. Mine was running parallel to my British neighbours, but the German anchor chain was at quite an angle to both of us — over mine and under his. So the disturbance created by my chain on the crossed chain was transmitted to the Brits chain via the German chain.

"Wait. I will start my engine and let off some chain," The skipper of the Jeanneau shouted.

"You don't need too."

"I do. You are across my chain. I can feel it."

"No, I'm not. I can see it. The rattling is being caused by the chain that is over mine and under yours."

But he turned away to confer and much of what I had said was probably borne away in the wind. So I started to pull in more anchor chain. That got his attention.

"Wait. Can't you wait. I just have to put something back together then I will start my engine."

"You don't, fucking need to."

"I do. You're crossed under my chain."

"No, I'm not."

This amusing debate carried on with me attempting to pick up chain until one of his crew had rowed out and confirmed that what I was telling him was indeed true. He then came aboard to see if he could help. The problem was quite bad because I had laid out a lot of chain — both a good and a bad thing. The more the chain, the better the holding but the greater the chance of somebody dropping their chain across it.

My anchor was way past the crossing point so, with no one on the German boat slackening chain, it was going to be impossible to simply pull up anchor and drop his chain from it. The only remedy was to detach my anchor chain from my boat having first tied a line to it on the anchor side of the cross over. I secured my boat on station by putting a line around the rogue chain — the German boat's anchor chain. Once secured, I could feed out my anchor chain under the rogue and, praying that the knot I had tied around my anchor line was a goodun and I wasn't about to lose my anchor and chain, pull my anchor chain back into the boat via the line I had attached to it. I was in the middle of this when I heard some shouting and looking up and towards the stern, I could see a Swedish flagged boat all but sat on my stern.

"Are you comink or goink?"

"I'm stuck-ink."

"Pardon?"

"I am stuck. I have a crossed chain. I am trying to deal with it."

"We want to moor there," he indicated the harbourside berth freshly vacated by the Danes. "And you are in our way."

"Right now, chum, I am in every fucker's way. You'll have to wait. And would you mind moving your boat off mine. You're not helping."

By now, the Germans were back on board and I was piling up chain on the deck and being shouted at.

"You are across our line."

"It's you who are across mine."

"Vot?"

"Oh, never mind."

"Be careful of our anchor."

"Thank you that's most helpful," I wished I had done German at school and could tell them to go forth and multiply or something, but I adopted the strategy of just letting them shout at me while I got on with it.

I pulled in the line that I had attached to my anchor chain and recovered the chain then fed it back through the rollers over the gypsy (the notched roller that feeds chain in or out and sometimes fails) and through the feed hole into the locker then secured the end in the locker. I was now in a position to pull in the anchor. I thanked the Brit for his help as he got aboard his tender and left. I then ceremoniously released my line to the German's anchor line blowing him a kiss as I waved bye bye. He waved both hands, one with four fingers held out, the other with just one. I knew he would not be able to resist talking about football for long. I also felt that had there been a poll for the most popular boat in the harbour, I would have difficulty making the top ten. Ha, well, at least I was out of it — nearly.

The anchor came up cleanly in so far as there were no more crossed lines but uncleanly in that it had, among other things, a discarded fisherman's net wrapped around it. Mud, weights, netting, and line were wrapped in and out of the curious curved protrusions of my bruce anchor. It was wound around so tight and the solid lumps of lead were so big that it was almost impossible to move. If I hauled the anchor in close there was not sufficient room between anchor and boat to wangle the netting and crap clear of the anchor flukes. If I released it a bit, the whole mess was difficult to reach without overbalancing and falling in the water — my final swansong of complete incompetence. I was drifting now. A 38 ft Bavaria with no one at the helm, but with a lump of mud drooped over the pulpit wrestling with another lump of mud that was wrapped around the anchor.

"You are rather near to me," this time British and upper crust with it — a smart blue 50 ft sloop. A smart blue ensign. Blue blazers and pink gins completed the picture.

"But I have missed you," I said as we slid past his tender leaving a gap you would have difficulty stuffing a cigarette paper into — 'phheww'. I finally got the whole mess free and dropped it into the water. I suppose I should have taken it aboard rather than drop it where someone else might pick it up but it was heavy and I was weary and I wasn't thinking straight. I walked back to the helm oozing mud all over the show and I distinctly heard:

"Didn't know Johnny negro types were allowed to drive yachts."

"Quite, what is the world coming to?"

"Care for another pink gin?"

"Do you know, I don't mind if I do."

I had fifteen minutes till the next bridge opening. I pootled around. I wasn't going to put my anchor down in Lefkas again. Not likely, you don't know what you are going to catch. The purpose of the exercise was to get up to Aktio try out a modification to the charging circuits on the one-hour trek and have a meet and a meal with a friend, Ian of Cariad a 36-foot Beneteau. The modification did not cure the problem, but a convivial evening in Aktio at Panos' taverna with Ian and a couple of his friends made up for that. And I did an oil and filter change on the engine and got dirty oil everywhere so that was good too.

I was up shortly after five the following morning with the nightclubs of Preveza across the water still thumping out their electronic pop stuff — 'bass 'n drums' or 'drum and bass' or something? I intended to head back to the Inland Sea.

Within ten minutes, I was off and away. The mountains on the mainland were shrouded in early morning mist and the eastern sky was cloudy and suffused in pink. As I left Preveza and Aktio behind, there were small fishing boats out to the north along the coast like a scattering of black ants in a silver sea. Early morning — I love it if I can get my backside out of bed. I have even got up at silly o'clock when heading to the west country in the UK just for the pleasure of seeing daybreak across the moors! I like spring too and I suppose that is more of the same, a fresh start — anyway, enough of this nonsense.

I was the only boat wanting through at the bridge so they didn't swing the bridge. They just lifted one of the ramps that span the gap between the land and the swinging ferry boat. I worried that the ramp would not clear the mast, but it ended up pretty much vertical — so plenty of room. I hurried through Lefkas hoping that nobody would notice that the bogey boat had returned, but nobody much was up and about. I continued on down the canal.

A couple of floating gin palaces were moored up on the marina fuel jetty. They do know how to live don't they? A smelly old fuel station one side, the town rubbish tip the other and a muddy old dredger alongside. Still, they probably need a drip feed from the fuel station to keep their air conditioning and champagne coolers going. I motored gently on down the canal relishing the quiet. There was no one else about apart from the odd fisherman and a brace of pelicans. I emerged from the south end of the canal into the Inland Sea and unfurled the genoa. Sundowner glided gently down the east coast of Lefkas.

As I closed on Nidri, I spotted some dolphins — biguns and a couple of small ones. I saw four of them side by side break water simultaneously. There must have been double that number in all. They were just off the coast. I stayed around for about quarter of an hour. They were going nowhere — just playing. One of them was launching himself, or herself of course, out of the water and slapping down on his side. I believe David Attenborough has a term for it. Breaching? Probably, "Launching out of the water and slapping down on his side."

I don't know why these creatures make me happy, but they do. Making me happy is a monumental task so Helen informs me, but seeing these creatures is always a joy. Attenborough tells us that they can be quite beastly beasts, brutalising and sodomising those from other gangs — they're almost human then — bless! But they are intelligent. They take it in turns to corral fish two or three of them driving the fish to leap out of the water and into another's already open maw. All he, the recipient, has to do is lie there with his mouth open and the fish are

285

driven in. Then, when he has had enough, he reaches for the Rennies and swaps places with one of his mates. How do they work that out? These are fish for God's sake (yes yes… I know they are not but…), is that what all these squeaks and trills are about? Are they saying:

"That's enough, Charlie, I'm stuffed. Your turn sunshine."

"No, it's Arthur next."

"No, that's all right old boy."

"No, I insist. It's your turn. We should stick to procedures otherwise where would we be."

"Fish that's where we'd be."

"Don't talk to me about fish. Anyone got some Rennies?"

Presenting Ships Papers in Sami

Sami on Keffalonia is a port where we find ourselves from time-to-time. It is a small busy town with good facilities — shops, water, showers. There are pleasant walks into the steep slopes behind the port or simply along the coastline. There are sites of archeological, historical and general interest. From time-to-time, I take my Dekpa in to get it stamped but they rarely seem to worry too much about it. On this occasion, a couple of 'uniforms' came down to the quayside taking boats names and asking boat owners to repair to the port police office with their ships papers and some dosh. Unusual? I had not had that done to me in Sami before. Vathi on Ithaca yes... Fiscardo on Keffalonia yes... but not Sami.

I foraged around and picked my usual folder of bits of paper up. I was not entirely sure what all the bits of paper were. Some of them were entirely in Greek and indecipherable, even apparently to some Greeks. I guess legal speak is like that in any language — purposefully incomprehensible to maintain the mystery of the trade and thus preserve the jobs of poor impecunious lawyers. It is an approach that has parallels in trade unionism and free masonry or am I being cynical here? The crucial documents were the insurance certificate, the SSR, the Dekpa itself. The port police seemed to be mainly interested in whether these three were in date.

When we got to the office, we were next in the queue after a delightful young girl, Marlise, who we learnt was from Friesland in Holland — home of the black and white Friesian cow, the world's milker of choice. She was part of the crew of the lead boat of a Dutch flotilla. She was the 'hostie' (hostess) and had been lumbered with the task of presenting the port police with the ship's papers of the seven boats that comprised the flotilla. She was overwhelmed by the amount of forms that had to be filled in and the amount of endorsing, signing and countersigning that went on.

There were four Greeks involved. The main man behind the desk — the customer facing operative so to speak — was quite charming, good looking, and, well, Helen took to him straight away. There was also a consultant who was continually consulted when there was a difficulty as there often appeared to be. He wore a gun, handcuffs and an air of authority so his opinion was respected. Then there was the man whose function seemed to be to refresh the endorsing pads with ink. It seemed to be a full-time job. The fourth man seemed to be some sort of reserve in case any of the other three was injured in the line of duty or was showing signs of being tired.

Marlise whispered to me, fairly loudly, "So much fuss and paper."

I pointed to his coffee mug stood on the desk in front of him. It was badged with a design that claimed that it belonged to the New York Police Department.

"That's why. We're in the wrong office. I knew my navigation was bad..."

"Ahh so. Same here. Skipper is hopeless. I thought we were a long time getting here from Ithaca."

There was a certain amount of giggling going on between Helen, I and Marlise and I had to explain myself to the good looking official, "Sorry, I thought we were at the port police office in Sami on the island of Keffalonia."

"You are," Mr Good-looking replied sternly.

"We think that says that we are looking at a NYPD officer," said Marlise pointing at the mug. "Oh, that is just my weekend job," he winked at Helen. "And you" he said looking at me with mock sternness. "What have you got for me?"

"Um Ship's papers," I pushed the Dekpa at him and he looked at it with its tea and coffee stains, and sticky tape mends where we had left a port open while cleaning the boat and the Dekpa had got covered with water, gone soggy and got torn.

"Have you a crew list?"

"Ah. No."

"Why not?"

"I don't know."

He laughed uproariously at that, "That is the right answer. Had you not replied in that way I would have had my man," he said pointing at the consultant. "Put you in handcuffs and club you with his revolver, but you are lucky because Tuesday is waterboarding and sadly is not allowed for crew list problems." He clicked his fingers and the first reserve produced a crew list form out of thin air. I filled it in omitting the passport number for myself and Helen, as we had not brought them, and hoped he would not notice. He didn't, or if he did, he didn't care. Eventually, he told Marlise, "You are free to go your papers are good." And, pointing at me, he continued, "But not this one. We have unfinished business."

"But first, I have a question — a very important question," Marlise told him.

He leant back in his leather chair, "Yes?"

Marlise got up, turned around and pointed at a large photograph on the wall behind us. It was a photograph of a fin whale, a large whale with a long, curved mouth. It dwarfed the large flatbed lorry that it had been craned up onto. "What is that? Is it local?"

Oh, Christ. No more snorkelling for me," moaned Helen who clearly had not noticed the photograph.

"It was found in Greek waters. We do have whales. This was a Fin Whale. There is a Fin Whale museum on the island of Kastos. This whale was ill — dying from cancer — so I think navigation was low on its list. The authorities tried to rescue it but... well... it did not work and he died. But no, you are unlikely to find one. You can snorkel safely," he smiled at Helen and Marlise.

We got off with a mild telling off at the state of our papers and were told report to the port police every time we were in a port — a different story each time. Twice before in other ports when proffering our papers for inspection and stamping we had been told to bugger off with the explanation, "We are very busy today." From where I was stood at the time, they certainly hadn't seemed to be — unless you count drinking coffee and smoking.

When we left Sami, we were originally going to head up to Polis Bay at the north end of Ithaca, but the conditions made the alternative of heading back along the south coast of Ithaca then cruising along the east coast looking in at one of the bays more attractive. It was August. Blue skies, blue waters and a light breeze that helped us along on a close reach off the south coast. We steered well clear of the shallows off the little chapel at the south east corner of the island and then sailed in towards 'rat island'. The bays in the vicinity of the island were crowded — it was about lunchtime — so we headed north along the coast and found Sarakiniko, a pleasant sheltered bay lightly populated with beach towels and sunbeds. It was surprisingly free of yachts and floating gin palaces.

We dropped anchor with the inviting thought of a swim, some lunch and maybe, the hell with it, maybe we would while away the afternoon reading and swimming and then stop overnight. Within a few minutes, however, half-a-dozen forty- to fifty-foot yachts arrived. Although they were not one of the holiday flotillas, they all seemed to be part of the same party. Each boat seemed to have about a dozen young Italians and Greeks many of whom clearly could not afford much in the way of clothing. They anchored noisily, running lines ashore with much shouting and yelling. It was clearly going to be party night. Nothing against parties, but... after a while, we pulled anchor and headed on up the east coast.

At the Gulf of Aetou, which lies between the north and the south parts of the island of Ithaca, we investigated the first bay that we came across on entering the gulf. It was large. There were a few yachts at anchor at various spots, but plenty of room so we found a spot; a small inlet on the west side of the bay and anchored for a belated lunch and a swim. I watched idly as two youths in their late teens slowly made their way around the bay in a pedalo visiting and talking to each boat in turn.

"Do you think they are some sort of officials?" asked Helen.

"In a pedalo? I know Greece is supposed to be making economies but..."

"They seem to be working their way around the anchored boats methodically — almost as if they are the port police."

"Port police — at their age — they look hardly out of school."

"Everybody seems to look that way to you."

"Yeah… but… port police! They've no uniform for a start. Do you think the port police have a plain clothes division that dress in Bermuda shorts and go around in pedalos?"

"I didn't say they were port police… it's just that they are visiting each boat in turn. It's almost as though they are some sort of official."

"No. This is a bay. There's only one house apart from that one on the foreland. There are only half-a-dozen boats. I can't think of any sort of official that would have any truck with the place."

By now, it was our turn. They were approaching Sundowner and we were about to find out.

"Hi, nice day. Where you from?" One of the two hailed as they approached us.

"Reading. You?"

"Harrow,"" — He had the upper crust accent associated with the school too.

"You staying on a boat?" Helen asked them.

"No in that house over there," They replied pointing to a house set among eucalyptus trees.

"Nice."

"Yes, it's OK, but the fridge is broke."

"Oh dear, that's a shame."

"Yes, it is," the second one butted in. "Have you got any ice cream?"

"Ice cream? There are more important things than that if your fridge isn't working," Helen said, needless to say. "No. Ice cream's essential," they said, all delivered in an impeccable Harrow accent.

"Well, we don't have ice cream on this boat even when our fridge is working — which it's not," said Helen, again.

"No ice cream on a boat with a fridge! That's just ludicrous," and off they pedaloed to badger the next boat in the bay.

Shortly after this encounter, the wind began to rise and I was not one hundred percent convinced of the holding. A nearby boat had difficulties with their anchor and eventually made off. We departed rather hastily — the swimming ladder was still down, the hatches were still open, and smalls were hanging from the taffrail.

The Emu has pointed out that you can anchor in the top north west corner of the gulf of Aetou. It sort of looked exposed, but we made our way over. There were a couple of yachts already laying at anchor there but there was room. Tucked right in the corner where the north Ithaca joins the narrow isthmus of land that links north to south was a 35 ft white catamaran, but the *piece de resistance* of this beautiful setting was a cream coloured 70- or 80-foot yacht. We anchored between the two and admired the yacht using the binoculars to pick out detail; probably to the chagrin of the elegantly dressed owners who were sipping cocktails in the sumptuous stern cockpit. There were servo motors at the foot of the mast and the forestays so sails were hauled in and out and reefed at the touch of a button.

It was late in the day and the locals were swimming in the balmy early evening sunshine. Some came out to us and said hello. We joined them in the water and a couple of small children, after asking our permission, clambered up the ladder to dive off Sundowner. The water was cool and very very clear. The only slightest of slight blemishes in this idyllic setting was.... not to put too fine a point on it was.... well... it was the rubbish tip.

It often happens in Greece. You are walking along a rough stone road high up on the hillside overlooking a beautiful azure sea with birdsong and the exotic scent of wild herbs transported to your ears and nose by the cooling breeze. The path takes you through the shade of overhanging conifer, maple, eucalyptus and it jinks pleasantly around the contours of the hillside then suddenly you are over a rubbish tip. They have only been backing up and tipping the rubbish onto the steep slope below the road. There it is... rubbish... like a run of scree but plastic bags, bottles, tins and other household detritus instead of the stones and earth of scree.

We couldn't see the tip from where we were anchored, it was the other side of the isthmus and was facing Keffalonia. But we could smell it. The reason we could smell it was that someone had recently put a match to it — or maybe the sun's rays had been focussed through waste glass onto paper and it had started that way. Nonetheless, it was on fire or at least smouldering. There is nowt as bad as the smell of burning rubbish. Other things burning are mostly OK. I used to love the smell of bonfires of burning leaves as a child. In fact, my enthusiasm knew no bounds and I set fire to a house once — but that's another story. We had noticed the rubbish burning a couple of days back when we had been sailing in the Ithaca/Keffalonia channel. In fact, they appeared to be trying to put the fire out at the time by pumping water and dumping earth on it from the road high above the tip. It had little lasting effect; in fact, the earth probably turned it into a natural slow cooker.

A change in the wind direction as the sun went down had the effect of gradually diminishing the smell of smouldering rubbish, but the change of wind also made it clear that the posh yacht was laying to one hell of a lot of chain. We found ourselves lying close under her beautiful long counter stern. Much closer and we could have helped ourselves to one of the cocktails or biscuity things that the flunkeys brought out on trays to the snappily dressed yotties in the cockpit. Now that would have been a result. Instead, what happened was that the light pollution increased as the yacht not only had cocktail-shaking, bumfreezer-clad flunkies, soft cream-coloured leather soft furnishings in the cockpit, but it also had subsea lighting just below the waterline all around the hull. The whole elaborate thing was floating in a field of light blue luminescence. Helen wondered whether it was the Beckhams on their annual seaside holiday. If so, they had aged considerably — but that's the stress of keeping up a celebrity lifestyle I suppose.

Petalas and the Long Low Island

Late in the season, we here heading down towards the Gulf of Patras and found ourselves a nice anchorage at the east side of the island of Petalas — a large peaceful anchorage with good holding. In spite of the peace and quiet, I awoke about three o'clock in the morning. I couldn't get back to sleep, but was attempting to do so in my usual place in the starboard cabin aft of the navigation station (a similar location to the one that I slept in my cherished Tethera curiously enough). The midges were making their presence known. I had a mosquito net for one of the hatches in my cabin so that I could close the door and open the hatch with the mosquito net fitted over it. This can give you some fresh air and a midge free cabin if you catch and kill those that were in there when you shut yourself in. But it was hot — far too hot. I opened the door and sat in front of the nav station. The batteries were not good so I was using a little LED light that I had. But then I got tired of reading and wanted to write something on the computer, but that meant using the boats lights for a while.

At first light there was a hazy, early-morning sky. By then I had been trying to assimilate the weather forecasts on the web. I was hot and swatting (and mostly missing) the mosquitos that were eating me alive. The others in the crew were asleep in their cabins and I had shut the doors so my battle with the mosquitos, rattling of the laptop keyboard and coffee making activities do not disturb them. That and the fear that the sight of an overweight, balding, grey old man who is semi-naked, scratching and typing might be too much for their delicate stomachs.

When I first gave up the struggle with insomnia, I switched on a light to read in the cooler air of the saloon, but immediately the midges fed on my bare feet and ankles. I sat sipping coffee in the cockpit at first light. We were in a tranquil bay. The fish were disturbing the water with a quiet slurp from time to time. Occasionally, there was the distant bleat of a goat (or tonk of its bell) on Petalas. Apart from that and the quiet creak of running rigging when a slight shift in the air gently moved the boom, there was nothing. No cocks a crowing. No dogs a barking. No mopeds a mopeding. No lords a leaping. It was so quiet you could hear the goats thinking.

I booted up my laptop to type up notes on an island that we had left the day before — a small low island that we frequently visited. The island has a population of about 30 people, 60 sheep and goats and quite a few chickens. Viewed from the sea as you sail along the shores the vegetation seems to be mainly scrub and the ubiquitous olive. Once ashore, along the lanes on the outskirts of the only town are tall eucalyptus with dry rustling aromatic leaves and there are blackberry bushes that promise an autumn harvest. Just like home really — well, not quite.

One of the tavernas on the island was run by Gianni and Maria. It is a climb up a hill. One route to it takes you up a steep narrow path between small charming stone houses their gardens cultivated with flowers, fruit and vegetables. Roses, lilies, large red tomatoes, glossy black aubergines, melons and courgettes grow in the gardens in company with olive, almond, pomegranate and lemon trees. Bougainvillea and vines of one sort and another are draped across pergolas or along wires strung along the front of the houses. The houses vary from weather beaten houses with stone or rendered walls and sunbleached timberwork to newly painted rendered houses with timberwork picked out in blue, green or chocolate brown. The walk up is sheltered by trees in which lights are set which make the walk quite magical by night. By day, in the summer, it is alive with the tumult of cicadas. When you get to the taverna the views are magnificent over the sea and the mountains of the nearby mainland. When we had visited it last year, Maria was not there. We missed her feminine touch to the evening; thin slices of crisp toasted bread with olive paté would appear at the table, immediately, as you sat down and then she would come and greet you and ask how you had been since she last saw you.

"The walk up doesn't get any easier Maria," I wipe not so imaginary sweat from my brow.

"Then you call me and I fetch you in my limousine," she tells us. "It says to do this on the notices we have put in the harbour. And our phone number is there too."

"Only joking. The walk is good for us… and it is very pretty. But where is this limousine you keep telling us about?"

"Over there," she said, pointing at a battered white Nissan van and tinkles with laughter.

But last year she was absent. We had asked Gianni, "Where is Maria?"

"Oh, she has some business to attend to," he told us somewhat enigmatically.

"In Athens?"

"In America."

"America?"

"Yes, America. We lived there for years. We have family there."

"Oh... Will she be back later in the season?"

"No not this year."

And that was as much as he was going to tell us. But then, another day, we saw his daughter who was over from America. She told us that Maria was donating one of her kidneys to her son, Nikos. We spoke to Gianni about it later. There were tears. 'Oh dear, are we being intrusive?' I thought. However, we had known him and Maria for some time and he seemed to want to unload. He was feeling the stress of keeping it to himself and having to run a business far from his beloved Maria with her undergoing an operation which would be painful and would call for a long recovery — "She is not as old as I, but she is not young," Gianni said. We talked and later our departure was marked by a bear-like hug and many "hank yous and promises to keep in touch.

We did keep in touch for the rest of that season but, the following season, the place was not open on the first couple of visits and we did not get up there for some reason on the third visit so when we got to the island on the fourth visit in the middle of July I told Sharon and Helen that I was going up there. On grounds of economy and spinning out our pension, we were eating aboard most nights and had determined to do so that night but I wanted to catch up. Once the boat was secure, the passerail run out from the stern, sails stowed and loose lines frapped down I went ashore. Sharon opted to come with me. Helen wanted to stay on the boat and chill. Sharon and I found Maria sat in the shade talking to her cousin. She greeted us with a smile on a face that was as pretty as ever but showed signs of the strain and pain of the last year.

"Go. Find a nice table with a view or some shade. Whatever you want. And I will bring you a drink. What you want?"

I opened my mouth to speak and she interrupted.

"No, not you. I know what you want. Cold beer. Big beer." She grinned, "Just the lady."

"Oh same same," Sharon grinned back. She had not met Maria before.

Maria came over to the table with two large Mythos and started to ask about our family, but we interrupted, "We want to hear about you Maria. How are you feeling? You are well? Your son is well? Why did you have to go to America for this?"

"You want to hear everything?" Maria asked.

'Oh dear. Am I being intrusive?' I asked myself, not for the first time. I looked at Sharon who can read body language like I can read a book. I am quite insensitive to it all. Sharon nodded at me. Go ahead.

"Yes, Maria, sit down and tell us."

She settled herself and paused for a little while seeming to gather strength.

"You know my country, Greece, it is a beautiful country. It is a very beautiful country. I was born here on this lovely island. When I married Gianni, we went to America to earn a living. I love America. We lived there for many years. Our children were born there. We have many friends there. But some years ago, we decided to come back to our beautiful Greek island and open a taverna here. Greece is beautiful," she paused and swallowed, "But there is corruption." She paused again for breath and the emotional strength to continue.

She told us that the problem had started four years ago when her son Nikos caught an infection. He was always a fit young man running marathons and establishing club records that stood for quite some time. Now he is a professional man. He works for the Cypriot embassy in Washington. But, suddenly, he was anything but fit in spite of a healthy life style and regular exercise.

The symptoms were considered and tests carried out. It was established that he had kidney virus. However, the treatment that the medics prescribed and carried out did nothing to abate it. It was leading inexorably to renal failure and a lifetime of dialysis.

Maria was in touch with the Greek healthcare system and undergoing tests to establish whether she could donate a kidney which she wanted to do before dialysis became necessary. The tests established that she could and she signed the necessary forms for the procedure to be put in place. There was then a period of waiting terminated by a phone call and a meeting at which she was told the procedure could not go ahead. She could donate a kidney and Nikos could go on the list of recipients, but her kidney would be unlikely to go to Nikos who would have to wait his turn in the queue and, indeed, might never get a kidney transplant…

She contested this and once money had changed hands, she eventually got her way. However, the testing regime had to be repeated and this time they found that she had some sort of infection and prescribed medication. Sharon being in the pharmaceutical industry was following all this. A lot of it was lost on me, but the degree of suffering was obvious.

Maria went to hospital for treatment which immediately made her unwell — dizziness, balance and other problems. She was advised that this was an unfortunate side effect that would eventually go. It didn't. She contacted her American doctor — they had kept up the healthcare insurance in America — very wisely it turned out. She described the drugs and the symptoms to her American doctor whose reaction was, "Refuse the drugs. Don't take any more. What they will do is damage you — maybe even kill you. Discharge yourself — get out of that hospital." This she did but by then, Nikos was on dialysis and suffering. Some mistreatment had led to paralysis in his legs. This had to be sorted out and it was, but it all took some considerable time and there was a long wait before the transplant could be effected in the United States.

The recovery from the eventual transplant was quicker for Nikos who had youth on his side so Maria had a long period of convalescence in America and was in regular touch with Gianni who was running their restaurant back on their Greek island. Towards the end of the summer, she lost contact with him. She phoned him at the restaurant — no reply. She phoned other numbers that might raise him — no result. She contacted her mother who investigated and reported back that the restaurant was closed and Gianni had left the island. Maria was still not fully recovered. She was frail and fraught with worry which wasn't helping her recovery. She contacted Gianni's brother in Athens who eventually found him in a hospital there.

During the summer, he had developed a lump on the side of his neck. He had not wanted to further stress her by telling her about it, but it had become so bad that he had eventually closed the restaurant early and gone to Athens for diagnosis. The diagnosis was cancer and the treatment immediate and extensive taking out nerves and body tissue on the side of the face and the eye and the side of his body. Skin transplants and plastic surgery were necessary. But he was now back on the island being looked after by Maria and her mother. Sharon and I were introduced to Nikos who had leave of absence from the embassy to help run the restaurant while his father recovered. The conversation went on and stories were swapped.

"Tell Sharon the story of the John brain. The car you stopped in the US," I said to Maria. (John is the anglicised equivalent of Gianni.) Her face lit up.

"We have a saying here. Insulting, but it is a joke. One rooster brain = 49 John brains. We were driving along a road in America — Route 66 actually — and I noticed that we were following a car with a number plate something like *1 RB 49 JB*," she giggled and went on. "I said to John, 'The man in the car in front is from our island'. He told me not to be silly, 'How can you know that?'

I said 'He is and I bet his name is John. Look at his number plate. 1 RB 49 JB. Hoot him and wave at him.' So John wound down his window and drove past the car hooting his horn, shouting and waving, then pulled off into a lay by. The man, whom we did not know from Adam, followed him and they both got out of the car and greeted each other slapping each other on the back like long lost brothers. It was so funny," and she dissolved in giggles taking Sharon and I with her.

Sharon and I wandered back down the stone path to the harbourside. There were two tavernas alongside the harbour. As we came to the first, I said to Sharon.

"Let's stop. I feel I need to catch my breath after that story."

"It's as good an excuse as any."

We sat talking to the owner, Panos, who, at the time, had us as his only customers. His little girl was playing around her push chair. An engaging and lively little girl.

"What's her name?" enquired Sharon.

Smiling and looking straight at us he said, "Her name is Zoe. It means life. You want to know why we call her that?"

"Of course."

"When she was still in her mother, there was a car accident. It was a bad accident. It may have been that neither of them survived. Both did. So we called her life."

So there it is, Kastos, a small low island with beautiful views, a handful of wonderful people in the winter and many visitors in the summer, tragedy, love, laughter, and beauty all mixed up — oh and the luxury of a single shop in the summer.

Tragically, Gianni died the following year.

Vonitsa to Sami

Early one season, Helen had planned a short sojourn in a villa. Incidentally, in the Greek part of Cyprus I was told that this word was slang for "prick" — languages, a veritable minefield. Sharon had booked the villa with her daughter Hollie and Hollie's daughter Maisie. So, four generations of the family under one roof in Karavamilos on Keffalonia. "The witches of Eastwick," I mused when I was first told about it and received a slap for my impertinence.

I was in Vonitsa on the mainland at the time of their arrival, and moved the boat to Aktio to pick up a boat part before I was due to meet them. A longish haul ahead of me the next day, I planned to make Ithaca and meet up with some friends in Frikes, and wanting to make an early start, I set alarms.

The first alarm went off at 0430. By 0500, I was underway feeling my way past the entry lights to Cleopatra marina and on to the Preveza channel. The route was marked by lit buoys so was quite easy. My only worry was unlit fisherman's buoys and I shouldn't come across any of them until I was out of the Preveza channel by which time it would be getting light enough to see. That was the theory anyway.

Sailing at night has always fascinated me I used to love a trip across the channel to France usually to Cherbourg or St Vaaste. My old countess was so slow that one part of the trip would always be in the dark. Usually through the shipping lanes trying to work out who was doing what and who looked likely to hit you and what you should do about it. Unfortunately, on one occasion, we ran over a fisherman's buoy which wrapped around our propeller and took out the flexible coupling between the drive and the prop shaft. We were shafted in more ways than one, but lessons were learned.

Anyway, I digress. Leaving the Lefkas channel, I headed south for the Lefkas Bridge and made it with a good twenty minutes to spare. I was out of the other end of the Lefkas canal by about 8.30. It was getting warm. I had started off in jeans, shirt, sweater, socks and deck shoes, but now I started to strip layers off. By the time I reached Nidri, a bit of a breeze had come up so I cut the engine and attempted to sail but, about halfway down the Lefkas/Meganissi channel, the wind died and low dark clouds enshrouded the heights to either side, even Meganissi which hasn't much in the way of height had dark clouds on higher ground. And it got colder. So I stowed the sails and put discarded clothes back on to the relief of all passers-by. At the other end of the Lefkas/Meganissi channel, the wind picked up and on a fine reach I roared past the uninhabited island of Akhoudi entering the bay of Frikes about 1300 where the wind, as usual, did not so much die as get very erratic in direction and strength. I dropped the sails and prepped for mooring alongside the mole, port side to.

Unfortunately, somebody else had nicked my favourite spot so I moored up at the east end of the forbidden new jetty where the ferry swell that hits that jetty, is minimal. I tidied the boat up, re-checked the mooring lines and went to have a beer and some gavros at my favourite watering hole. There I caught up on the local gossip before returning to Sundowner. The wind had now blown up and was howling into my stern. I helped a German-flagged boat, the helmsman making a complete pig's ear of it cracking his boat against the unforgiving concrete quay.

The following day, I had a nice easy sail to Sami on Keffalonia where they were waiting on the quayside, young Maisie in a great state of excitement.

We took Maisie for a day sail to Aghia Efimia for lunch. About halfway there were suddenly four or five dolphins playing around the boat. She had never seen dolphins before and stood on the bow of the boat with her mum. Both were entranced with the aquabatics of the dolphins rolling, leaping and diving around the bow of the boat.

Noisy Nidri and Celebrations in Kioni

Nidri on Lefkas has a selection of stores selling fruit and veg, bakeries selling bread, spinach pies and Greek cakes, chandlers selling boating equipment and bars, tavernas or kaffenios in which to linger a while. We often restock there, but usually move on to spend the night at anchor somewhere peaceful like the lagoon at Vlicho or a bay on Meganissi. On one occasion, we had been re-stocking and lingering until fairly late. We clambered on board and I passed the provisions that we had bought down to Helen saying, "If you stow them, I'll start prepping to pull away."

"Where are we going? There's not a lot of the day left."

"I thought we would just drop anchor in the lagoon — off Geni."

"Do you know, let's not even bother to do that. Let's stay here for the night."

"Vlicho's only around the corner. It will only take five."

"Five what? We've got to take the passerail in and stow it."

"A minute and a half."

"Yeah. Then, as you use the main halyard to support it, you will have to fiddle around with that."

"All right, three minutes."

"Then we got to take in the shore lines, pull up the anchor... and you insist on the fenders coming in and being stowed."

"And that's the five," I said triumphantly.

"More than five... and there's all sorts of other fiddling and faddling about that you do."

"I don't fiddle and faddle."

"No? Just faddle then? It seems a quiet enough night. I'll start a spag bol now." She disappeared below with the words, "We'll be eating it in half an hour."

"I don't know. Swinging at anchor in the lagoon would be nicer."
I muttered to the vacuum that was Helen seconds ago.

I thought that I heard the soft pop of a cork being withdrawn from
a bottle followed by the comforting gurgle of wine being poured. She
who must be obeyed appeared in the companionway with a glass of
wine in her hand. "Here... chill why don't you? Sit in the cockpit.
Watch the world go by and savour this," and so it came to pass that my
sensible compulsion to go and find a nice anchorage disappeared —
sunk without trace.

That night there seemed to be a sort of conflict between bars and
night clubs. There was loud live Greek music from one of the tavernas,
loud pop music from a nearby bar and the undefinable, but loud output
from a night club. Each seemed determined to outgun the other with
their Mega/Giga/Teradecibel machinery. It was a long night and when
it all seemed to be quieting down with the glimmer of breaking day, the
clattering of garbage collecting trucks took over.

The forecast in the morning predicted light weather with a bit of a
breeze in the afternoon — force three, northish with a touch of west —
pretty much the prevailing wind. We left Nidri as the Meganissi ferry
was making its business-like way out to disgorge the sparse early
morning load of cars, lorries vans and foot passengers into Meganissi.
The sea was blue and wrinkled by the odd zephyr of wind. We headed
down the Meganissi/Lefkas channel under motor. Checking the engine,
I noticed that the raw water pump that draws seawater into the engine
cooling system was leaking seawater into the engine bay as we headed
for Ithaca.

"We had better turn back," said Helen when I gave her the good
news.

"Back to noisy Nidri; no, thank you. I want a quiet night tonight,"
I told her.

"But there are chandlers and IBA in Nidri."

"It's only a small leak."

"Define small."

"It's just seeping around the gasket on the pump. It will stop when
we are under sail."

"Does it look much like a sailing day?"

"No... but there is very little leakage and, anyway, I'll fix it this evening."

"And what do we do till then."

"Bail out if it becomes necessary — but it won't be."

"Better not be," she muttered darkly.

We dropped anchor in a quiet bay on Ithaca in the middle of the day. The village that rose into the steep slopes around the harbour was decked out in bunting and flags. Helen went ashore to investigate while I sponged half a bucketful of water out of the engine bay and made up a makeshift gasket.

"Did you know that it is St Elias day?" Helen said as she clambered aboard back from an exploration of the village. I confessed that I did not. "Well it is and St Elias is the named saint for this village."

A village usually celebrates its saint's day in a fairly robust fashion and this was no exception. The celebrations kicked off in the evening, but typically didn't really get into their stride until about midnight. Traditional Greek music, traditional Greek singing and dancing, traditional Greek eating and drinking all started around 10.00 p.m. It was certainly as noisy as Nidri, but it was a lot of fun. I celebrated my fixing of the leaky pump by joining in with some enthusiasm but, being a bit of a lightweight by comparison with the locals, I was in bed shortly after midnight as exhausted as a newt.

I thought that it would be going on until the small hours and that maybe we were in for a night of disturbed sleep as the walls of a boat are kind of thin compared to the bricks and mortar of a house. So there we were right on the harbourside where all the action seemed to be. However, we were tired from the previous interrupted night and slept through it all. We pulled out of the harbour about 10.30/11.00 a.m. the following morning. The partying was still going on. The diehards had decamped from the harbourside to a taverna on the hillside overlooking the harbour from which their revelry was broadcast and could be heard well out to sea.

Dolphins and Tuna

We were not long out of Kioni before I spotted dolphins. Their dorsal fins were a tiny black vertical strip appearing and disappearing in the water at quite some distance away. At that stage, it might have been my imagination or some other disturbance in the distant water, but a few minutes later we could see them clearly.

About a year back a sailing buddy, Mike, and his son were on Sundowner for a week. His son had a theory that if you knock on your hull with your fist, it will attract dolphins in the vicinity — inquisitive as they seem to be. He tried it out and we saw dolphins most days during their stay so I tried it now. We gradually crossed paths and pretty soon there were about a dozen of them playing around Sundowner, but whether my knocking attracted them or whether it would have happened anyway is anyone's guess. I ended up with a sore set of knuckles in any case.

Tuna are another frequent sighting though often, it seems to me, late in the season. Having left the dolphins half an hour back, our attention was caught by a maelstrom of white water below some wheeling, diving seabirds. As we got closer, we saw quite large tuna leaping clear of the water. Are our friends the dolphins in pursuit of their lunch? No, they are nowhere to be seen. Gulls wheeled and dived above them. "Are the gulls after the tuna?" Helen asked.

"Hardly. I would think that the tuna are too big for those birds. I guess that the gulls are after smaller fish that the tuna are pursuing and generally stirring up."

Aristotelis in Frikes — whose apartments we had stayed in on land-based holidays — had given me a hook for tuna last time we saw him in Frikes when he, his wife and young son, Konstantinos, had come aboard for a look around. It was a cruel looking hook the shank of which was threaded through a two-inch length of half inch clear plastic tubing. I looked at it puzzled.

"Tie the hook onto a line and trail it behind the boat after the first rain in September. If you are doing five or six knots you will catch tuna," he had told me. It was not September. It had not been raining. But there were clearly tuna about. I decided to give it a try and foraged around in a locker and produced a tatty plastic bag of fishing line and hooks. Helen watched me inexpertly tie off Aristotle's lure and a weight on the end of some nylon line that I had wound onto a block of polystyrene.

"What are you going to do if you catch one?" asked Helen.

"Give it to you to gut it, clean it and cook it," I said.

"Uh huh... Not me... You can do the killing and gutting bit."

"It won't be a problem. I can't see us catching one with a hook and a bit of plastic tubing."

"That's a relief then. You know how squeamish you are about taking hooks out of fish."

Much to my surprise, we caught two fat tuna. I had to dispatch them, but we barbecued them at anchor that night. It may be that the plastic tubing going through the water and catching the light gives the impression of a small fish flashing through the water — or maybe tuna simply like plastic.

We chose a quiet little bay to spend the night and barbecue our tuna. We anchored off a steep white rocky slope beneath which clear blue water enabled us to see enough to avoid dropping our anchor in weed. The anchor stuck firm giving an immediate positive tug when we stressed it. As we tidied the boat up for the night, we found ourselves in the company of a large herd of goats. They were making their way across and down the white cliff face finding footholds where none seemed to exist. Every now and then, a goat planted a hoof where the rock was not as firm as he thought and there would be a clatter of scree descending onto the heads of any goat unfortunate enough to be below him.

We ate our tuna with a glass of wine as the sun disappeared below the hills to the west and the goats seemingly ensconced on the pebble beach for the night.

I awoke at dawn and looked out. The goats were in a long line along the beach staring at us, silent apart from a very occasional bleat. The sea was flat and windless. We had some problems pulling up the anchor so I put on my mask and had a look. The anchor had caught under a rock. We put the engine on the outboard and put a metal loop (a jib halyard minus the rope tail off one of my ex dinghies) around the anchor chain. I weighted the loop with a couple of the largest bits of ironmongery that I could find and put a long line on it. I let the loop around the chain drop to the bottom. I drove off with the line attached to the tender to try and pull it from under the rock. My theory was that the loop would travel along the chain and up the shank of the anchor and act as a tripping line and hopefully pull the anchor from under the rock by its crown. The water was pretty choppy by now as the wind started to pile in and the dinghy took quite a lot of water. It took several pulls, but eventually it was free and Helen pulled the anchor and manned the helm while I pulled myself back to the boat on the line, piling the line back into the dinghy as I went. The wire loop dropped clear of the anchor as it cleared the water and we were sorted.

The forecast had predicted much the same weather as the previous day. We headed off in the direction of the island of Kalamos. The wind was anything but constant, but Sundowner ghosted along accelerating in patches of breeze until a more constant breeze set in and we took off on a nice easy reach to the island. We fetched up in Episcopi. We were going to re-acquaint ourselves with the young couple, Theodore and Stephanie who ran the taverna/snack bar there. We knew their plans last year were to get married this year. It turned out that it had all happened a fortnight ago and they had just re-opened the bar. They told us all about it. They were married in the little church above the bay then had the reception in the harbour — 300 guests, some making their way over the mountain road from Kalamos Town, many arriving in water busses, private launches, fishing boats and caiques from the mainland (Mitikas). Being a Greek wedding, it was probably great fun, doubtless very noisy, lasted well into the night and possibly into the following day.

A white catamaran pulled in next to us shortly after we had moored up in the small harbour. A hard chine hull and the chunky construction made it look as if it had been conceived and built by a fairly expert DIY enthusiast. The crew was a Greek family on their annual holiday. The two small children spent a lot of the time out with their mother, Maria, on the nearby beach. The father, Nikos, was often off fishing and after lunch collapsed into a noisy siesta. Maria apologised about the loud snoring. "I think Nikos is worse than the last earth tremor," she giggled. "I am used to it, but you must think Tsunami is on way." The eldest child rarely left the boat as she was spending her time reading and revising for exams. The fishing, when successful, provided them with supper and we often watched Maria descaling three or four fat fish on the quayside. He came back to the boat on one occasion with, as usual, a bucket with a cloth over it. The children, who had just come back from the beach, rushed up asking what he had caught to-day.

Although I could not fully follow his reply, the gist of it was, "Just you look in the bucket. You'll get a big surprise." The youngest, a girl of five or six, lifted the cloth and dropped it back squealing.

"Has he lots?"

"One. Only one. But…" the little girl stooped to the bucket and lifted the cloth again fishing around beneath it.

"It's big?"

"No, no, no… it's tiny," she fished out a tiddler and held it up between finger and thumb. With the other hand clasped over her mouth to, unsuccessfully, stifle her giggles.

I don't know what cooking facilities they had on board, but Maria produced a variety of meals for her family and occasionally shared some dish with us. On one occasion, some hot sweet doughnut-like sweets were brought over on a plate by her eldest girl. On another, she handed a plateful of unleavened bread — a pitta or similar — with olive oil, melted feta cheese and herbs. It was simple and delicious.

Greece — A Gastronomic Wasteland?

Greece has an unfair reputation as a bit of a gastronomic wasteland. A lot of tavernas stick largely to a tourist menu of souvlaki, moussaka, kalamares, pastitsio and the like. However, Greek cooking at best is excellent. One year, during our backpacking days, we found ourselves on Koufonisia in the Small Cyclades south of Naxos. We had found rooms at a charming place run by an equally charming lady called Sophie. She usually came and had afternoon coffee with us when we returned from our wanderings and snorkelling on that very small island. She spoke little English and we at that stage, little Greek. She arrived one afternoon proffering her mobile in an outstretched hand. I looked at her, unsure what exactly was going on. She thrust the phone at me again so I took it cautiously. I could hear a tinny voice coming from it and, following her signalled instruction, put it to my ear. I recognised the voice as a gay Athenian who occasionally stayed, together with his poodle, in one of her rooms.

"Mrs Kypriades apologises that she cannot speak English very well, but she would like you to come for a meal up on her balcony this evening," he told me.

"We'd love to," I told him and handed the phone back to Sophie who talked to him further then handed me the phone again.

"She will cook you fish. Is that OK?"

"It sounds lovely. Thank you very much er… Ef haristo poli," I told him and her, smiling and nodding as I handed the phone back to Sophie. She spoke further and then handed me the phone for the gay Athenian to tell me, "Seven thirty is OK?"

"Yes, it's fine."

And so we found ourselves sat on her balcony that evening eating delicious fish with herbs and flaked almonds in the company of Sophie, the gay Athenian (Marcos), and an Albanian youth called — well

Simon so we were told. Simon was doing some building work for Sophie and spoke no English and not much Greek. However, Sophie seemed to have some grasp of Albanian. Sophie's English and our Greek were exercised, but Marcos was called into service when we got stuck. Conversation with the Albanian, however, went from us to the Gay Athenian, to Sophie, to the Albanian and returned using the same route reversed.

We ate the fish and learned a great deal despite the language difficulties and watched the distant lights of Santorini emerge as night fell. The island was usually not noticeable from Koufonitsia during the day but, from Sophie's balcony at night, its lights glistened on the horizon like small diamonds set in dark blue-black velvet.

Greek cuisine was also called into question in the island of Samos in the Dodecanese during one holiday. We had been off visiting other islands and arrived back a few days before the flight home from Samos. We found rooms in the small village of Aghia Konstatinos. It boasted (in those days) just two tavernas a few houses and no shops. In the evening, we would watch an old lady making yoghurt from the milk of her goats in the yard behind the house next door. There were beautiful walks up to delightful villages in the hills above. The narrow country lane that led up to our favourite village followed the course of a stream of fast clear water tumbling over stones and rocks from the village down to the sea near Aghia Konstatinos.

Once we had found and installed ourselves in rooms run by an exotic sounding and delightfully eccentric Mrs Calypso, we explored the local facilities and sat at the nearest taverna for a cold beer. The proprietor introduced himself as Mikalis. He took our order for two beers and asked whether we wanted anything to eat.

"No thank you."

"Tonight?"

"What have you got?"

"Ah, delicious, souvlaki, moussaka, stifado, kleftico…" he faltered watching our faces. "Not good?"

"I'm sure your souvlaki is lovely and your moussaka the best in Greece," I said patronisingly.

"Of course, of course."

"But we've had three weeks of souvlaki, moussaka, pastitsio, kalamares, chicken, pork chops, lamb chops — all with chips — no vegetables."

"Potato chips is a salad… Is how you say — a Glasgow salad?"

"Yeah, but what have you got against vegetables?"

"Look look…. we make good Greek food. But we make from fresh. We cannot get all meats and vegetables in fresh then throw them away because the people just want pork chop and chips or souvlaki. If you want… if you promise that you come here… Well how many days you stay?"

"Three. We've got three more nights."

"Yes, well, if you promise that you come to me for each of those nights, I give you something different; something Greek, something delicious each night."

"What will you give us?" Helen asked suspiciously.

"Ah, that's for me to decide and surprise you, but it will be good. I promise."

Helen looked at me, "Do we want to?"

I shrugged, "Up to you." I said doing my usual slopey shoulder job.

"Listen," Mikalis interrupted. "You will like it. If you don't like, then you don't pay me."

It clinched the deal and he was as good as his word. There were three courses each night. There was a glass of wine with each course including the sweet and the wine was good — good enough to impress my much-abused palate anyway. Each course was tasty and new to us and inexpensive. Greek cooking is OK. Some tavernas seem to favour the traditional tourist menu, but most are improving their act all the time, especially those in the more popular tourist destinations.

One House Bay

It was mid-July morning and a gentle north west wind was ghosting us along in the expanse of water between Kalamos and Ithaca. We had Sharon on board and, as the tourist season was well under way, we had been overnighting in the less well-known bays of the Ionic. However, we had decided to head for Sami on Keffalonia for a bit of life and the opportunity to stock up with supplies and fuel. Sharon had her nose in Rod Heikel's 'Greek Waters Pilot' and looked across at a nearby island.

"That is Atako isn't it?" she asked.

"Yes, that's Atako."

"So this 'One House Bay' is on there."

"Yes, it is," I confirmed.

"Have you been in there?"

"Well I did look in once."

"Was it nice?"

"Yes, very pretty."

"Did you stay... put down your anchor?"

"Nope."

"Why not?"

"It was crowded."

"Well, let's have a look."

"It will be heaving with yachts and motor boats."

"Well, it must be worth a visit then if it's that popular."

"Hmm. It's just because the Emu says it is a pretty bay. In the height of the season, the trick is to find the places that he doesn't sing the praises of and go there."

"Is he always so miserable, Mum, or does he just save it for when I'm aboard?" Sharon asked Helen."

"Oh no, this is cheery compared with what I get."

I just knew that they would gang up on me so I changed course for One House Bay. The place has become known as One House Bay because it's got one house in it — imaginative or what? It is said that the house is occasionally occupied by a fisherman and his wife. The bay is pretty with a pebble beach, a backdrop of chalk-white cliffs and green vegetation and, of course, just the one house. The blue waters are as clear as crystal. At the height of the season, it is likely to be crowded with boats that range from big floating gin palaces to little outboard powered day hire boats with all shapes and sizes of motor and sailing yacht in between and, as we arrived, a half dozen canoeists were threading their way between it all.

"It's a zoo," I muttered. "I don't know why people come here"

"Because it's pretty, you cheerless old goat," came the response.

We found a spot where we thought we might anchor without fouling anyone else's mooring. Often, this is not difficult because most of the boats at anchor are pointing more or less into the wind unless they have a line ashore in which case they may not be. At any rate, you can hazard a guess where their anchor might be and, in waters this clear, you might actually be able to see anchors and chains. However, the bay was more or less in the lee of the island, the wind was curling around the headland and eddies of wind were pointing boats every which way. Boats were rafted together. Boats were milling in and out and trying to guess where to drop anchor. Boats that were already at anchor were twisting this way and that in the capricious wind that came from first one direction then another. To complicate it all, a boat occasionally lost its anchor and drifted wherever the wind felt it would send it.

"It's a bloody shambles," I grumbled.

"I think it's great," Sharon hooted as a large Beneteau came in carefully dropped anchor and, as the momentum of the boat and the swirling wind and the anchor line had their varying effects swung gracefully into another moored boat. In truth, the wind was light and people mostly seemed alert to the problems so everything was being coped with.

We had moored near a large blue French-flagged yacht who had watched apprehensively as we dropped the anchor and laid out an appropriate amount of chain.

"Have you seen that boat behind?" shouted Helen.

"The blue one — yes."

"We are getting rather close."

"I'm watching, I'm watching my little obergruppenfuhrer," I replied testily and thinking: 'bugger I thought I'd got that about right'. "Let's just see how it settles down," I said. My stern was quite close to his bow but we straightened up to lay parallel to the French boat and a respectable distance off. And when the wind changed so that the two boats lay in line there was still a respectable distance between my stern and his bow. "You see we got it about right," I said picking up some muttering which included the words "luck" and "judgement" and "more by".

"What were you muttering?"

"We said we really should trust your judgement more," they lied.

We swam and had a pleasant lunch. Sharon watched as a couple of 30-foot boats tried unsuccessfully to anchor between us and the cliff. It's surprising the entertainment that can be derived from other folk's difficulties. Schadenfreude, I believe they call it.

Eventually, we decided it was time to go and anyway a large charter boat that had parked a respectable distance away was edging towards us. "I think your anchor is slipping," I shouted.

They started taking appropriate action, but I still had to fend them off. The woman ran up to the bow and hauled up the anchor so that it would not catch on the network of anchor chains on the floor of the bay. The man at the helm was fiddling with the throttle/gearshift control. "I can't get it into gear," he shouted.

The anchor, a CQR, came up festooned with a large clump of weed which explained the slipping anchor thing a bit. The woman who seemed to be the cool-headed one of the pair released the furling line and pulled on the starboard jib sheet to run out the large genoa. As the genoa filled the boat picked up speed toward a tangled clump of boats on the other side of the bay.

"You're heading for us," came the rather unnecessary shout from a distant boat. The woman took the helm and steered the boat neatly through the mass of anchored boats and out to sea. We followed her out and hovered around to see if they wanted assistance, but they had rapidly sorted themselves out and were heading back into the fray.

"You OK?" I shouted.

"Yeah fine. All sorted."

"You're going back in there?" I asked incredulously.

"Got to really. Our children are still on the beach there."

We left One House Bay early afternoon with me vowing under my breath not to bother with the place again and Sharon chuckling at all the melodrama she had seen. We were moored in Sami by early evening and had a pleasant evening catching up with various people. I found Stefanos in his usual Kafenio. I had struck up a casual acquaintanceship with him a couple of years back and looked out for him whenever I was in town. He looked about ninety years old, but it might have just been due to the wear and tear of a hard life. He walked stooped with age and arthritis, but he still managed to get on and off his boat with the casual nonchalance of a much younger man and he always had a cheery greeting. Bright eyes shone mischievously from a countenance creased by age and weather and decorated with grey stubble. He still took his eighteen-foot fishing boat out each morning and was back at midday with fish. He waved as I entered the kafenio. I took a seat and ordered a cup of coffee.

"Catch many fish today?" I asked.

"Some, some. But not many."

"Oh dear."

"Ah — is overfished. No fish these days."

The proprietor came to the table with my coffee and placed it in front of me. "He waits for the weather forecast," he said with a wink and indicated a large television screen in the corner of the room.

I turned to Stefanos, "Is that true?" I asked him.

Stefanos laughed — a dry cackle. "Yes, true," he confirmed gleefully.

"I thought you fisherman know what's coming better than the weatherman."

"New weather man. Very good," he chuckled. "Look look."

The television switched to a weather map of the area and standing in front of it was a young and well-endowed girl wearing a very skimpy

316

bikini. She started talking animatedly in Greek and indicated weather movements on the projected map behind her with sweeping movements of her arms that had her whole body moving coquettishly to show off her considerable assets to their best advantage. Stefanos chuckled fruitily at each over-the-top gesture and, at the end, wiped tears of laughter from his eyes as he turned to me and said, "See. Much better weatherman."

"Was her forecast good?" I asked.

"I don't know. I don't care," Stefanos chuckled.

Messalonghi

The echo sounder went wrong while we were heading for the Gulf of Corinth hoping to explore places where the charts were covered with notes that effectively said: *this is what was found at the last survey but the depths are prone to change.* It was clearly going to be helpful to have a working echo sounder.

We had just radioed Ion Traffic and got permission to go under the massive Rrion/Andirrion bridge into the Gulf of Corinth when I looked down and the echo sounder display was dead. I carried out the obvious checks, but there was power at the appropriate places so I concluded that it was a failure in the electronics of the device and a new unit was probably the only practical answer. We radioed traffic control to cancel our last communication and headed for Patras — where the huge ferries from Italy head for. It is a large port. The main harbour is dirty and it smells. We moored there because we didn't want to pay marina dues for a fleeting visit, but could not find a chandler or engineer or anyone who could help us. We walked to the marina, but there was no one about. It was run down and there seemed to be no marina office. So we decided to make our way back ensuring the passage and the overnight stay en-route for Lefkada were known to be safe depth-wise.

From Patras, we made Messalonghi for an overnight stop. It seemed like an ideal place. The bouyed channel into the harbour meant no problems with shallows. The harbour is sheltered and, according to the charts and the pilot, yachts can anchor in the basin of the harbour and the holding is good. We had just got settled. The boat was moving peaceably at anchor. We had watched turtles surfacing and diving. We had just started cooking a supper around 8.00 p.m. when the port police were on us, and the other half dozen boats similarly at anchor. "You must move."

"What? Where?"

"Alongside on the harbour wall, or on the marina."

"Why?"

"It is dangerous?"

"How? To whom?"

"Dangerous..."

They wouldn't elucidate further so we reluctantly moved the boat on to the harbour wall which was entirely suitable for large commercial vessels, but unsuitable bordering on hazardous for us. One boat went onto the marina floating pontoon where he was charged exorbitantly for a mooring that did not provide any services such as water, electricity or a walkway to the shore. On the harbour wall where we were, there was fendering for large vessels. At intervals, a dozen big lorry tyres were threaded on an iron bar each end of which was shackled to a rusty fixing on the harbour wall. The mooring bollards were for large boats and were thus spaced at large intervals which meant either very long mooring lines or attempting to tie one line to a bollard and the other to one of the rusty fendering fixtures.

We got our heads down but, around one-thirty in the morning, I was woken by scrambling on the boat and I looked up to see someone raising the mosquito net over my hatch and a hand slid through clicking a cigarette lighter — presumably to see if there was anything worth stealing aboard. I had a partial glimpse of a boy's face, late teens, made a grab for the hand thinking I will pull him through the hatch, the bastard wouldn't fit and it would disadvantage him. He saw a naked elderly man making a grab for him and fled. I let out a yell that woke Helen up, pulled on my shorts and burst out of the main hatch, but he and his mate had gone.

In the morning, I went to the port police and asked them to explain their reasoning for moving us. I was handed from pillar to post. I eventually ended up with a bloke who, unlike the rest of them, was not in port police uniform. Obviously, the plain clothes man, or for all I knew the janitor. He repeated the "dangerous" argument. I repeated my, "How is it dangerous?" and "To whom is it dangerous?" questions. Eventually, he had an exchange in Greek with a good-looking woman in the Port Police uniform and then she told me in broken English, "This is a harbour and by Greek law boats are not permitted to anchor in the basin of a harbour because of restricting the movement of large commercial boats attempting to moor or leave the harbour."

"Do you have large boats calling in here?" I asked looking at the rundown harbourside.

She shrugged, "It's the law."

This was ringing a few bells. A few seasons back they attempted to ban anchoring in Lefkas town harbour. There was something about it in the Practical Boat Owner or some similar yotties mag. They gave up in the end. I think there are plenty of odd laws they can in theory invoke (some in conflict with EU laws). This is no different to the UK. A London copper told me a few years back that London cab drivers are still technically obliged by law to carry enough hay to replenish the horse that they no longer have! However, it is different in Greece in that law is invoked as and when they feel like it and it is often suggested that there are ulterior motives behind the invocation.

A fellow yottie had uncharitably suggested that the port police were in cahoots with the marina who wanted the anchored boats to tie up on their pontoons and pay their exorbitant fees. I thought it prudent not to express this conclusion to the port police.

I reported the attempted burglary. The officer listened patiently and, when I had finished said, "Oh yes. I am afraid that happens from time to time. Perhaps you would fill out a report? Would you recognise him?"

Were they saying they would set up an ID parade? I didn't think so. There were at least a dozen staff that I met during my conversations. I asked them whether there were officers on duty through the night, "Oh yes."

"But this sort of thing often happens and you haven't caught them yet?"

He shrugged, "Difficult. Gypsies."

Gipsies often get the blame if they are in the vicinity when this sort of incident occurs. Sometimes this may be deserved but they are easy scapegoats and the face that I saw didn't look very gypsy-like to me.

The next day saw us back in the vicinity of Lefkas. The following day, we were able to find an engineer trained and equipped to test our particular instrumentation (so his card said). He confirmed my diagnosis and sourced a replacement unit which we were able to buy and fit the next day.

A Wobbly Windlass

Early in the season, just after the launch, I called into Nidri to stock up. I moored on Nidri quayside in the early evening and watched a Russian flagged catamaran approach amid a lot of on-board pandemonium and shouting. It was presumably Russian pandemonium and shouting; at any rate, I understood not a thing. It was clear enough what their intent was, however, and that was to moor stern-to alongside me. They thanked me in broken English as I took their lines, but I thought quietly to myself: 'I want to be on Sundowner when they decide to depart.... just in case'.

The next morning, as I returned from the shops of Nidri, my Russian friends were pulling out and doing it rather untidily. They managed to pick up my chain with their anchor before I even got on board. So I started the engine to push Sundowner off the jetty against the mooring lines, switched the windlass on and ran to the bow to let out anchor chain so they could easily unhook my anchor (which they now had wrapped around theirs) and, hopefully, drop it somewhere out there in line with my bow.

No such luck. In spite of some vigorous yelling and gesticulating on my part, the helmsman just let the boat drift with the wind rather than keeping it on station. The more chain I let out, the further they drifted downwind, away from me and towards the mooring lines of the Christina (a traditionally styled day trip boat). I stopped letting chain out. There was no point. As fast as I was easing tension by paying out line, they were putting tension back on by drifting down wind and they were struggling to get my anchor off theirs. My stern lines were tied to the quayside rather than rigged to slip and the passerail was still down so I couldn't just slip the moorings to get the boat off the quayside. In any case, had I attempted to do so they were drifting downwind and would have pulled my boat across the anchor chains of boats moored

321

downwind — one of the problems with the Mediterranean penchant for mooring stern-to or bows-to the quayside.

The problem with not paying out chain was that the catamaran was now pulling my anchor chain and thus the bow of the boat downwind. I opened the throttle a bit to counter this but without a lot of effect. They finally untangled my anchor from theirs and dropped it uncomfortably close to one of Christina's mooring lines. I took in the passerail, untied the stern moorings and took Sundowner off the quayside. I moved her out cautiously picking up the anchor chain. Of course, picking up my anchor chain was now taking me on to Christina and her mooring lines so I was alternating between being at the stern of Sundowner to keep it clear of fouling Christina's moorings — I particularly didn't want the rudder or propeller near the mooring line that stretched tautly out from the bow of the Christina into the water.

At one point I rushed forward to take up more anchor chain and failed to notice that the chain had slipped off the bow roller, and jammed between the roller and the housing. As I pressed the button there was an almighty crack and the windlass canted forward as its powerful motor tried to pull the bow roller assembly into the chain locker.

I dropped the windlass control and wrestled the chain back onto the bow roller. This was not an easy task so that, by the time I freed it, the wind had taken me back into Christina's mooring lines. I hastened back to the stern to manoeuvre the boat away from the mooring line before returning to the bow to take in more anchor chain. As the wind was taking me back onto the Christina, there were several iterations of this with me charging backwards and forwards along the boat like a demented animal pacing to and fro in a cage. A bunch of spectators began to gather on the Nidri quayside to watch the fun and games. To their disappointment, I got the anchor up and moved the boat out to the open water to inspect the damage. It seemed to be mounted solidly enough. I always use a snubbing line when anchored to take the stress of the anchor chain on to a ship's cleat rather than the windlass.

'Reasonable care when hauling up the anchor should see us all right' I thought to myself. However, I found out later in the season that I was mistaken.

This "later in the season" was mid-July. The Ionic was getting rather hot and crowded and we were increasingly trying to find places away from the popular bays and harbours. We found a small bay in the Dragonera islands. It was a bit exposed for an overnight stop, but a nice place for lunch and a swim. The really sheltered bays seemed to be fully occupied often by fish farms and, in my experience, mooring near a fish farm meant the boat was infested by flies. When we pulled away in the early afternoon, we discovered that we had got the anchor planted under a rock and rather over stressed the windlass at one point. Not to put to finer point on it we managed to pull the bloody thing off its mounting. A 1,000-watt motor, a 20 kgm Bruce anchor, 8 mm chain and I discovered the weakest link — the windlass mounting. The two rear bolts complete with washers pulled through the base (two-and-a-half-inch thick ply — supposedly marine ply). One of the front bolts was bent the other had snapped.

We were going to have a few days in bays, but had to return to the heat of Nidri instead. We had quite a nice sail back and then had to find a place to moor alongside at about seven o'clock in the evening.

When I dismantled the windlass from the mounting, the underneath of the windlass was corroded to hell which was why one of the bolts snapped off. It took a lump off the base of the windlass with it. I didn't know how we were going to solve that. The windlass base is cast aluminium so might be beyond the local talent to do a welded repair.

We called IBA the following morning and Tom appeared within the half hour. He looked at the carnage.

"How the hell did you do that?"

"With the greatest of ease. How are you going to repair it?"

"No problem. I will make up two stainless steel plates to sandwich the suspect ply base (which looked fairly black with water infiltration) and act as two bloody great washers with the necessary holes for the windlass bolts and chain feed. It all sounds like a temporary repair, but we have done it before and it is known to do the job."

"If it's temporary, how long will it last?"

Tom grinned, "That largely depends on you. It should last quite a long time."

With the job done, we moved out to a nearby bay and stayed at anchor all the following day. "What if we get it stuck under a rock again?"

"Well, we'll have to pull the bloody thing up carefully!"

"Don't we usually do that."

"Apparently not."

"Oh dear."

"Well, look on the bright side."

"Which is?"

"It will test the repair."

Around Kastos and Mitikas

Kastos is a small attractive island surrounded by nice bays with clear water. There is one town — Kastos Town. The holding is poor inside the town port and it is a popular place so laying a longish anchor chain in the relatively shallow port means that there are almost invariably crossed lines when boats pull away in the morning. It's not an insurmountable problem, but it can be a nuisance if you want to slip away early in the morning.

The forecast showed settled weather. The sea in the bays near the port is crystal clear as it is pretty much all around Kastos so you can see what you are putting your anchor into. We dropped the anchor clear of the patches of weed and it seemed to hold as we gave the anchor a tug to check the holding and nervously stressed the newly-mounted windlass. Snorkelling around later, I could see the anchor planted clear of the weed in the soft sea bottom. As we washed up after the evening meal, we could see through the hatches that the sea was darkening. Helen went up for a look and shouted for me to come up.

"I thought that you said we were going to be OK here."

"Well, that's what Poseidon and Meteo were telling me on the web."

The sea was flat with regularly spaced little waves — not much more than ripples but further out it was striated with white horses — a regular pattern of them like some gigantic weave of foaming white on a back blue backdrop. The sky was overcast and the sea was bathed in a curious light.

"We are going to have to move."

"I don't think so. It seems to be passing to the south of the island and us. We are not in a strong wind here." That much was true. Although the wind had suddenly got up off the coast, we were relatively sheltered in the bay and the suddenness of the arrival of the ministorm meant that the sea had not had time to build a swell into the harbour.

"But what is that?" Helen pointed north east along the coast. The storm seemed to have originated in the mountains of the mainland and advancing along the coast in our direction was a boiling mist of spray. But what had caught her attention was a concentrated rosy glow in the centre of the boiling misty spray of rain that was heading our way. It looked as though someone had lit a bonfire in the midst of it all!

"Well, what is it? It's a bit scary… and the wind is strong now." The wind was snatching the bow about with some vigour. I walked up to the bow. The anchor chain was secured with a snubbing line so at least the windlass was unstressed. We were moving about a bit, but essentially staying on station. As I walked back the blasts of wind seemed to be diminishing. I looked at the mysterious red flare in the mist and noticed that it was now tinged with orange on one side. It was the start of a rainbow. I had not seen a rainbow manifest itself like that before. Some trick of the evening light and the way that rainstorm was moving across the water had caused the rainbow to start as a flare of red light at ground level. We watched it build into the familiar arch with the normal hues of colour as the rain moved across the water. Forty minutes later, the storm had passed and the tranquillity of the Ionian evening had returned.

The next day, we sailed around Kastos and Kalamos to Mitikas. The hinterland behind the mainland town of Mitikas is a large squarish plain which is bordered on two sides by mountains and the other two by the sea. The plain shimmers silver grey with olive trees and is backed by the pastel shades of the mountains. Mitikas is on a corner where the two sides of the plain that are bounded by the sea meet. From the sea, the buildings of Mitikas show as a line of predominantly bright white buildings on the water's edge. Inland, at the foot of the mountains, you can make out the red roofs of another town.

On one of the mountainsides there is a long horizontal splash of white. It reminded me of monastery at Amorgos in the small Cyclades which looked as if a Greek giant had thrown a massive handful of white plaster at the sheer face. From the sea, using binoculars, we could make out a cross painted on the rockface, a long man-made stone wall painted white and a white bell tower. So it is possibly a monastery built into the steep hillside — or just a church — or just some white-painted stones.

I was told at a later date that it was a Greek Orthodox church built into the mountainside during the days of Greek occupation by the Ottoman empire when the Greek Orthodox religion was banned. It had enabled the locals to carry on with their religious services surreptitiously. I do not know how true this is, but if it was not painted white when built it would have blended into the rocks of the mountainside.

Mitikas harbour is normally busy with small craft. Small ferries, caiques and other craft service the various ports on the islands of Kastos and Kalamos transporting people, building materials, vegetables, fruit, soft drinks, newspapers, bread, beer, ice cream, bottles of water by the hundred and, well, everything you can think of. Besides this commercial traffic, there are small private launches busying in and out in the holiday season. There is usually water available on the waterside. We called in for supplies and to refill our depleted water tanks with water. The quayside tap however, issued no water when we turned it on. I sought out the man who seemed to be the harbourmaster. There was, he explained, a water supply problem.

"No one in town has water," he told us.

"How long is the water going to be off for?"

He shrugged, "Maybe on later today. Maybe tomorrow — maybe not," he said.

"What do we do?" Helen asked.

"There's enough on board for now. Let's overnight here and if it is still a problem tomorrow, we'll head off for Lefkada or possibly Keffalonia as we originally planned. We can get water in Nidri or Sami."

Walking through the town in the afternoon, I realised that the Mediterranean siesta still lives. While it is subsumed by the need to cater for tourism in most popular destinations on the Mediterranean, in Mitikas the main street in the middle of the afternoon is as silent as a graveyard. It was like a scene from some science fiction film where an alien force had suddenly wiped out the human race. The shops were open but usually empty. Through a doorway the sound of snoring emerged from the stygian darkness. So they hadn't been taken by some alien force — they were just resting. If I wanted a loaf of bread, I could possibly help myself and leave the money on the counter. Disturbing the proprietor's sleep would probably get me lynched.

I walked on. Chairs and tables still stood outside kafenios and bars but the places were deserted. Some were clearly shut. Some were just uninhabited. My footsteps echoed in the unnatural quiet and the only other sound was the moaning of the wind and the occasional desultory crow of a cockerel who sounded as though he could not really be arsed, but felt that he should. Weird. I felt as though I was going to turn a corner and be confronted by a bunch of daleks chanting, "Exterminate! Exterminate!"

A Wedding on Keffalonia

No, this is not a tale of a traditional Greek wedding. One of my granddaughters, Hollie, had holidayed with us in Aghia Eufimia on the island of Keffalonia in Greece when she was very young. Many years later, when she and Stu decided to get wed, the wedding was to be in Aghia Eufimia. The small wedding party arrived in bits and pieces. Stu, Hollie, with Maisie and George (their two children) were already there when we sailed in from nearby Sami. So were my eldest daughter, Nicola, and her husband, Alan. Stu and Hollie were established in a charming little villa overlooking the harbour from where they could see our boat. Alan and Nicky were in a hotel on the edge of the town near Stavros' Paradise Beach Taverna. The mother of the bride, Sharon, had a room overlooking the harbour. On Stu's side, Bret and Jan arrived the next day and ensconced themselves in the same hotel as Alan and Nicky. Sue arrived the day after and found a room in the town.

The wedding was set for the last day of May and at the appointed hour (half past nine), we all met at the town hall and filed up the stairs to the registrar's office. Here, we were told that they were not quite ready for us. Dimitris, the facilitator told us, "Come back in half an hour." We repaired to a bar just across the road where our first "bracer" of the day was variously tea, coffee, beer, wine, and even ouzo (Helen). We shared the small bar with two hirsute Greeks chatting quietly over coffee. They seemed bemused by the sudden invasion.

At 10:00 am, we crossed the road to the town hall and up the stairs to the registrar's office followed by the two hairy Greeks who now seemed to be part of the wedding party. The office was small — only just large enough to accommodate even our small party. The registrar conducted the service in Greek pausing every now and then to allow Dimitris to translate into English. The low table in front of me had a large shallow ceramic bowl containing decorative stones. George took them out and dropped them one by one on to the tiled floor where they shimmied across the floor under people's feet. We tried to retrieve and replace them with as little fuss and noise as possible and quietly tried to restrain George without much success. In the middle of this, while the registrar was conducting the service sonorously in Greek and George was playing ten pin bowling with the stone ornaments, a mobile phone rang. The registrar fumbled in his pocket and Dimitris glared at him as he silenced the phone and stowed it back in his pocket.

The service continued with stifled giggles adding to George's ten pin bowling and the sonorous tones of the registrar. The phone rang again. The giggles became less stifled, the registrar cursed in Greek and wrestled in his pockets for the phone. There was a grunted couple of Greek words from the doorway and the arm of one of the hairy Greeks with outstretched hand appeared through the doorway. The registrar gave him the phone, muttered Greek and footsteps receded down the corridor as the hairy Greek answered the phone.

At the end of the service, photos were taken outside the Town Hall then we all adjourned to the Café Bar 1760. The place had tables under parasols in front of a grand official-looking building that was quite possibly built in 1760. Prosecco was served before we all made our way back to the boat and then went our separate ways to prepare for the wedding on the beach.

Stu and George appeared after a short while and came aboard to get dressed for the ceremony while Hollie and Maisie were preparing themselves in the Villa. The next event, at 13:30, was a photo shoot at the boat which we had decked out with bunting for the occasion. The photographers came down to the boat to photograph Stu and George.

Once our photography session was over, the photographers went up to the Villa to photograph Hollie and Maisie and we shut up the boat and made our way to the Paradise Beach taverna walking up the gentle slope of the coastal road overlooking stony coves and azure blue sea. We were early and so we sat around the table that Stavros family had prepared for us in the shade of the overhead grape vines. Sharon joined us looking a bit flustered.

"What's up?"

"Hmm. I got showered and made up and I felt nice, clean, fresh and fragrant so I thought I'd pour myself a cheeky little Bacardi and coke bracer and have five minutes chilling looking out over the harbour and the blue sea."

"Sounds good."

"Well, it would have been had I not dropped the fucking Bacardi bottle on the tiled floor."

"From your general demeanour, I guess it broke."

"Right first-time, Sherlock. So, there I am trying to clear up glass and mop up Bacardi with tears in my eyes — a bottle of Bacardi is not cheap — and I am no longer nice, clean, fresh and fragrant."

"Christ," said Sue blasphemously. "Never mind the broken glass; I'd have been on my hands and knees with a straw."

Meanwhile, Dimitris was carrying stuff down to the beach below, a table, some flowers in an ornamental arrangement for the table, more prosecco. The photographers were arriving, so we made our way down to the beach and waited for the bride and the bridesmaid to appear.

George was overjoyed. More stones to play with. We waited while finishing touches were put to the table and the general set up and a mandolin player who had quietly appeared tuned up his instrument.

Maisie appeared first down the stone steps that wandered down the steep cliff face. She looked resplendent in her long white dress and gappy-toothed smile. Then Hollie descended the stone staircase in a long white dress, the train flowing down the steps behind her and the veil floating in the light breeze.

The second service was in English with the mandolin playing gently in the background. After the service, a little prosecco on the beach and of course more photographs before we all ascended the stone steps to the Paradise Beach Taverna.

They had arranged, at Hollies request, the tables in a square set under grape vines and with a view to the south across Sami bay to distant Sami and to the east across blue water to the dark green mass of Southern Ithaca.

We asked the taverna owner about the grapes, "Do you make wine from them."

"We try, we try, but we are not so good at it. Most often it ends up as wine vinegar. Good wine vinegar. Very good wine vinegar."

"When do you pick the grapes?"

"When they are ripe. September maybe October. Always about three o'clock in the morning when the last customers and the wasps have left. Then, when we have picked them all, we all go for a swim in the sea."

A couple of days later, I filled up with fuel ready to leave Aghia Eufimia. Once full and paid up, George, who manned the diesel bowser, proffered me a yellow Post-it Note with something scrawled on it, "Do you know this?"

I read it, "Rovani, yes."

"No rovani," he said with the emphasis on the second vowel rather than the first.

"Ahh rovani," I said stressing the "a".

"No, rovani," he said with the final vowel short and rising.

"Rovani," I repeated dutifully.

"Yes, that's right," he said. "It's a speciality…"

"I know, it's special to Stavros on Ithaca, a cake or sweet meat made from rice, herbs, honey and other stuff."

"Ah, you know then the Margarita, the café, delicatessen, in the centre of Stavro."

"Ah… yes."

"Well, next time you are there and are going to be coming to Aghia Eufimia or Sami from there, could you get me four or five pieces. I will pay you for them. I love it, but I am busy here all of the season so cannot get to Ithaca. It's four years since I last had any!"

Ithaca and Ferries

It was a typical Greek summer's day — bright sunshine, blue glinting sea, clear cloudless sky and capricious winds. We decided to head for the beautiful island of Ithaca and anchor for an overnight stop in one of the bays on the east side of the island. We had a leisurely sail from Keffalonia around the south of Ithaca, and up the east coast. However, by the time we got there, the bays were crowded with the floating gin palaces that arrive in high summer occupying a lot of space and playing with their noisy toys — jet skis and the like. We went on to Vathi, the pretty main town of Ithaca built around a lagoon. It tends to admit the strong north westerlies sometimes making it an uncomfortable place to stay unless you can get into the north east corner. Towards the end of the afternoon, we dropped anchor in the head of the bay, near the town centre. It seemed to hold well. Holding is generally good but you can get unlucky in Vathi.

Once anchored securely, we set about tidying up for the overnight stop. There was a bit of a commotion on the shore. Whistles being blown and there was distant shouting. The source seemed to be two or three port police who were stood outside their building blowing whistles and waving to boats moored in the centre of the lagoon. From our position, near the head of the bay, it was difficult to tell who they were waving at and what they wanted. A smart Italian rib sped over to us and shouted, "The port police want you to move." As they circled round our boat, waiting for us to respond, I said that I doubted it and I was sure that they meant a couple of boats that lay at anchor nearer the centre of the lagoon where the car ferry would be turning its ponderous bulk. "Do they not have a launch? Can they not come out here and clearly state what it is that they want?" Helen wanted to know.

"They have a magnificent launch. A super rib," I told her. "It's over there on a trailer on the harbourside. What they possibly don't have is petrol — part of the austerity measures no doubt."

"That's stupid."

"I'm only guessing. It might simply be that they cannot be arsed to launch it."

I was listening on the VHF, but there seemed to be nothing in the way of instructions. The Italians shrugged at our lack of response to their demands and sped importantly on to take the message indiscriminately to all yotties at anchor anywhere in the lagoon. I moved the boat nearer the head of the bay but was fairly certain that it was not us the message had been intended for — we were way beyond the scope of the ferry — he'd be grounded if he even approached our position.

Soon after the port police disappeared, several boats anchored in the centre of the bay. We watched with some interest when the port police re-appeared and walked along the harbourside to the deep-water jetty at which the ferry would disgorge it cars and lorries. At the time, the car ferry was coming in late in the evening and stopping overnight for an early morning departure to wherever it went to — Sami on Keffalonia or Astakos on the mainland. When it appeared, it was much larger boat than the one we had seen before. "Ah so that's why the hullabaloo," I muttered to Helen. However, the ferry captain turned the large boat slowly on a sixpence — I suppose in really bad conditions he would need some extra room, but I had watched ferry captains park their cumbersome craft with spot-on accuracy even in quite horrid weather.

I have long been fascinated by the arrival and departure of the ferries that act as a lifeline to the islands of Greece and have developed a lot of respect for ferry crews and the port police alike. The first impressions are usually... well... bedlam. I can remember looking up at the huge bulk of a car ferry that we were waiting to get on to as it pulled into the small port of Folegandros on our first visit to that island many years back. We were surrounded by cars, vans, lorries, pickups, people, parcels and livestock. There was even a tractor with a high-sided trailer containing two scrawny confused looking sheep and a goat who had wangled his head out between the slats of the side panel and was contriving to eat the rather elaborate hat of a lady stood nearby. An old lady stood near us clutching a length of sisal string at the other end of which was another goat. A Greek Orthodox priest led a straggling line of small children down the road to the jetty. A man and a woman, each with a chicken under one arm carried a large lumpy brown paper parcel between them. Somewhere, I could hear a donkey. Above the braying, hooting and lorry engines, port police whistles regularly rent the air as they directed traffic or drew some driver's attention to the fact that he had parked in a spectacularly stupid place.

The ferry pulled in with two crewmen perched precariously on the end of the already lowered landing ramp. Beyond them a similar throng waited in the dark and gaping maw of the boat ready to surge forward as soon as the crew and port police would let them. "Hell, it's going to take an age to turn this lot around," I hissed to Helen, imagining a scene something like a medieval battle as those trying to get off conflicted with those trying to get on.

We were on our way to the island of Milos where Venus de Milo was famously found in the ancient city ruins, or by a farmer in a field depending on which story you believed. I was a little worried. If we arrived late in the evening, would we be able to find rooms? We had always managed on previous occasions when we had arrived at our destination late but it was still a cause for concern. The ramp clonked down on the quay and scraped along the concrete. The crew kicked and dragged a pad of coiled hemp over the edge of the ramp to soften the step from the concrete to the ramp for vehicles embarking or disembarking. Satisfied with their work they unclipped the chain that extended across the mouth of the ferry which several of the more intrepid disembarkers had already ducked under. At this signal, the embarkers pushed on to the ferry, the disembarkers surged off and the first disembarking lorry edged forwards. The police whistles rose to a crescendo and there was a lot of waving of arms.

My heart sank. It seemed as though it would take an age before we could be on our way to Milos. However, it took little more than ten minutes before the ferry pulled away. All of the vehicles that had wanted to get off had got off and had been directed by the port police to the road that led up to the main town. The waiting vehicles had been waved forwards in an orderly manner and directed to reverse into the ferry to be dealt with by the ferry crew. The foot passengers had threaded their way on or off the boat. It was all sorted out with a great deal of noise and apparent confusion but, despite all that, with a great deal of efficiency too.

Mitikas, Italian Parking and Sofia's Farm

Mitikas has always been one of Sharon's favourite stops. Near the end of one of her holidays with us, we entered the harbour and looked for a place to moor. There seemed to be a couple of slots between the boats moored on the town quay. One of them was between a 30-foot Canadian-flagged sloop and a 42-foot Austrian flagged Jenneau. They were moored close together, but I was fairly sure we could just about get in stern-to on the quayside between them. The second position was next to a Czech flagged boat. It was a more generous slot, but the Czech anchor chain was angled across the slot. This was inviting trouble if they wanted to depart before us. "Time for you to do a bit of Italian parking," I told Sharon who was at the helm.

"Oh. What does that mean?"

"We are going for the narrow slot."

She stopped Sundowner about halfway along the harbour and started going astern. Once the kick of the prop had been overcome and water was flowing over the rudder to give her good steerage, she had a nice line on the narrow slot and was able to approach it slowly despite the moderate crosswind.

"Ok, drop the anchor now," I shouted to Helen.

"No that's too small a gap."

"It's big enough."

"Surely it's too small."

"Just drop the fucking anchor."

Sharon at the helm beside me muttered, "The gap is a bit small, Dad."

"It's OK, Sharon. We are going in slowly. We can pull out again if it turns out to be too small."

We squeezed in with the fenders kissing and tumbling around, but no contact with the hulls on either side.

The crew of the Canadian boat praised Sharon's helming and the crew of the Austrian boat remained fairly taciturn having shouted at us, "You are too big. Go away."

There was quite an assortment of friends from the past few years moored up. Bill and Annemarie from Dublin on Goldeneye, Kevin and Morag flying the South African flag on Xinran and local residents Gerry and Lynne on Bristol Fashion also flying a South African flag alongside the red duster of the UK.

We had called in for water and some stores, but there was also the opportunity to pick up some diesel but, of course, bumping into old friends meant that there was catching up to do so an overnight stop seemed likely. Sharon got talking to her fans on the Canadian boat next door and got invited to a barbecue over on Episcopi the following evening. However, our first port of call once we got sorted out was O Faros (The Lighthouse) a waterfront ouzeri with views across the blue Ionian to beautiful pine-clad Kalamos island to the south and Meganissi, Scorpio and the heights of Lefkada to the west.

We sat admiring the view and savouring the cold beer and mezes and made plans. Sharon was due to catch her plane back to Blighty in a few days so we left the choice to her.

"Well Episcopi to see Theodorus and Stephanie. Haven't been into Episcopi this time around and it's a must really."

"It sounds like everyone is heading over there tomorrow so we will have to go early to get a place," cautioned Helen.

"Ah, they'll be looking for a place on the quayside. We'll anchor in the bay," I answered.

"The wind is north-west-ish so it means a swell. Do we risk it?"

"Heck yes. The holding is brilliant. It's not a strong wind. If the worst comes to the worst, we can up anchor and head back to Mitikas and drop the anchor behind the harbour — even in the harbour if there is a slot — it's well lit."

"Leaving Episcopi in the dark? There are always unlit fisherman's buoys. It would be awful to get a prop wrap in the dark."

"One of us will be in the bows with a torch."

We ate at Dimitri's that evening where his mother, Cleopatra, does the cooking. Dimitri and his sister Sofia wait tables. At the end of the meal, Sofia grabbed hold of me and bundled me into her car with Cleopatra. "You come see my farm," she told me firmly. So I did. A five-to-ten-minute drive got us there. She pulled onto the verge and signalled that I should get out of the car. I helped Cleopatra out of the back and in spite of her advancing years she seemed to need less help than I. The fenced off field that we entered contained olive and lemon trees among which scratched chickens, sheep and goats. At least, I think they were sheep then I remembered Grenada. Their rather scrawny brownish sheep looked very similar to their rather scrawny brownish goats until I was told, "Goat's tails stick up, and sheep's tails hang down."

One sheep was, as far as I could gather from Sofia, rather reluctant to feed her offspring. She held the ewe in question in a "feeding stance" stroking her gently while her young one suckled. When the lamb had enough, he emerged licking his lips which amused Sofia greatly pointing at the lamb and licking her own lips in imitation.

Most of the goats were quite obviously goats rather than sheep and one in particular was tethered to a post.

"Not near him," Sofia warned me. The goat in question was large and his face had an even more wicked look about him than the satanic look of your average goat. I heeded Sofia's advice.

Once the feeding of the chickens was over and they had been ushered into their coop, Sofia opened the door of a brick-built shed in the corner of her field and took one of the large buckets of feed that she had brought with her. With this, she enticed most of the sheep and goats into the shed and slammed the door shut behind them. They obviously got locked up during the night to keep them safe from some sort of predator I suppose. Human? Animal? I was unable to establish what.

After having shut the bulk of her flock up, Sofia set about capturing the more reluctant goats and sheep. She enticed them with food and grabbed at them when she thought they were off their guard. It took several attempts to capture some of them. But she worked through them bundling them one or two at a time into the shed. This wasn't easy. She had to open the shed door while blocking the escape route for those inside who realised that they had been conned. Meanwhile, she had to manhandle the new interns into the shed while existing interns tried to squeeze out between her legs.

Eventually, all that was left to go in the shed was the big bad satanic billy goat. Seeing Sofia sizing up this big bad tan coloured goat, I felt I should step in and help but I was pushed away. "He hurt you," she told me. Smarting a little from this unintended slur on my masculinity I decided that, nonetheless, discretion was the better part of valour. When stood on his hind legs, the goat was as tall or taller than Sofia. I watched as she wrestled the goat into submission and into the shed. She slammed the door shut, locked it firmly and then stood leaning with her back on the door panting for breath and grinning.

Cleopatra emerged from a small fenced off garden in which aubergines, tomatoes, peppers, beans, and all manner of other vegetables were in evidence. She was clutching a carrier bag and opened it to show me what she had picked. A couple of large tomatoes, a cucumber, some aubergines and peppers. "Oh, they look good," I said admiringly.

"For you, for you," she said.

"No, really, I can't. We have stocked up," I said but she insisted with the generosity that is so typical of the Greeks.

From Dimitri's taverna, we walked back along the main street calling in at the Compass where AnneMarie and Bill had said they would meet us. They introduced us to the proprietor George who was in mid rant about the government.

He referred to them as "those lazy fucks in Athens," much to Annemarie's amusement.

"What do you think of our Georgio?" she asked.

I looked at Bill. "Do you remember the TV series from the USA with Sergeant Bilko in it? In the fifties I think."

"The Phil Silvers Show... Yes."

"Well, isn't he a dead ringer for Bilko?" It wasn't the looks, but the animation with which George and Bilko made their pronouncements.

Bill turned back to look again, "You're right. You are absolutely right."

So Georgio was christened Bilko and, when he asked, "Who is this Bilko then," we told him to look up Phil Silvers on YouTube which he had done by the time we next called in on him and he did a very good impression of the man.

Episcopi and the Barbeque

I put water on board first thing the following morning. "Are you off today," the skipper of the neighbouring boat asked.

"Ah, yeah."

"Where to?"

"We're not quite sure yet," Helen intervened.

"Uh oh... I thought we were going to Episcopi..."

"Change of plan," Helen said mysteriously.

The skipper went below and Helen turned to me, "We don't want everyone to know. There are folks planning barbecues. I think quite a few of them are going so we want to get there first to anchor in our normal spot."

"So you envisage a mass exodus. A marine version of Whacky Races with boats of all shapes and sizes creaming across the water to Episcopi..."

"You know what I mean," hissed Helen.

We anchored in our usual spot in the shallow bay outside Episcopi harbour around the middle of the morning and watched the other boats streaming in from Mitikas.

The few places on the quayside were soon taken up and the Canadian flag once again became our neighbour anchoring on top of us first time.

"Sorry about that. I thought I had got it right... But... There you go," he grunted as he took up his anchor. "How much chain have you got down? Where do you think your anchor is?"

I walked up to the bow and looked down. I could see the run of the chain through the clear water. It was all over the place as the boat had moved this way and that since I had planted the anchor and the anchor itself was about half a boat length off to our right at the end of great whirls of anchor chain. "It is actually about five or six metres off our starboard bow and there is about eighteen metres of chain down there."

"Oh ta," he shouted back as his anchor broke the surface. He relaid it off to our port side and reversed back to stress the anchor and dig it in. Once settled down his boat came to rest a respectable distance away.

We swam and idled the day away. At one point the Canadian flag rowed up to the boat. "Are you coming to the barbecue then? Bring your own meat and beer. We'll provide the Barbie."

"No, we're planning to go up and see Stephanie and Theo tonight. Thanks though."

"Ah… Pity… My crew's brought a couple of friends across from Mitikas and another friend of his is coming across from Kalamos Town and, well I don't know them." he grinned. "I don't know my crew awfully well."

"How come?"

"Well, he just joined me at Mitikas. Answered an advert of mine."

"Oh, how long's he with you?"

"Just the week."

"Oh, well, you should know him well enough by then. Sharing a small boat with him and all that…"

That evening, as planned, we went up to the small taverna above the harbour. We were greeted like old friends by Theodorus and Stephanie.

AnneMarie and Bill together with Morag off Xinran joined us as we finished our meal.

"Where's Kevin?" Helen asked Morag who responded by collapsing in laughter.

"He's entertaining," explained Bill after several attempts to explain by AnneMarie and Morag were vanquished by hysterical laughter.

"What? Singing bawdy songs? Music Hall stuff?"

"No no," gasped AnneMarie flapping her hands around. "You know those folks who were going to barbecue."

"The Canada flag?" interjected Helen.

"Yes, them. Well they did the barbecue on the harbourside but ended up on board Xinran," said AnneMarie.

"Oh... ah..." I was unsure why this was a cause of so much hysteria.

"Well, you know there isn't really anywhere to sit down comfortably and eat," said Morag.

"There's the harbour wall."

"Not really comfortable with stinky fishing nets and other rubbish."

"It is a harbour."

"Well, anyway, I felt sorry for them," Explained Morag. "They were stood around eating... like a finger buffet at a civic reception but instead of manageable food, bits of cheese, little sausages on sticks, that sort of thing, they were trying to cope with large badly cooked steaks, those enormous Greek pork chops and great dollops of some sort of glutinous mix of... I don't know tzatziki and shredded carrots."

"Tzaziki and shredded carrot?"

"Well, that's what it looked like to me. Anyway, they were struggling so I invited them aboard so they could eat in comfort in our cockpit. So there we sat, Kevin and I, watching them eat. There was hardly any conversation. We did not know them very well. I don't think they knew each other very well, so the conversation was that sort of sorry exploratory exchanges that happen between strangers if they don't hit it off."

"You and Kevin were not hitting it off with them very well and you invited them aboard?" asked Sharon.

"Well, we felt sorry for them standing around trying to eat barbecued stuff off floppy cardboard plates."

"Yeah, but if you didn't get on with them?"

"Well, we didn't not get on with them — if you know what I mean."

"Well, no. I'm struggling with the double negative."

"The conversation was stilted because they were eating. You would say something that invited a response from someone you didn't know who had to cope with an uncooperative lump of badly cooked steak that he (or she) had to clear before they could respond. As they didn't know you, they were slightly embarrassed by their inability to respond straight away so tried to clear their steak or whatever quickly and ended up choking."

"To death?"

"If only! No. But it was awkward, and we didn't really want to slow down their eating process because we had planned to come up here for something to eat."

"So are they still there?"

"Yes. I had to get away because we were both sat there saying very little and watching a bunch of strangers eating in our cockpit and I kept catching Kevin's eye and getting the giggles. So, eventually, I said, 'Look Kevin I have just got to have a word with AnneMarie and Bill — I'll be back in five'. He nodded at me with an expression on his face that told me he was either cross at me for inviting them on board or he was trying to suppress the giggles or he had got chronic wind or something. So I fled and I have overstayed my five minutes by about twenty-five."

Theodorus came by, "You enjoying yourselfs?" so AnneMarie tried to explain why all the laughter while I got another beer for Bill and myself.

Morag sloped off back to Xinran, "I had better try and rescue Kevin."

As Bill and I settled down to our beer and general gossip AnneMarie muttered that she had to go and have a word with Barbara, a lady she had been in fairly intense conversation with when we arrived. "She lives just up the hill. I'll only be five minutes."

"Hopefully, a bit of a shorter five than Morag's," muttered Bill.

By the time Helen, Sharon and I decided that we had better get back to the boat because failing light and the incoming swell would make getting back on board a bit of a performance, AnneMarie had been gone about forty minutes. "I had better go and find her," said Bill picking up the cockpit cushions from Goldeneye that he had strewn around him.

"What on earth have you got all those here for?"

"Well, we had been down on the beach swimming and we take them down to sit on and we were on our way back to the boat and it took us past this place."

"Fatal."

"Quite so. And we haven't eaten yet. AnneMarie is still in her swim wear under that pashmina… The wet seat doesn't indicate incontinence you know."

"Ah… yes… but leave the cushions behind. We'll look after them."

"Thank you, but no. We Irish don't find it easy to trust the English. History and all that."

Bill set off up the slope with what appeared to be all the soft furnishings from Goldeneye clasped around him.

"He looks a bit like Michelin man," said Helen. "But hadn't you better go up after him. He's got a bit of an affinity with those brambles that line the road." She was referring to the previous year when Bill, returning from Kalamos town on his folding bike had taken the final downhill strait into Episcopi at speed, the bike had folded and he had ended up in the hedge.

I set off after him, relieved him of some of his soft furnishings and walked beside him. Halfway up the slope, he opened a wrought iron gate and knocked on the door of the stone cottage that stood inside a tidily kept garden.

The person who opened the door seemed surprised to see him and after an exchange in what appeared to be a mixture of Greek, Italian and Gaelic the man closed the door and Bill came back out.

"No AnneMarie?"

"Wrong house … I think … at least they did not seem to recognise the name AnneMarie."

"Have you not been there before?"

"I think so, but it was a long time ago and it was dark."

"Well, it's dark now so you should recognise it."

"Ah, for an Englishman, that's a particularly Irish piece of logic."

"Well what are we going to do now?"

"Carry on up the street."

"Well there are not too many houses up the street so I suppose enquiring at each one won't take too long."

"Oh, I'll recognise it when I see it."

"Just like that last one I suppose. Are you sure it's on this side of the street? Are you sure we haven't passed it already?"

"Oh, ye of little faith," he paused outside a house about three houses further up the road. "Well here we are then."

"Really?"

"Yes, hold my cushions while I go and get her. I think my being wrapped in cushions startled that last boy quite a bit." Bill went off and started what seemed a more meaningful conversation with the occupant. Maybe he had got it right.

"Hey, Rob. What are you doing wrapped in all those cushions?" Kevin appeared from the gloom.

"They keep the cold out."

"But it's hot, very hot."

"Well, never mind. What are you doing here?"

"Well, we've finally come up for our supper and Helen was sat all alone. She said you had gone to give Bill a hand. She also said you'd got some sort of painful feet and I thought I had better come and rescue you two old invalids."

Getting back on our boat when the evening eventually ended was a bit of a challenge because of the swell now entering the bay. Kevin had stationed himself on the end of the harbour wall with a high intensity torch to help us by illuminating things from afar.

"The swell has not died back at all," Helen said quite unnecessarily as she and Sharon clambered back on the boat trying to time their transfer at a point when boat and dinghy seemed to be in synch, sort of. "Do you think we'll be all right?"

"It'll be alright. I have put on a snubber to put the load on the cleats rather than the windlass and the rubber on the snubber will absorb some of the snatched loads."

"Well, you haven't had the windlass mounting mended since Tom carried out that temporary mend."

"It's sound for goodness sake. The shelf that the windlass is mounted on is really thick marine ply and is sandwiched between two big stainless-steel plates."

"Yeah, but you said it wasn't very *marine* ply."

"Ach, take no notice of my grumbles."

"Well, I try not to."

I put the snubber on. I had been down with a face mask to check the anchor when we first arrived. It was well and truly buried on the sea bottom.

Getting back on Sundowner in the dark and getting the outboard back onto its bracket on Sundowner had been a bit of a struggle, but we eventually settled down for a bit of a bumpy night.

A Broken Windlass

In the morning there was, unusually, still a swell coming into the bay.

"We seem to have slipped back a bit."

"I don't believe it. The anchor was in good and buried when I checked."

I switched the instruments on. The echo sounder showed us in little more than 3 metres of water. A little bit less than last night but the seabed undulated a bit in the bay.

"Ah, well, we had better get off," I went to remove the snubber but the bloody thing had broken. An eye had been whipped into the end and the whipping wasn't up to the job, the eye had come undone and the hook that normally clipped on to the 8 mm chain was lost. The chain had dropped us back towards the shore as the slack was taken up.

Sharon drove the boat forward to give us slack chain and Helen went forward to use the windlass. I heard the starting whine of the electric motor and almost immediately Helen let out an almighty shriek.

"It's broken!" She yelled.

"What's broken?"

"The thingummy," she shouted pointing down to the anchor locker.

I rushed up to the bow and looked down to find that the supposedly solid shelf that the windlass was mounted on had collapsed. The Lofrans windlass had descended into the bowels of the anchor locker. I went back to the stern and explained what had happened to Sharon and told her, "Your task is to keep the boat off this lee shore. I have to tidy things up a bit then I will be pulling the anchor up by hand so I will want the boat over the anchor."

"How the hell will I know where that is?" she asked me looking at the still vigorous swell that was tossing the boat about.

"Your mother will be up there. She will signal what I want you to do and, meanwhile, keep your eye on the echo sounder and keep us out

348

of trouble. When we tell you the anchor is off the bottom just head out of the bay and in the general direction of Nidri."

I took some line up to the bow and started taking up the anchor by hand with Helen indicating to Sharon if I wanted the bow turned to port or starboard or the boat moved forward or astern. The anchor was well buried. I was unable to raise it by hand so I tied a line to the chain with a few half hitches and fed the line back to a winch. Helen went back into the cockpit to winch in the line while I hauled on the chain by hand. We broke the anchor out of the sea bed with ease. I signalled to Sharon that we were free and she set off out of the bay heading towards Scorpio and Meganissi as she cleared the headland to the southwest.

I secured the anchor on the bow roller, tidied up the mess a bit and walked back to the cockpit.

"Well, what are we going to do now, without an anchor?" Helen asked.

"We've got an anchor; we just can't use the windlass. We can go in bow to or..."

"We don't do bow to."

"Well we should."

"How do I get over the bows, especially on to a pontoon? It's a big drop."

"Oh, there will be someone there to take the lines. There always is."

"Not always."

"Well I'll call Iliana... make sure there is."

I fetched the kedge anchor — a Danforth — out from its place. It was buried in the port cockpit locker. Unused for many a season, it was well buried and a struggle to get out. The kedge chain and line were neatly coiled into a container which seemed to be falling to bits. I measured out the line along the boat, about two boat lengths. A bit short, but the holding was good and the water shallow. I checked out the splice that joined the chain to the rope line. It looked sound. We went through the procedure as we sailed on past Meganissi.

At the pontoon, Sharon lined up on a spare slot and motored slowly and steadily in. As I dropped the kedge, Sharon shouted, "The boat on the right of our berth is coming out."

"That's not nice of him, but carry on."

"I can't. He is cutting across us."

I could now see that his anchor line was at an angle to the normal and that was why, seeing us coming in, he had hastened up his intended departure. Sharon put the boat into reverse and I took in the kedge line so that we didn't wrap it around the propeller.

"Are you going to take the kedge up? Do we do it all over again?"

"No, it's planted OK. He will be clear in a minute. I've got the kedge line taut and I will keep my eye on it so we don't wrap it around the prop."

In fact, the other boat seemed to take an age to get his anchor up but soon we were approaching our berth again. Illiana and the skipper of a Maltese flagged boat on the left of our berth stood ready to take our bow lines but, less than a boat length off the pontoon, it became obvious that the kedge line was going to be short.

"Sharon, sorry we've got to go out again. I've got to put another line on sorry." So I explained to Helen and the guys on the shore what we were doing and Sharon reversed the boat out again with me taking line in to prevent prop wrap while tying another long line on so when we started our third approach we had plenty of line on the kedge.

Unflustered, Sharon took the boat in for the third approach. Well, she was unflustered until an old boy, an old girl and an old dog in a rubber dinghy, appeared from nowhere and unhurriedly pop-pop-popped across our path. For the third time, Sharon put the boat into reverse and using terminology that would have made a marine blush, asked them to get out of her way, fast. I tried to get the line in. The engine stopped.

"Oh no. Now the engine is fucking broken," she shouted.

"No, I think we've wrapped the line around the prop," I told her.

"What do we do now?" asked Helen.

"Yes, I am wondering the same thing," but I rapidly came to the conclusion that it was mask and snorkel time. We dropped the swimming ladder and in I went.

"Are you going to unwrap it? Can you do that?"

"Well, I'm going to have a look."

The water was murky, but I could see the wrap clearly enough. I took a deep breath and, conscious that I could not hold my breath for long, swam (or rather scrambled) under the boat and was able to unwrap one turn before heading back to the surface.

"Are you going to be able to unwrap it?

"I think so."

"Shall we slacken the line for you?"

"No, the boat will just drift off, probably towards the shallows, and the line will be taut again."

In the second dive I almost cleared the prop. The line was now just hooked around two of the propeller blades and the rudder post. When I came up for air Helen said "Your head is all blue"

Sharon, aware that I had a very minor stroke some three years ago, thought I was having some sort of seizure and began shouting "Mother, get him out of the water he is having a heart attack."

In fact, it was antifouling. Some of the stuff had rubbed off on my head, back and feet as I scrambled about under the boat trying to brace myself against various bits of the hull while I unwound line from around the prop. Once we had sorted this minor panic out, another dive cleared the rope from the prop and the rudder and we were free. We sorted ourselves out and went in bows-to for the fourth time. Illiana, still patiently waiting, took our starboard bow line and the skipper of the other yacht took the port line.

"I am impressed," he told us. "I don't know what I would have done. I would have panicked. You all seemed so calm when the line went around the prop. I would have been panicking."

"You clearly were not near enough to see and hear the panic that was going on," I told him. "I was panicking big time and Sharon thought I was having a heart attack."

There was a car hire firm in Nidri who would let me have a car for the airport run for a song so I had booked up several through the season to get visitors to or from the airport. Even factoring in fuel for the short run, it was about the same price as the taxi and enabled Helen to meet and greet or say goodbye at the airport and enabled us to do a shopping run. It must be said that some of the cars we had hired were a bit near the end of their useful life. One had an air conditioning switch but, if you used it, smoke smelling of melting plastic came curling out of the vents — so we opened the windows for air conditioning.

I had booked one of the cars to get Sharon to the airport at Preveza. I walked into town to just check with our car man that the booking was still on. It wasn't.

"What do you mean you don't have a car for us. I booked it up a month ago."

"I know. Sorry. No car," he shrugged.

We remonstrated but soon realised that we were wasting time which would be better spent searching for taxis or hire cars.

We phoned the various firms we knew about without much luck. It was changeover day near the height of the season and was beginning to look like the only option was the local bus service. This was a tortuous route involving a change and wait at Lefkas bus station and we were not sure whether the connections were good for a 1200 flight on Sunday.

"Look, let's get showered, changed and head into the town for something to eat," I suggested.

"How can you think of your stomach at a time like this?"

"There are taxi and car hire firms we haven't tried and we can call in at one of the travel agencies and check out the times of the bus."

"The bus service isn't going to be an option on a Sunday."

We went anyway and Upside-down George greeted us as we approached his taverna the Ola Kala on the main street of Nidri.

"Hullo darlings."

"George; we seem to have a problem. We want to get Sharon to the airport tomorrow and we have been let down. Do you have phone numbers for taxis? We've tried all the ones we know but... perhaps... you..."

"Don't worry. I'll get you sorted geezer."

I heaved a sigh of relief, "Thanks, George, that's good of you. We'll sit down and have a drink..."

"A drink? Not till we have transport organised," Helen interrupted.

"Look... while he's phoning around for us."

"Well, I'm up for it," grinned Sharon who seemed less perturbed by the situation than her mother.

So we found a table and ordered drinks and were half way through them when George re-appeared.

"Any luck?"

He shook his head, "No cars. No taxis."

"Oh hell, what are we going to do?" implored Helen.

George shrugged, "No worries. I take you. What time you want to go?"

Arrangements were made, telephone numbers were exchanged and we settled down for a meal. Helen was still worrying, however. "Supposing he doesn't wake up?" she hissed in a stage whisper. "Is he reliable? He is Greek."

"That's a bit racist isn't it?"

"No. That's not what I... I mean you know how laid back they can be... mañana, that sort of thing."

"Rubbish... anyway he's not Greek he's Albanian."

"Same thing."

"I'm not sure whether he would like that."

"Well, you know what I mean."

"No."

"Well supposing he is hung over in the morning."

"He doesn't drink."

"Well, he will be tired. He probably doesn't close his taverna till three or four in the morning."

"You worry too much, Mum," put in Sharon.

"Well, after all that's gone on today... are you surprised?"

"Look; he's OK is George. Under that veneer of complete and utter lunacy he is a perfectly dependable chap. He has said to phone him. He's given us telephone numbers. Landline and mobile."

In the morning, Helen phoned George at 0800. The phone was answered promptly. "When do you want me darling?" She dissolved into giggles of relief.

George arrived just a little bit after the appointed hour, "Sorry I'm late. My car wouldn't start."

"Oh, you've got it going now though?"

George grinned, "No, I had to borrow my neighbour's car. The key was in the ignition and I don't think he is up till the afternoon on a Sunday, the lazy bastard."

When she reached the airport, Sharon phoned as Helen had asked her to… "Here in plenty of time, Mum. George was brilliant. I left him picking and eating blackberries outside the airport. I'm checked in and just going to the taverna opposite for a cuppa."

Helen heaved a sigh of relief and we turned our minds to the windlass problem.

Goodbye Frikes

Towards the end of one season, we found ourselves in Frikes at the north end of Ithaca. From there, we were making our way back to Lefkada then on to the boatyard to pack Sundowner away before leaving for home. We were going to call in to one or two favourite places on the homeward journey and Frikes was one of them.

Surprisingly, we found our favoured slot on the harbourside unoccupied and so were able to moor up for a couple of days which we occupied with walks up to the village of Stavros and along the coast to Kioni as well as taking the opportunity for a bit of socialising. On the last day, I wandered around the harbour to say cheerio to the crew of Mehalah who I knew were leaving later that afternoon. About half way around the harbour, I heard, "Yassoo, Robin." I looked over to locate the greeting and greeter and there were Dionisis and Andreas sat under a tree outside the Rementzo with someone I didn't know. I went over, "You like a beer?" enquired Dionisis.

I wondered whether it would offend him if I said no and continued around the harbour to catch Mehalah before she left, but concluded that it was probably not worth the risk, so I said, "Thank you. Yes."

I sat with him and soon a large man in a dark T-shirt joined us. It was Gianni, Dionisis' cousin.

"He captains a cargo vessel 350 metres long," Dionisis told me.

After a confusing exchange of Greek between Gianni and Dionisis, Gianni turned to me and said, "I understand you are a captain too."

"Ah, err, yes," I replied hesitantly.

"Oh, what sort of a boat?" he asked.

"A 38-foot Bavaria," I told him.

"A what?" he enquired.

"Look, there, it is over there," I pointed to my boat moored in splendid isolation at the end of the new quayside. "It is a bit shorter than yours".

He looked at it, "So it is. So it is." He laughed uproariously. Meanwhile, Stathis arrived and winked and chinked glasses with me "Yammas" and started to tell everybody how bad the fishing is compared to twenty years ago. I was unable to understand much of it... and I've known the bloke for years.

Makis joined us. His band had been part of some celebrations the previous evening. The celebrations were to do with a young man getting married, or about to get married, or maybe thinking of getting married sometime. I never fully understood, though I met the gentleman in question. Tzantenos hosted the celebration at the Ulysseus. He had spit roasted two lambs and his wife Barbara had prepared gavros, cheese pies, pastitsio, stifado and numerous other dishes for 120 or so people. The celebrations were still in full swing at five thirty when I woke up in the morning. The last guest left at seven.

The party was growing and I felt it was time to move on, but the problem was that I had had a number of drinks brought me by now and felt I ought to have contributed. I called over Nektarios, who with his wife, Poppy, runs the Rementzo. "Look can I pay my share?"

He spoke to Dionisis and Gianni and there was a fierce exchange of Greek. "What they are saying" Nektarios explained, "Is that they shouted you over, so the drinks are their responsibility. It is not like in England where you buy your rounds... now it's his turn, now it's your turn... In Greece, if you have shouted someone over, then you pay. No further obligation."

"Endaksi... so... avrio," I suggested to Dionisis and Gianni.

Telis lowered his sunglasses and looked at me over them. "Ah well," he said with a grin. "If your sensitivity will be offended, perhaps I will have a drink with you."

We had another and Gianni had an argument with a second Gianni who had turned up. As far as I could gather, the argument went something like this:

Gianni1 (the sea captain): "Gianni, why you build that wall over there?"

Gianni2 (who apparently worked for the council): "To make the harbourside look tidy."

"But I can no longer park my car under the tree outside my house."

"But the place looks better."

"But I cannot park my car there anymore; I have always parked my car there, outside my house. And my father did before me."

"Outside your house is not your land."

"Pah. This is Greece. My father parked there. My grandfather before him and my great grandfather. Of course it's my land... In principle."

"What fucking principle?"

"The traditions of Greece. We have always parked there so it's ours. My father before me."

"Yes, and what he parked there was his donkey, in the shade of the tree. It needed the shade. You parked your big BMW off road monster..."

"Is same. Needs the shade."

"Does it really. Well, you tell that to the council. They tell me to build a wall."

"Ah. the council. They are a pack of bastards. Every one of them."

Andreas intervened, "Hey. You sit here shouting. Is hot. Why don't you have a cold beer and shut up."

"Yeah OK."

An hour later, I felt I really ought to leave. "Will you explain to your friends," I started to say to Nektarios. "That I enjoyed their company, but I was walking around the harbour to see my friends on *Mehala* and to buy something from Kiki, but now I am suddenly taken drunk for some reason... the friend has sailed off to wherever he is going to... and I quite forget what I was going to buy from Kiki... so I have to go and lay down somewhere quiet for a while."

I find Frikes difficult to leave... but it may be kinder to my liver if I do.

We had lift-out booked for early October so we found ourselves overnighting in a bay at the north of the Inland Sea in order to make a leisurely passage up to the boatyard the next day. The following morning was a perfect September day. Warm with, in the morning, a nice gentle wind. We breakfasted in the cockpit watching the other boats in the bay turning slowly on their anchors in response to changes in wind direction and strength. We were in no hurry to get going so we had a further cup of coffee as the sun climbed and warmed the air.

About ten, I started the engine and walked to the bow to haul up enough of the anchor chain to release the snubbing line. I hauled it up by hand and noticed what I took to be a little bit of seaweed on the chain just below the snubber but then I realised it was a sea horse. I took it gently off the chain, showed it to Helen and then put it back in the water. It was motionless for a few seconds and I thought it was dead, but then it stretched out and swam off in that rather peculiar way they have of getting themselves through the water looking rather like a small formation swimmer practising his part in some complicated routine. I was relieved as I thought he might have been damaged — pinched between two links of the chain as I lifted it. So, there you go. Pull in your anchor by hand. It's exercise so it's good for you. And you may save a seahorse's life!

We motored up the Lefkas canal through a busy, but no longer manic, Lefkas harbour and pootled along the final stretch listening for the siren and watching for the lifting of the swing bridge ramps. The road traffic stopped and the bridge opened pretty much on time. The marine traffic was light and the bridge had only just parked in its fully open position as we passed through. Already, there were long queues of road traffic each side of the bridge. We motored around the buoys that marked the shifting shallows and watched the depth on the echo sounder to keep clear. We had seen a few groundings along this short stretch in years past and we had been told that there had been a few this season. Out in the open, we hoisted the mainsail for the last time of the current season and set across the rolling water on a fine reach to the outer marks of the Preveza channel from whence it was a right turn then follow the marked channel in to the boatyards that lay on the south side of the entry to the intriguing inland Gulf of Amvrakikos.

Aktio was busy. Some boats were being launched, but mainly boats were being sailed in for lift out, jet wash and winter storage. Boat owners and helpers were busying themselves with end of the season repairs or packing the boats away for the winter. We tied up to the eastern jetty beside the slipway and I pumped out the engine oil while it was still warm and easy to pump. Gianni's machine appeared as I finished and half an hour later Sundowner was parked on her keel in a metal cradle with a ladder placed against her sugar-scoop stern ready for us to board and start to "winterise" her.

At Aktio, and doubtless other yards, there was a communal barbecue. Scrap wood or charcoal was heaped on it. Occasionally, someone would rap on the side of your boat, "We're leaving tomorrow. We're having a goodbye do at the barbecue tonight." The usual arrangement was to bring your own food and drink for a communal cook up and binge. By the end of the evening, you had normally had a sample of what everyone else had brought with them and they had in turn sampled your own offerings which could be somewhat bizarre if you were trying to make something of the various stores that needed using up before you left.

We said goodbye to bunch of folks leaving Aktio one Thursday in late September. The chosen venue on this occasion was Panos' taverna where tables were pushed together to accommodate something over twenty yotties. Panos place is known somewhat disparagingly as "the greasy spoon" by some of the Brits. It is in fact a respectable taverna serving excellent food cooked by Panos himself. The gathering was mainly Brits, but with a smattering of French, Italians and Greeks. The conversation was always highly technical about things that have mystified yotties through the years. How do you keep gout at bay? What are you going to do if they bring in drink driving rules for yotties?

An Unlikely Story

"I heard an interesting story this season," reported Patrick and waited for entreaties for him to continue. When they didn't come, he continued anyway. His story went something like this:

Many years ago, when the Ionian was just being discovered by the flotillas, one of the flotillas was moored in a small harbour one night when the crew of one of the boats heard sounds which they interpreted as rumpy bumpy on their neighbouring boat. This was followed by shrieks and screams which sounded a bit above and beyond the climax of even fairly noisy sex. Eventually, they went up to check what was amiss.

The lady on the neighbouring boat was in hysterics but, when they brought her back down to earth, it appeared that her large husband had passed out and she could not revive him. They went to investigate and it appeared that their first impression was correct, it had been rumpy bumpy. He was laying flat on his back, stark naked, with de-tumescence in process but their inexpert analysis had him dead, very dead.

"What the hell do we do now?" they asked each other as they struggled to try and placate the wife.

"Get the crew of the lead boat on the case that's what."

The crew who had heard the carry on had appeared on the quayside. They rapidly organised someone to feed the distressed wife with coffee, or brandy, "or whatever she damn well wants." They scrambled on board and the skipper checked the body.

"He's only bloody dead," he whispered to his mate.

"Strewth. What do we do now?"

"Phone the office."

"What this time of night?"

"Yes, this time of night."

"We need a box or coffin to put him in first off."

A box of sorts was drummed up from somewhere, but the man was big and the box was not. So he didn't fit.

"Cripes. We can't deal with him like this. What do we do?"

"Sleeping bag that's what."

"He's too big for a sleeping bag."

"We'll use several."

And so the body was wrapped and tied up like a quilted Christmas parcel.

"OK, so let's get him off the boat. You two take his feet. We'll take his top end and let's get him out into the cockpit."

"Yeah, but what then?"

"Oh fuck. We can't leave him in the boat. Let's worry about the next step when we've got him out of the boat. Ruthie phone home and ask what we do." The hostie (lead boat hostess) went off to raise someone in the head office for instructions while the skipper and the engineer off the lead boat and two "volunteers" set about getting the trussed-up body out of the cabin. They struggled and struggled.

"Look we can't do it, not unless we chop him to bits and stitch him together at the other side."

"We can't do that!"

"I'm joking man."

"At a time like this?"

"Yes, at a time like this."

"Well, how the fucking hell did he get through when he was alive?"

"Well, he wasn't trussed up in half a dozen sleeping bags then."

"You don't mean…"

"Yes, we gotta get him out of the bags, get him through the hatch naked and wrap him up outside." So, they busied themselves about doing that.

"Jesus Christ, he's leaking."

"Well deal with it."

"How?"

"I don't know. How do they deal with it at the undertakers or the morgue? Ruthie. Didn't you train as a nurse? Did you have to lay out any stiffs… er bodies?" The skipper had popped his head out of the cabin. The hostess had re-appeared and he noticed that they were beginning to get a bit of an audience — even in the early hours — and he wondered how he would explain it to the Greek police if they appeared.

Ruth, listening intently to the lack of response on her mobile put it on speaker and moved it away from her ear. "Ah yes, I did time in the winter gardens — the morgue — when I was training. We had to bung a swab in every orifice."

"Did you hear that Bruce?" he shouted to the engineer struggling with the problem below.

"Yeah, but what do you do with his old man for Christ's sake?"

"Tie a knot in it," Ruthie shouted.

"Strewth mate. I'm not doing that."

"Joking. Tie a bit of string around it... Tight."

"Another bloody joker. Jesus Christ, this wasn't in the job spec," grumbled the engineer.

"I think you'll find the small print covers it," retorted the skipper.

"Huh. What next? Delivering babies?"

"Don't even joke about it mate!"

Ruthie reported the instructions she got over the phone. "We've got to get him into one of our vans, someone's bringing one across, and then we have to get him to the morgue in the nearest hospital that is equipped with one."

At the hospital, they were turned away on the grounds that the stiff wasn't one of theirs. "Take him to the airport. They will have an officer to deal with this sort of thing."

At the airport, the parcel was unwrapped to verify the content then hastily wrapped up again, labelled up for the next flight to London and was dispatched to be loaded with the flight luggage into the hold of the aeroplane.

"Is that it?"

"Yes." The official said with a grin, "No longer a problem for Greece; now England's problem."

The news was imparted back to HQ "...So, mid afternoon you, or somebody will have this quilted trussed up parcel to collect off the luggage carousel at Gatwick."

"You are joking."

"No."

At HQ, they looked up contact details and tried his home number. A woman answered.

"We have some bad news, I am afraid. Your son, David, he and his wife are on holiday with us in Greece… or was that is. Well he died in the early hours of this morning, I'm afraid."

There was silence at the far end of the line. 'Oh hell', thought the poor office wallah, 'I could have done that a bit better'.

"Well," the voice at the other end interrupted the silence suddenly and sharply. "There's several problems there. I haven't got a son. David is the name of my husband who is supposed to be on a business trip in Bulgaria. The bastard." And the phone was slammed down.

"Patrick, I've heard quite a lot of old cobblers from you in the past, but that caps the lot," said Rory expressing the consensus of opinion around the table.

"It's true, it's true… I mean, I may have put in some detail just to clothe the bare bones of the story."

"Story is right. I can't believe they just popped him onto the plane."

"That part is absolutely true. Absolutely."

A Choral Finale

The conversation continued and got wilder as the evening progressed. It ranged around what one would and could do with a dead body, what one would do with a heart attack at sea, general health pointers and eventually back to gout and drinking.

"Do you stick to your 21 units per week?" Charlie asked me.

"Oh yes," Helen answered for me. "He regards it as a target to be hit as soon as possible each week."

"That's rubbish," I protested.

"Well, why have you got gout then?"

"I haven't got gout. I had it once…"

"Twice."

"Well twice."

"What brings it on?" asked Charlie.

"Booze," answered Helen.

"Well, I'm told to avoid red wine, shell fish and oily fish — whatever oily fish may be," I told him.

"Surely there are tablets you can take," said Charlie.

"Why? Have you got gout too?" interjected Helen.

"No no. Oh no…" Charlie defiantly took another slug of the red wine he was holding.

"Me thinks the lady doth protest too much," someone intervened.

"Didn't have you down as a Shakespeare scholar."

"I don't know about tablets. I have had it but not for years. I have a remedy," Ian intervened.

"What's that?"

"Avoid red wine, drink white," he answered.

"Huh," snorted Charlie seeing the chance of a panacea fade away. "I don't know how they come up with 21 units anyway. I know folks who habitually drink more and they seem OK."

"Yeah, they'll develop cirrhosis of the liver or diabetes or cancer and be a burden on the state eventually."

"It's being so cheerful that keeps you going."

"Yeah, well, all these things are on the increase."

"Yes, why is there so much drinking today?" asked Helen.

"It's probably no worse than it ever was. It's newspapers generating the sort of stories that sell copy."

"It's definitely on the increase. You hear about so many celebrities that have problems with it these days…"

"They always have had…"

"Well, there never used to be so much in the papers about celebrities drying out and going into rehab… It must be on the increase."

"No, they used to keep schtumm about those sorts of things. The newspapers were more deferential then than they are now — especially when it came to celebrities, particularly politicians."

"What do you mean?"

"Well, George Brown was notorious for it but I don't think it was ever directly reported while he was alive."

"Don't you mean Gordon Brown? Is he dead then?"

"No, George Brown — Harold Wilson's sidekick."

"Harold Wilson? Who's he?"

"Our Prime Minister in the sixties."

"I don't remember the sixties."

"Not a lot of people do."

"No, I mean, I'm too young."

"No, come on. I'm interested. And what do you mean *directly reported?*"

"Well, the newspapers used a sort of code of their own. 'tired and emotional' — that was the euphemism some of them used. They would report *'George Brown, returning from his conference in Copenhagen, was tired and emotional as he stepped off the plane'*. It meant he had fallen down the steps pissed on duty-free."

"No!"

"Yes. The rumour was that he was notorious for drinking. That and peering down women's cleavages. That and emotional oratory was what he did best."

"My Charlie is as bad…" from Sophie at the other side of the table.

"No, I'm not. I've never fallen down an aircraft steps in my life."

"Peering down women's necklines. You can't keep your eyes off them if they are on display. If there's a plunging neckline you might be talking to the owner, but your eyes are popping out on stalks." Sophie made a comic bug-eyed face peering in a downwards direction and letting her tongue hang from the corner of her mouth.

"No, I don't."

"You do. Remember Hattie with the big boobs and she always wears low cut tops so they're hanging out almost."

"Ah, yes, well."

"Well nothing. You had your nose down her cleavage every time you spoke to her. I don't think that you would recognise her face. You've lost your glasses down there before now."

"You do exaggerate."

"Well, I think you've got to..." I sprang to the defence of poor beleaguered Charlie ignoring the fact that I was launching into a PC minefield — you've got to back your friends, haven't you? "I mean if they're on display, it's obvious that they are there to be admired and it would be most rude not to."

"Typical. Trust you to defend Charlie," Helen interposed.

"C'mon, the human body is a beautiful thing. That's why all those artists paint nudes." I said digging myself ever deeper.

"The artists are men and the models are women is why."

"Not always." Charlie said springing to my defence not sensing a lost cause when it was about to consume him, "There are plenty of famous paintings and sculptures of the male nude. Come on Sophie… If you saw Rob here stripped down to his bathing trunks…"

"Bathing trunks?" shrieked Sophie.

"Well, budgie smugglers then. If you saw Rob here in his budgie smugglers you know your heart would give a little flutter."

"I have and it didn't"

"Ach, you just don't appreciate the beauty of the human form."

"Well, there's appreciating and then there's... well lecherising."

"That's not even a word!"

"It is. I've just invented it."

"Well, I was very worried about Amstel and Bill," AnneMarie chimed in. "I went to Athens on a course, on an archeology and history course, a month or so back. I left them moored side-by-side on Vonitsa town quay. I could see them, two grey haired old farts, running about the town and pursuing the local bimbos."

"Oh, very Benny Hill," I said dryly.

"Der-der diddle-dum der-der-diddle-dum" — Helen could not resist chanting the Benny Hill theme for old farts in pursuit of young tarts and AnneMarie collapsed in laughter.

"I hadn't quite thought of it that way," she gasped in between fits of laughter. "I'm going to have difficulty getting rid of that image now. I shall keep seeing them both hobbling along trying to catch a gang of shrieking bimbos in short skirts running along in front of them arms outstretched and squealing like pigs at a trough."

Photographs were taken. Jokes were told. There was singing: English, Irish, Scottish and French folk songs, smutty songs and, well, any old songs.

"What about a song from Essex?" I was asked — by this time, Helen and I had been labelled Essex man and Essex woman.

"Naah, we don't have songs in Essex. Besides, we're residents of Berkshire now," I said trying to posh up my voice and failing.

"Are there any Berkshire songs?"

"No. And if there were, they would all be about BMWs."

"You must... Haven't you any favourite songs?" AnneMarie persisted.

"Naah don't do songs," I was petrified that I might be bamboozled into attempting to sing something. And my singing usually contravenes some health and safety regulation or other.

"What about that song you're always singing when you go to rugby?" Helen said helpfully. I attempted to kick her under the table and only succeeded in hurting my toe on the table leg.

"What's that? Do you play rugby?" asked Bill, who among his other accomplishments is a rugby referee.

"Jesus, no. Games at my age? What do you think? Poker's as close as I get to physical activity these days."

"He watches London Irish," Helen said helpfully.

"Ah well. That'll be 'The fields of Athenry' then," with which Bill, AnneMarie and Jeff launched into a quite respectable:

By a lonely prison wall, I heard a young girl ca... aaa... alling:
"Michael, they have taken you away,

For you stole Trevelyan's corn,

So the young might see the morn.

Now a prison ship lies waiting in the bay.

Which rapidly degraded, as others joined in and the words were fumbled, hummed and got wrong:

Low lie the fields of Athenry,

Where once we watched the small free birds fly;

Our love was on the wing,

We had dreams and songs to sing;

It's so lonely round the fields of Athenry.

But it was, nonetheless, a harmonious end to the evening and the season.